Springer Books on Professional Computing

Springer Books on Professional Computing

Computer Confidence: A Human Approach to Computers
Bruce D. Sanders. viii, 90 pages. 23 figures. 1984. ISBN 0-387-90917-6

The Unix System Guidebook: An Introductory Guide for Serious Users
Peter P. Silvester. xi, 207 pages. 6 figures. 1984. ISBN 0-387-90906-0

The American Pascal Standard: With Annotations
Henry Ledgard. vii, 97 pages. 1984. ISBN 0-387-91248-7

Modula-2 for Pascal Programmers
Richard Gleaves. x, 145 pages. 18 figures. 1984. ISBN 0-387-96051-1

Ada® in Practice
Christine N. Ausnit, Normam H. Cohen, John B. Goodenough, R. Sterling Eanes. xv, 192 pages. 79 figures. 1985. ISBN 0-387-96182-8

The World of Programming Languages
Michael Marcotty, Henry Ledgard. xvi, 360 pages. 30 figures. 1986. ISBN 0-387-96440-1

Taming the Tiger: Software Engineering and Software Economics
Leon S. Levy. viii, 248 pages. 9 figures. 1987. ISBN 0-387-96468-1

Software Engineering in C
Peter A. Darnell, Philip E. Margolis. xv, 612 pages. 62 figures. 1988. ISBN 0-387-96574-2

The Unix System Guidebook: Second Edition
Peter P. Silvester. xiv, 334 pages. 16 figures. 1988. ISBN 0-387-96489-4

Peter P. Silvester

The UNIX™ System Guidebook

Second Edition

With 16 Illustrations

Springer-Verlag
New York Berlin Heidelberg
London Paris Tokyo

Peter P. Silvester
Department of Electrical Engineering
McGill University
Montreal, Quebec
Canada H3A 2A7

Library of Congress Cataloging in Publication Data
Silvester, Peter P.
The UNIX system guidebook / Peter P. Silvester.—2nd ed.
p. cm. — (Springer books on professional computing)
Bibliography: p.
Includes index.
ISBN 0-387-96489-4
1. UNIX (Computer operating system) I. Title. II. Series.
QA76.76.063S5585 1988
005.4′3—dc19 87-32136

Media Conversion by David E. Seham Associaties, Inc., Metuchen, New Jersey.
Printed and bound by R.R. Donnelley & Sons, Harrisonburg, Virginia.
Printed in the United States of America.

9 8 7 6 5 4 3 2 1

ISBN 0-387-96489-4 Springer-Verlag New York Berlin Heidelberg
ISBN 3-540-96489-4 Springer-Verlag Berlin Heidelberg New York

Preface

Well suited to medium-scale general purpose computing, the Unix time-sharing operating system is deservedly popular with academic institutions, research laboratories, and commercial establishments alike. Its user community, until recently a brotherhood of experienced computer professionals, it now attracting many people concerned with computer applications rather than the computer systems themselves. This book is intended for that new audience, people who have never encountered the Unix system before but who do have some acquaintance with computing.

While helping beginning users get started is the primary aim of this book, it is also intended to serve as a handy reference subsequently. However, it is not designed to replace the definitive Unix system documentation. Unix operating systems now installed in computing centers, offices, and personal computers come in three related but distinct breeds: Seventh Edition Unix, Berkeley 4.2 BSD, and System V. These differ from each other in details, even though their family resemblance is strong. This book emphasizes System V, while paying heed to its two popular cousins. It also includes a few facilities in wide use, but not included in the normal system releases. Individual details, of course, must be found in the manuals supplied with each system.

This second edition of *Unix System Guidebook* is in many ways like Unix itself. Although it resembles its earlier edition in structure and layout, it is much bigger and extensively rewritten, even in those parts which may superficially seem similar. About three quarters of the text is entirely new. Practically every example has been tried out on three systems derived from Seventh Edition Unix, System V, and 4.2 BSD.

Many people have been instrumental in shaping this book, and all richly deserve the author's gratitude. Particular thanks are due to David Lowther, for our many helpful discussions; and to the many students whose suggestions enlivened the task.

Peter P. Silvester

Contents

Chapter 1

Introduction

The Unix time-sharing system is rapidly becoming the most popular computer operating system ever designed. Its unique popularity may be the result of portability: Unix systems are available for various different computers, while practically all other operating systems are tied to specific machines. Whether for this reason or another, the Unix system is tending to become universal, much as Fortran became the universal language in its day. And just as Fortran influenced the style of other programming languages, so Unix software characteristics are becoming visible—both by emulation and deliberate avoidance—in other operating systems. For computer users, some acquaintance with the Unix system is therefore taking on increasing importance.

A Multimachine Operating System

Although it was originally intended for the PDP-11 family of computers, Unix software has been recreated for use on many other machines both smaller and larger. There now exist versions of the Unix system, or other operating systems which closely resemble it, for many widely used small computers based on 16-bit microprocessor chips. Upmarket from the PDP-11, Unix systems, in some cases several, exist for all Hewlett-Packard computers, for the VAX-11 family, and many other—indeed probably most—large minicomputers. Large-scale individual workstations such as the Sun use Unix either exclusively or as an option. Other versions run on large mainframe computers like the Amdahl. At the opposite end of the computer spectrum, Unix or Unix-like operating systems are available for personal computers such as the IBM PC series.

System Characteristics

Three main reasons are usually cited for the current popularity of Unix and Unix-like operating systems with users. First, they provide a simple and logically almost consistent command language through which the user can interact with the system; a language easy to learn, fairly easy to understand, and not very easy to forget. Second, Unix systems provide a very wide variety of software tools and services, so that program development can progress rapidly. Third, and perhaps most important, is that both system services and user programs are insured against too rapid obsolescence, by being nearly machine independent. Programs can be moved to new computers along with the operating system, while new system services become available on practically all versions of the Unix system at once.

Traditionally, many computer manufacturers have regarded operating system software as an unpleasant hurdle to be overcome before a new machine could be marketed. The relative portability of the Unix system has endeared it to hardware makers, for computers can be designed to run under this operating system by investing only a modest amount of software effort. New hardware can be made ready for the market not only quickly, but with all the sureness of an already accepted product. To the user, a knowledge of Unix software structure and command language is of long-term value, for it is very likely that his next computer will employ a close cousin of the same system. Relative machine independence also enriches the range of general utility programs available; because programs can migrate to new computers along with the operating system, development of good general-purpose programs becomes attractive.

Not surprisingly, the Unix operating system is less than perfect. Its major shortcoming is that it assumes a friendly user community. There are ways that one user can cause the system to halt, or to run very slowly; such situations are perceived by most users as a nuisance to be laughed off if they happen occasionally on a computer shared by three people in the same terminal room, but they can become major gripes among a hundred strangers. Next, many of the command structures and conventions of Unix bear the marks of having been developed by a circle of friends, without much regard for subsequent distribution to others. For instance, many commands are abbreviated to extremely short forms and appear easy to confuse with others. Finally, protection against operator error is imperfect; certain users can even accidentally destroy all files on the system, including the operating system itself. This latter disadvantage can be serious, especially in commercial or financial applications. But fortunately it only matters to highly experienced users, who have gradually acquired a knowledge of pretty well everything the system can do. Novices are unlikely ever to have access to quite so much destructive power.

Portability

Because Unix programs are almost entirely written in a high-level programming language called C, this system is practically guaranteed to become available on many future computers as well as already existing ones. To install a Unix system on yet another computer, two main things are necessary: a C compiler and a modest amount of machine-dependent coding. A compiler for the C language is always required, to permit translating the Unix operating system itself to the native language of the new machine. Construction of such a compiler generally takes a few man-months or perhaps a man-year of programming effort. In addition to the compiler, transporting Unix to another machine requires a few machine-dependent input-output hardware service routines. These must necessarily be written in the native language of the new machine, so that they are strictly locked to that computer. Fortunately, they are usually short so that not much programming effort is needed. Usually, a matter of man-weeks or, at worst, man-months, is involved. These amounts of time are tiny when compared to the investment required to design and write a new operating system. The initial effort that produced the Unix kernel amounted to two or three man-years, but the addition of the many utility programs that make Unix systems useful has taken much, much more.

Most Unix system services now available—editors, compilers, file sorting and merging programs, and much else—are written in high-level languages, with C the most widely used language by far. New utility programs constructed by the now widespread Unix user community are also written in high-level languages, C being again the most frequent choice. As a result, the new programs can be incorporated in almost any Unix installation without alteration.

Portability of source programs from one Unix version to another unfortunately does not extend to the binary modules ordinarily delivered to end users by software suppliers. Executable program modules are necessarily compiled for one type of machine so they are clearly not usable on a different hardware configuration. But worse is yet to come: often several variants of Unix are available for a particular machine, over half a dozen different ones for the IBM PC. Program modules runnable under one are not normally runnable under another. Every implementor has attempted to produce the best possible software, curing known problems and introducing desirable enhancements. Unfortunately, the result occasionally verges on a mild form of chaos. Standardization is clearly desirable and there have been two attempts to define a standard, one by the

IEEE and the other by AT&T. The IEEE standard is a far-reaching effort which very likely will lead to national and international standards in a few years. The AT&T approach is more pragmatic: it consists of publishing a precisely detailed statement, nearly 700 pages of it, on its System V. It is likely that these efforts at standardization will enjoy widespread support and will improve the portability of Unix software further.

Past and Future

Although it has gained wide popularity only recently, the Unix system is mature software, the product of years of testing and rewriting. To assess its probable future, its history may deserve at least brief mention.

Ancient History

The first Unix system was written by D. M. Ritchie and K. Thompson at Bell Laboratories some time in 1969, to run on the now all but forgotten PDP-7 and PDP-9 computers. Its authors' primary objective was to produce a system convenient for inexperienced users; in this they succeeded at least well enough to be encouraged to construct an improved version to run on a much more modern machine, the PDP-11/20. It became operative in 1971 and was accompanied by a booklet that subsequently turned out to be the first, but far from the last, edition of the *Unix Programmer's Manual*. The second edition appeared in 1972; it introduced the notion and mechanism of interprocess pipes and therewith assumed more or less the external appearance that all Unix systems have presented to the user since. Because the PDP-11 family of computers became enormously popular in the 1970s, a third version of Unix, again fully rewritten, appeared in due course; it supported the PDP-11/34, /40, /45, /60, and /70. By 1973 the system authors had abandoned assembler language coding, for it was becoming clear that transportability from machine to machine would be easiest to achieve if a major part (ideally, but impossibly, all) of the system were written in a high-level language. A language called C was developed for the purpose. C remains the principal language of the Unix operating system; it is well suited to writing operating systems, while retaining most other characteristics of good high-level languages such as Fortran or Pascal. C resembles Pascal in many respects, but it does allow programming a little closer to the machine register level—as if Pascal were to recognize the existence of registers and bits! The structure and capabilities of C thus allowed building the Unix system in a fashion which made it largely independent of the machine hardware structure: at least transportable, if not actually portable.

The name Unix appears to have been coined by Kernighan and was the accepted name of this system by some time in 1970. It appears to have originated as a diminutive of Multics, the name of a large multiuser system then in use by several of the members of the original Unix programming group. It has been suspected (probably wrongly) of having served initially as a deliberately misleading cover name, for Unix hardly sounds a likely name for a multiuser system!

A paper on the Unix operating system was published by Ritchie and Thompson in 1974, in the *Communications of the Association for Computing Machinery*. This paper quickly became a defining landmark for the system. It outlined the basic system structure and methods of work; although these have been refined considerably since that time, the basic notions have remained almost unchanged. What has changed, to be sure, is the range of system services and utilities available. Unix probably contains a better selection of software tools than any other operating system. Not only is their range wide, but they have for the most part been written to go together well. Four years later, in July 1978, the *Bell System Technical Journal* produced a special issue on Unix, thereby forever establishing the system structure as set out in the Ritchie and Thompson paper.

Unix Goes Public

Even before the landmark paper of Ritchie and Thompson, there were persistent rumors about the interesting new system being developed at Bell Laboratories. After its publication interest became widespread, particularly in the academic community. Bell Laboratories therefore took the decision to release the then current version to universities practically free of charge, with the proviso that it be used for nonprofit academic work only. That system, first released in 1975, was popularly though somewhat incorrectly referred to as Version 6, or more correctly as Sixth Edition Unix. The number in either case refers to the system manuals, which had by that time reached their sixth edition.

The seventh edition, widely called Version 7 or V7, of the system was released to universities in 1979, although it is known to have been operational within Bell Laboratories as early as 1977. The delay was probably occasioned by the preparation of the Seventh Edition of the *Unix Programmer's Manual*, a book about the size and shape of the Manhattan telephone directory! This version came to be known as *the* Unix system to thousands of computer science students, for it rapidly spread to practically all computers in the PDP-11 family, including the PDP-11/23, /24, /44, and other latter-day additions.

A significant and continuing influence on the course of Unix software development came in the late 1970s: a major development project was begun at the University of California, Berkeley. It produced another sequence of Unix systems. The Berkeley Unix systems adhered closely to the spirit and objectives of their Bell Laboratories ancestors but introduced substantial extensions and improvements. Many of the improvements were internal, invisible to the casual user. Others, however, are immediately visible. They include the **vi** text editor and an alternative command interpreter, support for the Pascal and Lisp programming languages, and Ingres, a now widespread data base management system.

The Modern Age

Unix systems for computers other than the PDP-11 started appearing in the late 1970s. A version for the Interdata 8/32 computer was undertaken by Ritchie and Johnson as early as 1976, and one for the VAX-11/780 came not long thereafter. Several versions for other processors, notably the model 68000 and Z8000 16-bit microprocessor chips and thus for the many computers built around them, followed. By 1983, quite a few smaller manufacturers had chosen to design computers suitable for running Unix, rather than to look for operating systems appropriate to their hardware. The IBM System/34, intended for small and medium business data processing, was supplied with Unix under license from AT&T, though the potential rivalry of AT&T and IBM in both the computer and communications businesses must have caused considerable worry on both sides. By 1984, IBM even offered a modified Seventh Edition for its extremely successful PC personal computer under the name of PC/IX; to round out matters, it was followed by VM/IX for large IBM mainframes.

Medium-sized computer companies took to the Unix system rapidly in the 1980s and to small companies it must have come as a godsend. Gone were the worries about software compatibility, of having to persuade customers to accept yet another new operating system—well, nearly gone, anyhow. The initial acceptance of Unix by large computer manufacturers, on the other hand, was slow and grudging. After all, the system was owned by a potential commercial rival! Laying aside doubts and hesitations, Hewlett-Packard formally adopted HP-UX (yet another name for Unix!) in 1983 as the company's main operating system, the same year as Digital Equipment Corporation began to furnish Ultrix on its VAX range as an alternative to its own proprietary operating systems. After some hesitation, IBM took up Unix in the scientific computing area in 1986, choosing it as the only operating system supplied with the Personal Computer PC/RT, a large and powerful machine despite its modest name.

Between 1978 and 1982, other operating systems similar to Unix appeared, developed independently but with a remarkable similarity to Version 7 (and the predecessor Version 6) Unix systems. Some resemble Version 7 only in what the system looks like to the user at the terminal. In others, the similarity extends to such internal details as file formats and system calls, so that not only programs but even disk or tape files can be moved between systems. There have been a few Unix look-alike systems for computers based on 8-bit microprocessor chips, but Unix is really too large to fit into their restricted memory and slow speed; most look-alikes are intended for computers that employ 16-bit processors.

Until 1980-1981, the creation and marketing of look-alike Unix systems were lent strong encouragement by the fact that the Bell Laboratories Unix system itself was, for all practical purposes, available to outsiders only for academic research and teaching use. Look-alike systems therefore appeared to fill the commercial gap. For example, the Coherent, Idris, and Unix systems are independent, but look similar to the user, and are largely compatible with each other. Around 1981, there was a change in distribution policy; although the Unix name has been retained exclusively for use by AT&T, the Unix operating system has been made available commercially through licenses granted to various independent repackagers and to computer manufacturers. Unix is therefore available under a variety of computer makers' names such as HP-UX, Zeus, or Ultrix, as well as under names given to it by repackagers: Xenix, Venix, Unisis, Unity, and many others. These are not look-alikes, but Unix itself dressed in a commercial suit. They are not only entirely compatible with Unix systems; they *are* Unix systems. Most such derivative systems are enhanced, modified, or adapted to perform well in particular environments.

Both the independently developed systems and the licensed variants of the original appear on the market under names other than Unix. Different names are used for both commercial and legal reasons, among which trademark protection probably ranks high. With Unix systems coming into widespread use, and commercially available almost everywhere short of drugstore counters, AT&T is presumably concerned lest its trademark pass into the public domain through excessively great success—along with aspirin, bakelite, and many others. At present, there is no generic name to cover Unix, Xenix, Coherent, Onyx, Zeus, Omnix, Cromix, Flex, Qunix,. . . and much of the computer press refers to them all as "Unix-like operating systems".

Versions and Derivatives

During the 1970s AT&T was thought to be a holding company for telephone utilities, which in many respects is precisely what it was. Computer operating systems were seen as an incidental though important part of the telephone business, not as products in their own right. Copies of the Sixth Edition (popularly called Version 6) were therefore released to universities, sparking among academics the interest in Unix which has remained alive ever since. It was distributed as modifiable source code, so that almost every academic institution with a Unix license actually used a maverick "improved" version rather than the original Bell Laboratories system. The Seventh Edition, which came later with various improvements over its predecessor, was still distributed as source code, so it too formed the starting point for new offshoots. Careful control over the terms of user licenses by AT&T, however, prevented the many maverick versions from travelling very far. The only derivative versions to reach a wide audience were those emanating from the Berkeley Unix project whose products were again disseminated to universities but not released for commercial use. The most commonly known Berkeley release goes by the curious name 4.2 BSD; the letters are said to stand for Berkeley Software Distribution.

While the Berkeley project gained speed and spawned a whole new breed of system programmers, the AT&T Bell organization, well aware of the potential commercial value of Unix, went to work on a new version of Unix which eventually came to be System III. It was the first version not to be distributed to academic institutions for study and emulation. System III was followed quickly by System V and then, as illustrated in the rough sketch of a Unix family tree in Figure 1.1, by its Release 2. This release is also called System V.2 (pronounced five-dot-two), presumably as the result of someone's inability to tell arabic numerals from roman. The most noteworthy children of System III include the near-abortive PC/IX system and Xenix 3. Latterly, many of the derivative system suppliers and repackagers have adopted numbering schemes parallelling those of AT&T, so that system names are suggestive of their origins, as, for example, Venix 7 and Venix V. The naming of systems, however, is no less complicated than the naming of wines—except that wines are at least partly controlled by governments and viticultural councils, but no such supervising authority exists for software. To illustrate the pitfalls for

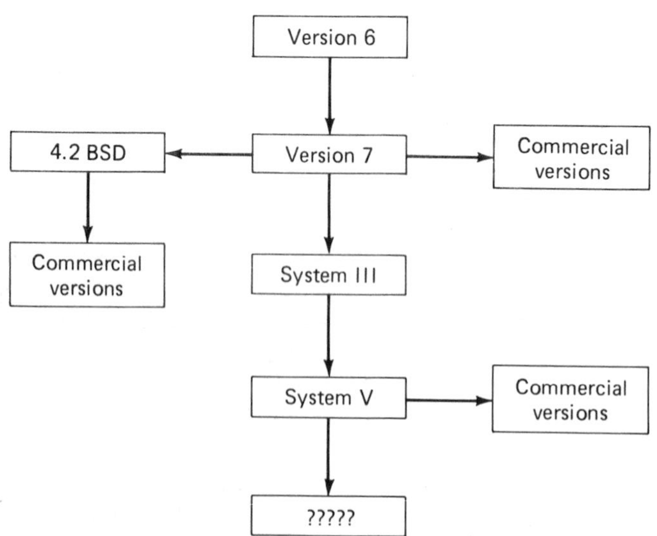

FIGURE 1.1. Approximate family tree of Unix systems.

the unwary: one look-alike system not derived from any version of Unix has chosen to call itself Version 4.2. *Caveat emptor!*

Through a Glass Darkly

Will the Unix operating system prove sufficiently long-lived and sufficiently universal to merit study and practice? No one can tell for sure, but since Unix installations now number in the millions the answer may already be yes. This system is no longer new; it has been seasoned by more than a decade of development, through several stages, and has settled down. There is an American national standard (and quite possibly an ISO standard) in prospect. The future of Unix systems in the 1980s and 1990s may well resemble that of the Fortran language in the 1960s and 1970s. Both Unix and Fortran were initially developed with particular computer systems in mind but quickly outgrew their original hosts. Both suffer from structural and logical deficiencies, which seemed minor or unimportant at the outset but became irksome after the first decade. Both have had to put up with numerous well-meant but nonstandard and standard-destroying improvements. Both seem better suited to their tasks (warts and all) than any currently available competitor. Both may therefore live on long after better languages and more portable systems become available—like the English language, with its constrictive syntax, underhandedly difficult grammar, incomprehensible spelling,... and two or three billion people who continue to use it simply because they all understand it.

Getting Acquainted with Unix

The Unix system is not hard to learn and fairly easy to get used to. Until serious commercial distribution began in the early 1980s, however, beginning users experienced some difficulty because most members of the then existing user community were in fact system programmers and system modifiers, sometimes unable to grasp that there actually could be people who just wanted to use Unix, not to improve it. That day, however, has passed. Concerns for the intending Unix user today are a bit different: they include choosing some reading material to get started with and learning to live with the idiosyncrasies of the system.

Things to Read

Until about 1982-1983, little reading material was available to provide a simple introduction to the Unix operating system. Most beginners were expected to cut their teeth on photocopies of the admittedly excellent brief articles that survey the system characteristics—and by perusal of the *Unix Programmer's Manual,* which resembles the telephone directory of a major city. Indeed, it is the definitive work, but hardly easy for the beginner.

With the growing popularity of Unix systems, a substantial number of textbooks and descriptions of a tutorial nature have appeared. These tend to be a good deal more readable than the full manual and should constitute the major reference point for the beginner. Others treat specialized topics within Unix, like system management, text editing, or systems programming. A bibliography listing most of these, annotated to give some idea of their contents, appears at the end of this book.

The *Unix Programmer's Manual* is the defining document of the system. It is normally furnished both as paper copy and in machine-readable form. Provision is made in Unix systems for keeping much of the user documentation available as disk files, so that users can read particular portions of the manual without having access to a printed copy or without even needing one. Keeping the system manuals in computer-readable form, and therefore easy to modify, is vital for most Unix installations, for there are probably no two installations exactly alike. While every system manager strives to keep documentation current, in many places no up-to-date paper manual exists; the disk-file version is the only true version.

Typographic and Lexical Curios

The words used in Unix system commands, the ways words are abbreviated, and occasionally the ways they are spelled are a bit idiosyncratic. Presumably, this is the result of having been developed initially within a circle of friends prepared to put up with each other's foibles. Some users take to the strange habits of Unix like a duck takes to water; others show enthusiasm more appropriate to a cat. There is no choice; Unix commands come the way they come.

Lowercase letters are used almost exclusively in Unix system commands, naming conventions, and programming languages. Although they are comparatively rare, exceptions do exist where uppercase characters are used instead. Thus, it is not simply a matter of using lower case instead of upper; both are used, but for some reason capital letters occur much less frequently than they do in English. A particularly irksome idiosyncrasy to some is the failure to use initial capitals even where the conventions of English demand it. The author, for example, will probably never grow completely accustomed to identifying himself to the system as *peter,* without a capital *P*.

The almost, but not quite, total use of lower case causes certain problems when documentation is written in natural languages. For example, the Unix text editor program is called **vi,** and the phototypesetter program has the name **troff.** (Not unreasonably, some users would have preferred mnemonically more useful names, e.g., *Editor* and *Phototype*.) They are never called *Vi* and *Troff*, because the system regards the letters *V* and *v* as simply two different, unrelated, characters. But what should one do when a sentence begins "**troff** is a program for. . ."? In this book, the Unix program naming convention is followed strictly: program names exist in one case only, so that names in lower case do not acquire initial capitals even if they occur at the beginnings of sentences. Much Unix system literature, occasionally even including the system manuals, is somewhat inconsistent (and confusing) about this point of usage.

Word usage in the Unix system shows up curious details rooted in history and often difficult for the newcomer. For example, the word "print" is used almost everywhere in the manuals to imply that output is to be sent to the user terminal. That verb may have been accurate at some past time, but today few users employ printing terminals; display screens are much more common. (The verb "print" to most computer users implies use of a line printer, not the user terminal.) As another example, the verbs "move" and "remove", when referring to files, are employed to mean "rename" and "delete". The reference here is to the software technique employed: deletion is achieved by removing a linking pointer.

Using This Book

The best way of learning to use an operating system is to use it. To allow the beginner to learn in this natural way, the first (short) part of this book contains an introduction to the system and its use, in brief and simple form. It is sufficiently concise to be usable while sitting at the terminal, trying out the commands. The main part of this book is longer. It is intended for reading away from the terminal and for reference; it therefore consists of a few explanatory chapters, followed by a summary description of the more important system commands.

Chapter 2

Getting Started

The Unix operating system is generally considered reasonably easy to learn and quite easy to use. But even the easiest operating system takes a little getting used to, especially at the very start when nothing looks even remotely familiar and every response from the system appears vaguely ominous—if indeed the system responds at all! Most computer users dislike the first hour or so spent with a new operating system, when the initial difficulties of a new command language, new name conventions, and new protocol rules all appear together. This chapter is intended to provide a launching pad for the novice user and to help overcome the problems of that first hour. It is brief enough to be read at the terminal, trying out the various commands on the spot. Or it can be read at another time and place, in preparation for that first hour.

Communicating with the System

Several users can be logged in to the same computer at the same time under a Unix time-sharing operating system. Learning to use Unix therefore begins with becoming an authorized system user, then acquiring familiarity with the procedures for communication with the system. Procedures and practices for doing so are described very briefly in this chapter, by way of a rapid introduction and overview. Details then follow elsewhere.

The System Manager

To keep track of users and their needs, every Unix system has a human *system manager*. In large computing centers, the system manager may well consist of a whole office establishment with receptionists and secretaries to cater to the needs of milling thousands. In small installations, an experienced user is often conscripted to fill this role. The choice generally falls on someone who happens to be particularly knowledgeable about the system and who is prepared to undertake the bureaucratic chores of management willingly. Whoever he may be, this individual authorizes users, issues passwords and user group affiliations, creates file directories, and takes care of all the other administrative needs that always arise when numerous people attempt to share the same computer. The intending user's first requirement is therefore a visit to the system manager, not only to obtain the necessary authorizations but also to obtain a briefing on the social customs of the establishment.

Although the official functions of the system manager form the most visible point of contact for the new user, the manager also has various duties of a more technical nature. An important one is system backup, a detail even neophyte users ought to know about early along. Computers do malfunction from time to time, so in most installations the manager, as part of everyday housekeeping routines, makes a complete copy of everything in the system at regular intervals. If machine problems, power outages, software failures, or other forms of disaster should strike, the system can be restarted and all files restored as they were at the time of the last backup. Who does the backing up? and how often? are questions to be asked of the system manager; how reliably they are done might be better asked of some other users.

User Names and Passwords

The Unix system manager issues every user a *login name* (also called the *user id*) and (on most systems) a password. The login name is just a name in the ordinary sense of the word, except for being limited in length (usually to eight characters). In many installations, it is actually the user's real name; in any case, it is publicly known. The password, on the other hand, is only known to the user and can be changed by the user himself at any time so as to maintain confidentiality. System managers often assign new users a blank password (i.e., no password at all) or a string of nonsense characters like zyS3qP, in the expectation that the user's first action on the system will be to change to a more easily remembered password. Passwords really are secret; even the system manager cannot find out what the user's current password is. Like all other password-based security systems, Unix presents the user with an irresolvable dilemma: it seems desirable to write down the password in lots of accessible places (to avoid forgetting it), yet it is undesirable to have it written down at all (to keep it secret).

Users of Unix systems can communicate with each other over the system through various message-passing techniques, described later in this book. The user login name serves as the address for all communications. Wherever there is any choice of login name, as there is in most installations, it pays to use a name that almost everybody else can understand and remember. Just the opposite holds for passwords: it is not a good idea to employ easily guessed items like birthdate, telephone number, or spouse's first name.

Passwords and user login names may make use of both uppercase and lowercase characters. Here, as elsewhere in the Unix system, lowercase characters are considered to be totally distinct from their uppercase brothers; Unix has no idea at all that there is any relationship between the letters X and x. The user passwords *Butch* and *butch* are therefore different and will not be taken as substitutes for one another. Some Unix systems do not believe in uppercase characters in user names and everything is done in lower case only. In any case, the uppers/lowers distinction must be observed carefully in all login names and passwords and indeed everywhere throughout the Unix system.

In many Unix installations, the system manager also assigns a user group affiliation to each user. User groups are generally just what the word implies: groups of people associated in common goals or common administrative frameworks. In industrial programming environments, groups are usually people working on the same projects. In an educational setting, a user group might be all the students in a particular course. Broadly speaking, groups are people needing access to a common pool of files.

Logging In

When a Unix system is started up, all the terminals connected to it display a *login prompt* and wait for users to log in. The prompt is displayed at the left margin of the terminal. It may take different forms in different systems, sometimes even including a message for the day or recent system news. In the simplest version, it consists of the request

```
login:
```

To log in, a valid user name is typed, all lowercase in most systems (it does look strange, but it works), followed by a carriage return. The system will then ask for the password, which is typed exactly as agreed with the system manager—in upper or lower case, or a mixture—again followed by a carriage return. On most terminals, the password will refuse to show on the screen or paper, to guard its secrecy, but it will be received by the system all the same. If the password is correct, the login attempt is accepted and the user's terminal is permitted access to the system itself. If the password is not correct, or the user name is not valid, access to the system is refused. Unix does not tell the user whether it objected to the password or the login name; it merely refuses.

Once the login procedure is complete, Unix signals the user that it is ready to accept commands, by placing a brief message called the *shell prompt* at the left margin. (Its strange name comes about because the program that actually sends out this character is called *shell*). The shell prompt, which often consists of just a single character, can be changed easily and therefore varies from installation to installation. In most systems, users can even adopt individual shell prompts. Historically, the dollar sign $ has been commonly used and the percent sign % is another popular choice. In this book, the dollar sign is used, except where it is necessary to distinguish between two different situations.

Many system managers like to have messages of general interest broadcast as part of the login procedure. Such messages follow validation of the user password and precede the first shell prompt.

Logging Out

Logging out is probably the most important single activity in learning to use a new operating system—just as the beginning pilot must master landing at an early time. Most operating system designers have tried to make the task easy by providing a command such as "bye" or "exit". Not so Unix!

Logging out of most Unix systems is done by typing control-D in response to the shell prompt, i.e., by striking the D key while holding down the CONTROL key on the terminal. Like the SHIFT key, the CONTROL key by itself does nothing; it only modifies the behavior of other keys. Control-D is usually written as ^D or ↑ D in books on Unix; it normally does not echo on the terminal screen as anything at all. Although some systems may send out a brief message to indicate disconnection, the usual response to control-D is simply

```
login:
```

showing that the system has disconnected itself, is not talking to anybody, but is prepared to initiate a new login sequence.

The idiosyncratic and unexpected logout procedure of Unix may seem irrational at first glance, but it makes sense after a certain fashion. The control-D character (ASCII octal 004) is employed almost everywhere in Unix software as an end-of-transmission mark. Many utility programs that expect input from the keyboard use ^D in this way. Consistent with this usage, a control-D sent from the terminal is taken to mean "end of transmission from the keyboard"—in other words, "good-bye". Despite its consistency with the rest of Unix, this scheme has two unfortunate flaws. First, some users find it all a little strange and certainly not easy to remember. Second, most modern terminals are equipped with a feature called auto-repeat, meaning that they will keep sending the same character over and over again as long as a key remains pressed. Slight carelessness with the keyboard can therefore result in sending not just one control-D but several, so the user intending only to leave a utility program may suddenly and unexpectedly end up logged out as well!

A note to the unwary: There do exist a few Unix systems which accept control-Z instead of control-D as the end-of-activity marker. All the above comments still apply, since control-Z is used for everything in such cases.

Because the control-D logout procedure is hardly obvious and can be a nuisance, one popular category of Unix installations provides a logout command, called simply "logout". There are also some mavericks which use "off", "goodbye", "arrivederci",. . . or whatever the imagination of the local programming support staff dictates. Attempts to log out using control-D are then usually refused.

Whether logging out is done by a single control-D or by a logout command, escaping from individual Unix programs is normally effected by typing control-D or DELETE. The control-D keystroke signals that no more keyboard input will be sent, a clear signal to most programs that activity should continue to completion. The DELETE keystroke, on the other hand, is an emergency brake: it stops anything and stops it immediately, without enquiring about possible consequences. Beginning users sometimes experience the dreadful situation of getting mired in a program, unable to escape and unable to log out. Under Unix, a DELETE keystroke, perhaps interspersed with a few control-Ds, ought to do the trick in a hurry.

The Terminal

One striking and unusual fact about Unix commands is that Unix insists on working with lowercase characters even where the normal conventions of English clearly demand capitals (e.g., user names, initial words of command sentences). However, uppercase characters are used in some cases. A terminal capable of using lower as well as upper case is therefore essential. Some versions of Unix do provide for automatic character conversion from upper to lower case, so that capitals-only terminals can be used; but these are messy at best. Anyhow, there are not many modern terminals incapable of handling lowercase characters!

Practically every terminal is equipped with a whole row of little switches somewhere. These switches set the various terminal characteristics: communication speed (baud rate), full/half duplex communication, upper/lower case, treatment of line terminators, tab characters, and a host of other matters. Of course, the switches must be set up in precisely the way the system expects. If they are not, logging in may be impossible or may result in incomprehensible strings of apparently random characters on the screen. Because there are many types of terminal and many variations on the acceptable switch settings for each, it is almost impossible to give any firm rules—except that if the terminal is used only for communicating with the Unix system, it is likely to be set up correctly and to remain so, since nobody has an interest in altering the switch settings. Problems ordinarily arise only in computer installations where the same terminal is used with several different operating systems.

Sometimes it happens that resetting the terminal switches has no effect at all. In most new, modern, microprocessor-controlled terminals, the switches do not control any electronic circuits directly; instead, the microprocessor reads the switch settings when it is first turned on and then controls all terminal functions in accordance with the switch settings as they were at the time they were read. Changing switch settings alters nothing unless the microprocessor is forced to read the switch settings again. The easiest way of doing so is to turn the terminal power off and on again after a few seconds, whenever any switch setting is altered.

The Unix internal software maintains a record of the characteristics of each terminal, a record which can be changed by users and in some circumstances by programs. Obviously, the characteristics that the system has on record must correspond to the actual nature of the terminal. If a terminal refuses to log in, then either the terminal switches are set wrong or the operating system records are wrong. Sending a control-D or two should reset the internal system records and allow logging in to proceed; switch-twiddling should only be resorted to in extreme cases.

Typing at the Keyboard

Characters entered at the keyboard are not immediately acted upon; they are merely stored until a carriage return is typed (with the RETURN key) to signify termination of the line. The Unix system only attempts to read and understand a keyboard line once it has been terminated. This allows typing mistakes to be corrected on the spot.

If a wrong character is typed at the keyboard, it can be corrected with the BACKSPACE key, which works in the obvious way on screen-type terminals. But when printing terminals are used, there is no way of erasing a character once it has been printed. When such terminals are used, a character is considered to have been erased if it is followed by a special character, the *erase character*. Usually, the # character is employed for this purpose. When decoding, any character will be ignored if it is immediately followed by the erase character. Thus `la#of#gim#n` is interpreted as `login`, the characters `a`, `f`, and `m` having been "erased" by the `#` sign. Similarly, a *kill character*, usually but not always `@`, is used to "kill" everything typed since the beginning of the line, so that `kif@login` is interpreted as `login`. If either of the characters `#` or `@` is actually wanted as part of a line, it must be preceded by the backslash character `\` to avoid erasure. In other words, `A\#B` is decoded as `A#B`, not `AB`.

Because typed characters are not decoded on the spot but merely stored for decoding when a carriage return is sent, it is both possible and permissible to "type ahead", that is, to keep typing even though the screen echo of the typed characters does not keep up. (It will come eventually.) But this practice is not generally to be encouraged, because typing without an immediate screen echo can leave typing errors unnoticed, with possible unexpected consequences to come!

Like many other computer operating systems, Unix employs all the printable ordinary keyboard characters, as well as a set of control characters which are not printable. The latter are formed by striking the appropriate key while holding down the CONTROL key. (One such, the control-D character used for terminating activity, has already been discussed.) The CONTROL key works much like the SHIFT key, that is, it alters the meanings of the other keys. Simply striking the CONTROL key by itself produces nothing whatever, just like striking the SHIFT key. Consequently, it is normal to press and hold down the CONTROL or SHIFT key, as appropriate, before striking the character key required. Control characters are unprintable, that is, there is no printed character that corresponds to the internal computer representation of any control character. When it is desired to indicate a control character in print, the character is shown preceded by a caret (as in ^D) or an upward arrow (as in ↑ D); alternatively, one writes "control-D" or "ctrl-D". The most commonly used control characters are probably control-D, which generally denotes an end-of-activity and therefore also serves for logging out; control-S, which allows terminal display to be halted temporarily; and control-Q, which allows terminal display to continue after being halted by control-S.

Running the System

All actions which the Unix operating system is able to perform are requested by the user through the Unix command language, which is both rich and flexible. The Unix system provides the user with an unusually wide variety of utilities—text editors, language translators, file management tools, and much else. These tools, like actions by the system itself, are also controlled by keyboard commands.

Commands

When the shell prompt is displayed at the left screen edge, the Unix command decoder is awaiting instructions. Nearly all Unix commands are actually requests to run particular programs. For example, the command

```
$ who
```

causes the system to find the program named **who** and to execute it. (This particular program looks in the system tables to find out which users are logged in at which terminals and displays their particulars on the terminal screen.) When execution is complete, the shell prompt is displayed again to show that another command is expected. Execution of any program may be stopped by pressing the DELETE key (sometimes labelled RUBOUT) on the terminal, so errors in typing need not be disasters. The DELETE key is one of a select few whose effect is immediate, i.e., it is not necessary to send a carriage return for it to take effect.

There is nothing particularly magic about Unix commands, for the set of commands can be extended at any time simply by adding more programs capable of being executed. The standard system-provided set of commands totals well over 100 in small Unix systems and easily reaches several hundred in large ones. Those most likely to be of immediate interest to beginning users are

cat	concatenate files and display on screen
cp	copy contents of one file to another
date	display correct date and time
f77	run the Fortran 77 compiler
lpr	queue files for sending to line printer
ls	list the contents of a directory
mkdir	make a new directory
mv	move (rename) a file
nroff	run the nroff text formatter
passwd	change the login password
rm	remove (delete) a file
tty	display the terminal name
vi	run the full-screen editor
who	display who is logged in to the system

Many of the commands listed above have to be augmented by file specifications. For example, to move a file to another name with **mv**, it is (reasonably enough) necessary to specify which file, and what its new name is to be. Other commands permit (or require) additional qualifiers to specify how and where the desired action is to be taken. In other words, the commands are really command verbs and may need to be augmented by other words so as to form coherent sentences. Some informal illustrations will be found in the examples below. More or less complete descriptions of the above commands, and quite a few others, will be found in a later chapter. Full details on each command appear in the *Unix Programmer's Manual* or in the system manuals available at each installation.

Any user can add more commands easily, since no distinction is made between a command and an executable program. Every command corresponds to an executable program and the name of every executable program is automatically a command, simply by virtue of being there. In fact, the only way of executing a program under the Unix system is to type its name, as a command, when the shell prompt shows. There is just one significant distinction between user-added commands and those supplied by the system: programs added by a user are ordinarily accessible to that user and that user only, inaccessible to other users unless special arrangements are made. System commands, on the other hand, are always equally available to everybody.

What happens if the user, not knowing any better, introduces a new program with the same name as an existing system command? No serious interference results, for the system always searches for the command first in the user's own directory of programs. Only if the command is not found in the user's directory does the system search elsewhere. Thus the duplication of a name already in use as a system command causes only one inconvenience: the system command becomes unavailable. It might be expected, however, that users who unwittingly use names of system commands are unlikely to want or need those commands in any case!

Because new commands are easily added and existing commands can be modified almost as easily, there are probably no two Unix installations with precisely the same set of available commands and precisely the same usage of the existing commands. This great flexibility allows tailoring every computer system to serve its user community to best advantage. Yet flexibility can also confuse users, because every Unix system seems forever fluid, forever almost as the manual describes it, but never exactly like that. There is no known cure for this ailment; all one can do is watch for unexpected behavior and to enquire whether it arises from a recent local system modification.

Files and File Names

The Unix operating system is designed to process files, so it regards practically every assemblage of information as a file, no matter what its physical form or storage medium. The formal definition of a file is about as simple as it could be: a file is a string of characters. Often enough, it is desirable to organize a Unix file as a set of "lines". This form of file subdivision is accepted as perfectly reasonable; indeed many Unix utility programs expect files to be collections of lines, every one terminated by a *newline* character which is generated at the keyboard by pressing the RETURN key. However, such a subdivision is a matter of convenience; there is no requirement for a file to have any particular internal structure.

Files are identified by file names and are kept track of by recording their names in file directories. Every user is allocated a personal file directory when his login name and password are authorized. Although there may be many files belonging to many users on the system, the allocation of a separate directory to each user means that he can ordinarily work in a universe of files which includes (1) those he created himself and (2) those supplied by the system, as system commands. No user need ever be aware of the names, or even of the existence, of any other users' files. Only rarely will there be any interference between files listed in directories belonging to different users. On logging in, a user gains full access automatically to all the files listed in his own directory, and only to those files, unless some special arrangements are made. A listing of all files in this directory is always available by means of the **ls** command.

File names may contain up to 14 characters. The characters may include almost anything printable, the blank character being a notable exception. Even the erase and kill characters are acceptable. For example, it is perfectly proper to use `file#27` as a file name. However, if a printing terminal is used, the # character may be understood to denote an erasure. Thus, it is usually wise to name files using only lowercase letters and numerals, because several of the special characters and punctuation marks have peculiar special uses that may cause grief.

The period (the . character) is usable and permissible within file names and causes no unexpected bad effects. It is used by many experienced programmers, and by many system-provided programs, to differentiate between related files. For example, the Unix Fortran compiler expects Fortran source file names to end in `.f`, as in `program.f`; it produces output files with the same names but substitutes `.o` for `.f` at the end. Thus `program.o` would be the compiled (object code) version of `program.f`. It must be emphasized, however, that characters preceding and following the period do not have any special significance to the Unix system, even though some programs (some provided with the system, as well as those created by the user) may attach particular meanings to them. In contrast to some other popular operating systems, file names are not divided into two parts separated by a period, with the two parts treated separately. The period is simply another character, as far as the Unix system itself is concerned, and several may well be included in a file name, as, for example, `file....a.y`.

File names occur in command sentences frequently. For example, suppose it is desired to remove file `program.o`. ("Removal" means that the file name is removed from the directory and the file space is released for reuse; in other words, the file is deleted.) To do so, the command

```
$ rm program.o
```

is typed in response to the shell prompt. Most other Unix command sentences are constructed in an analogous fashion. Some actions, of course, will require more than one file name to be specified. As an example of a command with two file references, consider the **mv** ("move") command, which moves a file from one name to another (i.e., it renames the file). Entering

```
$ mv a.out program.x
```

"moves" the file around in a directory, by reassigning its name from a.out to program.x.

Wild-Card File Names

File name references may be unique, or they may use wild-card characters, that is, characters understood to stand for several others. Wild cards are convenient and useful when several files with similar names must be referred to. For example, suppose it is desired to remove a whole set of files, whose names are all of the form problemfile.... One may issue a string of commands

```
$ rm problemfile01
$ rm problemfile02
$ rm problemfile03
```

and so on, but it is easier to type

```
$ rm problemfile*
```

The * character in file references is understood to mean "any and every string of characters". In other words, every file whose name begins problemfile and terminates in any characters whatever (or indeed none) will be removed by the above command. Similarly, the command line

```
$ rm *fil*
```

will remove all files whose names contain the character string fil anywhere—with anything at all, or even nothing, preceding and following. In effect, the * character in a file reference means "any, or no, characters". In a similar way, the question mark ? can be used as a wild card standing for a single character. The difference between * and ? is that the former stands for a character string of any length, while the latter signifies one and exactly one character. For example, ?fil? denotes any file name containing exactly five characters, the middle three of which are fil.

A Session at the Terminal

The foregoing explanations and examples should suffice to permit even a rank novice to try out a Unix system. The timid may wish to try the sample terminal sessions shown here by following them through step by step; the intrepid may prefer to rush in and attempt something more imaginative. The first example, shown in Figure 2.1, is very simple.

Several interesting points emerge in the session of Figure 2.1. To begin, the login prompt (which asks for the user name and password) displays a message identifying the computer system, then asks the user to log in. The user's login name is restricted to eight characters, of which the first must be a lowercase letter; this rule causes a bit of pain for those with long surnames! The password is not echoed on the screen, of course; the user can tell that it has been accepted because the shell prompt % appears next. The actions which follow in this session are typical of any terminal session and require little comment. The logout process, however, is noteworthy; the user enters ↑D at the terminal, which the system echoes as *logout,* not ^D, and the cycle begins over again with a new login message.

It may be of interest to examine the same, or rather a very similar, session carried out on a larger Unix system. The terminal conversation runs as shown in Figure 2.2. Here the login process is enriched by the inclusion of a message-of-the-day from the system manager. The **who** enquiry yields a larger haul of users than in the small system example but is otherwise similar. The commands and operations do not differ markedly, except that the shell prompt is different ($ instead of %) and that the attempt to log out by typing ↑D fails. However, there is little confusion because

```
McEEucl - Simian system with Unix V7

login: peter
Password:

% who
rcs       console Feb 10 11:01
peter tty7     Feb 10 16:11
% date
Mon Feb 10 16:11:46 EST 1986
% ls
helloprog.f
% cat helloprog.f
      write (6,100)
  100 format (" Hello!")
      stop
      end
% logout

McEEucl - Simian system with Unix V7

login:
```

System identifies itself,
asks for login name and password.
Note % shell prompt:
Who is logged in right now?
(just we two)
What is the right time and date?
List my files!
(there's just one)
Display it on the terminal screen
(it's a Fortran program)
Logout with ^D echoed as "logout"
System identifies itself,
asks for login name.

FIGURE 2.1. Brief terminal session on a small Unix system.

```
4.2 BSD UNIX (VLSI Lab)                          System identifies
                                                   itself,
login: peter                                     asks for login name
Password:                                          and password.
Last login: Mon Feb 10 10:52:31 on tty00         Login accepted!

*******************************************
  System shutdown today at 2300 hours.           Message of the day.
*******************************************

$ who                                            Who is logged in
peter    tty00  Feb 10 16:16                       right now?
michael  tty01  Feb 10 14:32
nora     tty02  Feb 10 14:19
boss     tty03  Feb 10 09:29
cleo     tty05  Feb 10 15:15
benny    ttyh3  Feb 10 15:14
wurzel   ttyh4  Feb 10 16:06
adler    ttyh8  Feb 10 15:21
$ date                                           What is the right
Mon Feb 10 16:19:48 EST 1986                       time and date?
$ ls                                             List my files!
helloprog.f                                        (there's just one)
$ mv helloprog.f hello.f                         Change its name
$ ls                                               then list again
hello.f                                            (OK, new name)
$ cat hello.f                                    Display it on the
      write (6,100)                                terminal screen
  100 format ("Hello!")
      stop
      end
$ ^D                                             Logout with ^D
Use "logout" to logout.                            not accepted
$ logout
4.2 BSD UNIX (VLSI Lab)                          System identifies
                                                   itself,
login:                                           asks for login name
```

FIGURE 2.2. Terminal session similar to that of Figure 2.1, but on a larger Unix system with more users.

the refusal to log out is accompanied by a clear instruction to show what the proper logout procedure is.

Writing and Running Programs

Development of applications programs is a truly common activity of computer users. Development work generally begins with the design and initial writing of a program, followed by testing and gradual correction of errors. Typically, this kind of work requires repeated program compilation and trial execution, interspersed with editing sessions to eliminate from the source file whatever errors turned up.

Program development requires at least two distinct facilities: a language compiler and loader for running the program and a text editor to permit preparation and correction of source programs. The Unix family of operating systems provides compilers for several computer languages, several text editors, and a host of advanced debugging aids for serious programmers.

Running Fortran Programs

The full Fortran 77 language and several other programming languages are supported by Unix systems. To illustrate how Fortran programs are tested and executed, suppose the file `mainprogram.f` contains a source program in the usual form. The command

```
$ f77 mainprogram.f
```

causes the Fortran 77 compiler to be run. The compiler translates the source program into the corresponding object program, which is left in file `mainprogram.o`. Because users most often wish to link the compiled object program with library modules and to execute it, the Fortran 77 compiler is automatically followed up by the linking loader, unless instructed otherwise. The loader assigns memory locations to the program and performs other housekeeping tasks that permit the program to be actually run. Loader output is always placed in a file named **a.out**. Any previous contents of **a.out** will be destroyed, so that if it is desired to save the executable object module for the long run, it should be moved to another name:

```
$ mv a.out mainprogram.x
```

Next, it is desired to execute the program. In Unix systems there is no distinction between commands and executable program modules, so that to execute the program it suffices to issue its own name as a command:

```
$ mainprogram.x
```

The Fortran program should now run and produce whatever output it might. When its execution has terminated, the shell prompt will again appear to signify readiness for further commands. To check what files have been generated in the process, the **ls** command may be issued; it produces on the terminal screen a listing of the files currently listed in the user's directory.

If compilation had been wanted without linking—as often happens when subroutines are developed and compiled individually—the additional argument `-c` would be included in the request to compile, signifying "compile only":

```
$ f77 -c mainprogram.f
```

Other program modules, such as subroutines developed separately, may then be combined with the compiled program by asking for the linking loader **ld** explicitly:

```
$ ld mainprogram.o subprogram.o
```

The system will respond by running the linkage editor (linking loader), again producing an executable output file called **a.out**. All files named in the command will be linked, together with any system library components that may be necessary. Execution, perhaps moving of the file to a more memorable name, and examination of output then follow as above.

The **vi** Text Editor

Preparation of text such as source programs is generally done using the text editor **vi**. This editor manipulates text stored in files by reading the file content into a text buffer (an area of computer memory), manipulating it in accordance with user commands, then rewriting it into the file. **vi** is a line-oriented editor which works much like word processing programs: it regards text as being composed of lines, each of which is made up of characters. This line-oriented approach makes **vi** well suited to preparing computer programs. Of course, **vi** knows nothing of the programs or programming languages; it only handles lines composed of characters. It is therefore not restricted to program preparation and is often used for other textual matter as well.

The **vi** editor is invoked by a simple command. In response to the shell prompt, one types (and follows with a carriage return)

```
$ vi filename
```

where `filename` is the name of the file to be edited. The editor responds by reading the file and displaying the first screenful of it. If the file is being newly created, there are of course no characters in it. In that case, **vi** does its best in these trying circumstances, by showing a screenful of empty lines, each with a tilde ~ at the left margin. The file name appears at the bottom of the screen, in the last line which is generally reserved for messages rather than text. **vi** then awaits commands.

All operations of the **vi** editor are controlled by keyboard commands.

Commands generally consist of single letters, though these short forms are often augmented by some additional information. Editor commands are expected and understood by **vi**, not by the shell, so that their form is totally different from shell commands. When ready to accept commands, **vi** does not issue a prompt, but simply waits patiently. If there is serious question about whether **vi** is listening, or something bad has happened, one possible action is to type an ESCAPE or two. The ESCAPE keystroke is understood by **vi** as a request to drop everything and listen for commands. If already in the proper mode for accepting commands, **vi** says so by tinkling the terminal bell. Two or more ESCAPEs should therefore produce a reassuring little noise.

If alterations to a file are desired, the file is fetched and opened for editing just as a new file would; the only difference is that the screen will not show blank lines but the first screenful of text. When alterations have been completed, the changed text must be written back to a file. To write out the text and exit from **vi**, the ZZ command (one of the few made up of more than just a single character) is used:

```
ZZ
```

This command replaces the file content with whatever was there previously. Until the ZZ command is issued, the altered file resides only in the editing buffer, an area of computer memory employed as a temporary scratchpad area, as it were; the original copy of the file is still in the archival file store and can be resurrected if necessary. Once the ZZ command is accepted, however, the old version of the file is destroyed and replaced by the edited version. While doing the replacement operation, **vi** shows the number of lines and characters in the new version.

When the editing session is finished with a ZZ command, **vi** stops running and the shell prompt appears again, to signify that the Unix system itself (rather than **vi**) is awaiting further instructions.

Creating and Modifying Text

There exist various ways for **vi** to modify text. But curiously, there is no explicit facility for creating text in the first place. When a new file is started, **vi** assigns it its name and immediately considers it to be a perfectly normal and proper text file, one that just happens to contain zero characters of text. These zero characters are displayed on the screen. Despite its meager content, the file is formally valid and may be modified. Of course, the only modification that makes any sense at this point is the insertion of additional characters. In other words, the only new file that can be created is an empty file, all further operations being regarded as merely modifications of an existing file.

Most of the editing operations using **vi** refer to positions in the text identified by the editing cursor, in a way similar to most office word processors. The cursor is a mark attached to one character in the text; it can be moved by the user and serves as a pointing tool to say, in effect, "this one here". The precise nature of the cursor is dependent on the terminal type; blinking underscores and highlighted characters are often used. For example, text insertion is performed at the cursor location, characters to be deleted are identified by pointing at them with the cursor, and so on.

Text can be entered into the workspace (usually called the text buffer) of **vi** with the `i` command ("insert"). Typing the single character `i` warns **vi** that the characters to follow are to be taken literally and placed into the text buffer: they are not to be understood as commands. The string of text continues on and on, until an ESCAPE character is encountered; vi takes the ESCAPE to signify the end of the text to be inserted. To insert the word *write* in the text buffer, one types

```
iwriteESC
```

where ESC denotes the ESCAPE keystroke. Similarly, to enter the small Fortran program shown earlier, one types

```
i       write (6,100)RET
   100 format (" Hello!")RET
        stopRET
        endRET
ESC
```

Here RET denotes the RETURN key. What shows on the screen is the program as it normally reads, for initial `i` and ESCAPE keystrokes do not give any visual echo, while the RETURN key echoes as a new line beginning, exactly as it would on a typewriter:

```
      write (6,100)
  100 format (" Hello!")
      stop
      end
```

The entire text need not be entered in one stream; it is perfectly all right to stop from time to time with an ESCAPE, then to resume insertion elsewhere. Insertion always takes place at the left-hand edge of the cursor, just ahead of the character over which the cursor is placed. Text can also be entered by using the a ("append") command. It works exactly like `i`, except that the new characters are placed at the right of the cursor character. The two commands act identically otherwise; both are needed because the `i` command cannot append at the end of a text line (beyond the rightmost character), while the a command cannot insert ahead of the leftmost character in the a line.

To move the cursor around, four keys suffice for the four compass directions. The cursor moving commands must be issued, of course, while **vi** is listening for commands, not while it is inserting text; if necessary, an ESCAPE character will get it to command mode. The four are

h	moves the cursor left one position
j	moves the cursor up one line
k	moves the cursor down one line
l	moves the cursor right one position

Some terminals actually have little arrows painted on these four keytops as a reminder, for there are software systems other than Unix which employ the same cursor motions.

When typing errors occur, correction can be effected by deleting the incorrect characters and inserting new ones. Deletion is effected by taking aim with the cursor, then issuing the command character x. Voilà, the character under the cursor disappears and its right-hand neighbors move over to fill the vacant space. If the deletion was wrong —or for that matter, if the last insertion contained a bad error—the last text alteration can always be undone with the command u. In fact, even the nasty effect of an erroneous u can be reversed with another u!

The a, i, x, u, ZZ commands and the h, j, k, l cursor movements actually suffice to prepare simple programs. However, **vi** can use much more sophisticated command forms and greater familiarity with it should be acquired at an early stage if any substantial program preparation is contemplated. A much more detailed description of **vi** will be found in a later chapter of this book.

	User types ^D to reset,
`login:  bftsplk`	responds to login,
`Password:`	gives password (blind!)
`$  ls`	Lists current catalogue;
`hello.f`	it contains one file.
`$  cat hello.f`	Displays it on screen:
`      write (6,100)`	it is the
`  100 format  ("Hello!")`	"hello" program
`      stop`	written in
`      end`	Fortran
`$  f77 hello.f`	Requests compilation:
`hello.f:`	compiler echoes name,
`   MAIN:`	compiles main program.
`$  ls`	Lists current catalogue;
`a.out   hello.f  hello.o`	two new files appear!
`$  mv a.out hello.x`	move (rename) a.out
`$  hello.x`	Executes "hello" program:
` Hello!`	it produces output.
`$  rm hello.o`	Removes intermediate file,
`$  ls`	lists catalogue again:
`hello.f  hello.x`	Fortran and executable.
`$`	User now logs out!

FIGURE 2.3. Working session involving program compilation.

Sample Terminal Session

It may be useful for the beginner to examine a sample terminal session and perhaps to try duplicating it under Unix, thereby acquiring some feel for how the system works and how it responds. The example of Figure 2.3, which follows on the editing example given earlier, may serve. Here once more the terminal conversation is printed at the left-hand margin; the right-hand column contains explanatory comments.

The program involved here is uncommonly short. Its extreme shortness may perhaps explain why it compiled and executed correctly the first time—something that even short programs rarely do! The terminal conversation, however, is precisely what would be involved in a more ambitious program. Even readers not very familiar with Fortran should find it easy to substitute equivalent programs in their own favorite languages.

Chapter 3

Files in the Unix System

An important function of any operating system is to house, safeguard, and manage various files. To be useful, files must be easy to store and easy to find again. To be practical, files must fit conveniently onto the available physical media. These requirements imply that the file system must have a logical structure that makes sense to users in terms of their needs and a physical structure chosen to suit the devices used for file storage.

The Unix System File Structure

The Unix system allows complex structures of files to be managed with ease. Its ease of use results mainly from separating the physical organization of files (their form of storage) from their logical organization, which deals with their content and purpose and therefore concerns the user directly.

There are three kinds of Unix files: ordinary files, special files, and directory files. Ordinary files are what most people think of when they use the word "files": programs, manuscripts, collections of data. Directories are just what their name implies, listings of files with information for the operating system about where and how to find them. Special files contain the rules for managing input-output devices so that most other

Unix programs need not concern themselves with such details as how the keyboard handles characters and where on the screen output is to be placed.

Ordinary Disk Files

Ordinary files are the type users are most often interested in. They include both the files created by users and the files that come as part of the Unix system itself; neither is accorded any distinctive privileges. The normal storage medium for Unix files is a magnetic disk, a random access medium to which files can be written and read back with equal ease. However, the structure of any Unix file is independent of the physical medium on which it is written; files on magnetic tape, for example, are laid out in the same fashion and contain the same characters as they would on a disk.

As far as the Unix system is concerned, an ordinary file is simply a string of bytes, stored on disk or on some other physical medium. There is no distinction between program files, data files, or any others; all files are merely strings of bytes. The bytes in the file may represent printable characters; in that case, the file is termed a *text* file. Characters stored in a text file do not have any particular significance to the system itself, though they presumably mean something to the user or to some particular programs. There is one exception to this general rule: when files are transmitted, the control-D character (in some maverick systems, control-Z) is employed as an end-of-transmission marker. Some confusion may arise when files containing such characters are transmitted between devices, so it is usually wise to avoid such privileged characters in text files.

No special form of internal organization is prescribed for an ordinary file. However, it is often convenient to subdivide text files into lines, separated from each other with the newline character (ASCII 012 octal). The lines need not be of any particular length so that a text file may quite properly consist of a single "line". Of course, individual programs may be quite fussy about the internal structure of files; for example, Fortran programs that read data usually expect specific data items to be located in predefined positions in the input line. But in such cases the structural requirements are imposed by the Fortran program, not by the Unix operating system.

While no particular logical structure is imposed on files, the physical structure of a file must be precisely defined—otherwise the operating system could not find files and could not know how to read them. Fortunately, most system users are never concerned with exactly how the reading and writing of files is actually carried out. They need only be aware of the internal logical structure of files and know the rules for naming files.

Special Files

One interesting peculiarity of the Unix operating system is that under Unix all input-output devices are made to look like files to the programmer; there is no distinction between writing to a file, writing to the screen, or writing characters into a telephone coupler for transmission elsewhere. Programs that transfer data to and from files can with equal ease transfer data to input-output devices. In fact, the programs themselves cannot even tell what their data sources and sinks are. For example, to print a file the system may be instructed to copy its contents into another file, called `/dev/lp`. The latter is a special file—special in the sense that the instruction to copy into it does not overwrite the original content of file `/dev/lp`, but causes the line printer to be activated. The special file itself contains the rules according to which characters are treated by the peripheral device. In other words, an attempt to copy into file `/dev/lp` does not result in its content being overwritten by a new character string, as would be the case if `/dev/lp` were an ordinary file. Instead, the Unix system identifies `/dev/lp` as being a special file and uses its contents as a rule book for determining what should be done with the characters copied (in this case, they are simply passed on to the line printer). Of course, the physical file `/dev/lp` must never actually be written into, otherwise the rule book will be destroyed!

Every input-output device on the system is associated with at least one special file. It could be associated with several, however. If a line printer is also to be used for graphic plotting, for instance, the plotting routines may conveniently be placed in a special file, say `/dev/lpplot`. Copying to this special file will then cause character strings to be interpreted in such a way as to produce graphic output; copying to `/dev/lp` will print out the characters themselves. Thus, the two special files appear to the programmer like two distinct output files, although only one physical device is actually in use.

Directories

Once a file has been written on the magnetic disk, a way must exist to find it again when required. Files are stored on disk in some convenient fashion, not necessarily in the order of their creation. They are made easy to find by name by creating an additional file called a directory, which shows where to find the individual files. Like a city directory, a file directory contains the file names and their physical addresses on the disk. Directories are files with a strictly prescribed internal structure, for they must be comprehensible to numerous system routines. However, there is no physical difference at all between a directory and any ordinary file. Every directory is itself a file, stored on disk like any other file.

To furnish a simple example, suppose a disk has room for 960 blocks

of 512 characters. At a particular moment, it contains the following layout of files:

Blocks	000–028	unused
	029–112	file, number 003
	113–219	file, number 002
	220–227	unused
	228–473	file, number 001
	474–478	unused
	479–480	file, number 004
	481–960	. . . other files . . .

The numbers assigned to the files are not related to the file contents in any way, but are assigned as needed. They can be made visible to users, if desired, but they rarely are, for few users consider them to have any value. Users always access files by their names. In fact, the main purpose of a directory is just precisely to keep track of which name corresponds to which index number, so that users may be spared the bother of knowing about index numbers. If file 004 in the present example is a directory, it might contain (among other things) the entries

```
datafile          001
matrixprogram     002
matrixoutput      003
.                 004
..                265
```

showing the correspondence between file names and index numbers. The user only ever refers to `matrixprogram`; the system itself will take care of looking in the directory, determining the index number, and finding out just where on the disk this program file is located. In addition, it will also determine whether the file is an ordinary file or not, whether the user has the right to access it, and a host of other administrative details.

The directory itself is listed as a directory entry, with the curious special name . (the dot, or period, character) assigned to it. It might seem pointless to list it, for the location of the directory itself must be known in order to consult the directory! However, the entry is conventionally included because it simplifies such system operations as calculating how much unused space is left on the disk. When users list the directory contents, which they normally do with the **ls** command, this special entry is suppressed to avoid clutter and confusion, unless the user specifically requests that it be made visible.

Directory Hierarchies

Since a directory is a file, it is readily possible to construct directories of directories. In fact, Unix assigns a personal directory to each user and lists that directory as an entry in a directory of user directories, which in its turn is listed as an entry in a system directory. (Fortunately, it really isn't quite so complicated as it first sounds.) In other words, each user's directory appears as a file when viewed from the system. The user in turn can create subdirectories which appear as entries in his own directory. The tip of this hierarchical pyramid is found in the *root* directory, which is maintained by the system. This directory structure is a great strength of Unix systems, for it implies that large numbers of users may create large numbers of files but still find them easily. Each user need only be aware of his own private universe of files and need not even know that any other users exist.

The Unix file directory structure always has the form of a tree, with the root directory at its root. That is, every directory must be listed in exactly one, and only one, predecessor directory. Such a relationship is illustrated in Figure 3.1. All files shown in this diagram are directories; to keep the picture simple, any ordinary files listed in them are not shown. By the tree structure rule, none of the directories listed as subdirectories under `jones` (`joe`, bob, `jim`) can appear as a subdirectory under `smith`; they are subdirectories under `jones` and a given directory may be listed in only one predecessor directory. However, there may exist another directory called `joe`, entered as a subdirectory under `smith`. The analogy with people's names is apt: the Jones family may have only one son named Joe, but there is nothing wrong with the Smith family also having a son named Joe. Despite the similarity of their names, the two Joes are altogether distinct individuals who have nothing to do with each other. Correspondingly, the two directories named `joe` are distinct and unrelated. The rule that directories must have a tree structure permits creating one subdirectory named `joe` under every single directory, if users so desire.

Two special entries appear in every directory as `.` (dot) and `..` (two dots). The first refers to the directory itself—it is a file, after all —while the second identifies the parent directory in the tree structure, i.e., the directory of which the present one is a subdirectory. (The root directory, which has no parent, is considered to be its own parent.) The **ls** directory listing command normally suppresses display of these entries. However, if the user wishes, an option exists to call for them to be shown.

The tree structure rule—every directory must be listed in exactly one

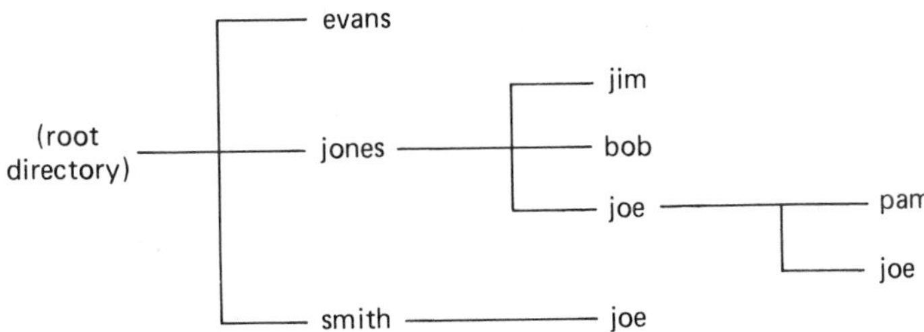

FIGURE 3.1. Hierarchical structure of a directory tree.

predecessor directory—prevents circular listings. Were it not for this rule, directory A could be a subdirectory of B, B a subdirectory of A. But this rule applies only to directories, not to ordinary files. In other words, an ordinary file may be listed in any number of directories while a directory must always be listed in one, and only one, predecessor directory. The ability to list an ordinary file in many directories means that it can be made available to many users. It can be exploited to allow many users to read a communal data file or to make use of a single copy of a program file. On the other hand, it can sometimes also create confusion if several users wish to write into the file at the same time!

File Names and Paths

Any file may be accessed by specifying the path to it through the directory tree. The path specification is the full and proper name of the file; it is known as the pathname of the file. It is the list of directory tree nodes which must be traversed to reach the desired file. Successive tree nodes (i.e., subdirectories) are separated by the slant character (also called a *slash* or *oblique stroke*) so that a typical file reference takes the form

```
direc1/direc2/direc3/.../name
```

Here name is the desired ordinary file and `direc1` must be a directory file currently accessible, that is, a subdirectory listed within the user's current directory. Files not listed in some subdirectory of the current user directory can be sought out by beginning the path at the root directory. The root directory is the only directory not to have a name, so that the path

```
/jones/joe/pam
```

will be interpreted as beginning at the root: no name, followed by the / delimiter, is taken as specifying the unnamed, i.e., the root, directory as the start. In contrast,

```
jones/joe/pam
```

causes a search to start at the current user directory. If `jones` is not a subdirectory of the current user directory, the search will fail.

To state the matter in slightly different words, every Unix file is uniquely defined by specifying the path from the root directory to the file. But since the path is always downward through the structure, the rules permit the user to omit, as a matter of convenience, all those portions of the path which lie above the current directory. Thus

```
/usr/jones/joe/pam
```

would be a full specification of a file, valid in all circumstances, but

```
joe/pam
```

is its proper and complete specification, if the current directory happens to be `/usr/jones`. Because `.` used as a file name always refers to the current directory,

```
./joe/pam
```

would be equally acceptable and would produce the same result.

Extensions and Suffixes

File names under Unix are simply character strings; the system does not classify files by any feature of the file name. This contrasts with various other operating systems in which data files, text files, executable programs, and other file types are made recognizable by suffixing a name extension of a few letters to the file name proper.

Saying that the Unix system does not recognize file name tags or extensions, however, does not imply that individual programs may not do so, nor that users might not occasionally like to. There is no objection to such a practice; indeed, it is conventional to follow it in many aspects of work under Unix. Frequently, names of ordinary files are given a one-character suffix, separated from the file name proper by a dot, as in

```
/lib/mseg.o
```

Tagging characters may be made up by users to suit themselves. However, several tags are recognized by commonly used programs:

`.a`	archives (often of system data)
`.c`	C language source files
`.d`	data files for utility programs
`.f`	Fortran language source files
`.h`	data files for system services (''headers'')
`.i`	C preprocessor output (C source) files
`.o`	relocatable object files
`.p`	Pascal language source files
`.r`	Ratfor language source files
`.s`	assembler language source files
`.z`	compacted files produced by **pack**

It must be kept in mind that to the Unix system itself the dot and the suffixing character are simply part of an ordinary file name. They constitute two characters, so the other characters preceding them must number 12 or fewer for the file name as a whole to fit within the permissible maximum of 14 characters.

The System Directory Structure

Although at first glance the Unix file system may seem to be complicated, familiarity makes it seem less so. Most Unix systems adhere to (roughly) similar structures of the root file system, so it is worthwhile to examine a typical file system at least briefly.

A diagrammatic view of the directory tree for a typical Unix system is shown in Figure 3.2. Only the portion near the root directory is given in detail; the farther from the root, the more individual implementations diverge from each other. It must be kept in mind that almost every installation involves not only a different hardware configuration but also a

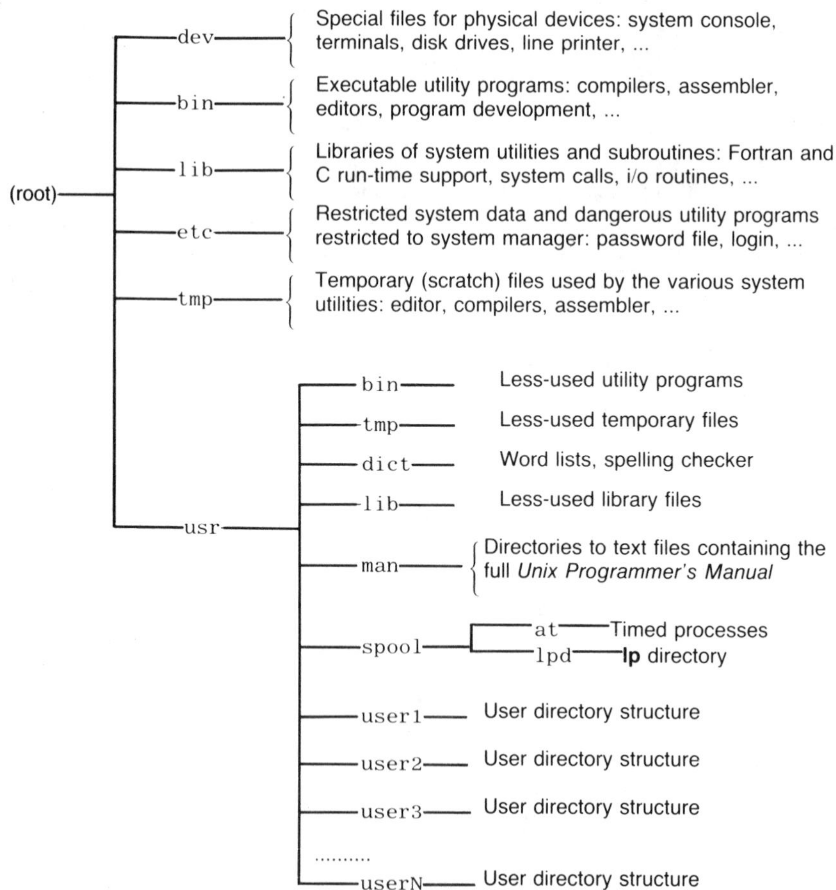

FIGURE 3.2. A typical Unix system directory structure.

different user community, so that the system manager most often will have had to restructure the file directories to suit local needs. For example, in a user community with few Fortran programmers but a large amount of text processing to be done, the file system may well be set up to have the text editor and spelling checker quickly available, while the Fortran compiler may even reside on a slower physical device. Nevertheless, most installations resemble each other closely near the root directory and adhere to the same organizational principles elsewhere.

As may be seen in Figure 3.2, the root directory has several subdirectories, with each containing more or less logically related matter. The first five directories shown—`/dev`, `/bin`, `/lib`, `/etc`, `/tmp`—are generally used by the system itself in carrying out user commands or by the system manager in maintaining administrative files and system software. The files are grouped within these directories primarily by the access permissions granted to users. For example, the general public is ordinarily given execute permission for files in `/bin` but not in `/etc`. It is usual to keep these five directories on a high-speed disk, so that users have rapid access to the files as they require them. The sixth subdirectory `/usr` shown in the diagram is generally the largest. The home directory of every authorized user is normally attached to `/usr` as a subdirectory, which can easily account for hundreds of entries in `/usr` even in modest-sized systems. In addition, `/usr` is employed to house system utilities of the same kind as found in `/bin`, `/lib`, and `/tmp` but needed less frequently. `/usr` is physically housed on a large, but possibly slower, disk drive in many installations. There is considerable incentive to keep the most commonly used items (which usually amount to a small percentage of the whole) in a small but rapidly accessible place, while the less often used larger part of the system resides on a slower but bigger device.

Working with the File Structure

The hierarchical arrangement of files within the Unix system is a valuable tool for maintaining and using large file structures in a tidy and orderly fashion. Getting around in this hierarchical maze, however, presupposes some familiarity with the actions that users are able to carry out. This section therefore outlines the main activities possible, indicating what can be done, how to do it, and who is allowed to do it.

Changing Directories

When a login name is first authorized, a home directory is associated with it and that directory is opened whenever the user logs in. Any file names used in commands then refer to files within the home directory, including any subdirectories attached to it. The thousands of files owned by others are thus invisible to any one user so order prevails despite the large number of files resident in the Unix file structure.

On many occasions it is useful to group various files containing logically related material into subdirectories. For example, Fortran programmers often find it convenient to store the source code for the subroutines of a large program in a directory structure that resembles the calling sequence of the subroutines themselves. Similarly, the author of a book may store individual subsections in separate files small enough to edit conveniently and to join them together through a hierarchy of directories. For example, `book/chapt3/sect4/subsec2` might be one file in such a hierarchy. The disadvantage of such a structure is evident at once: file names become awkward and unwieldy even if the individual file names do not come anywhere near the 14-character length permitted under Unix. For the book-writer to work on the subsections of a particular section, for example, it would be best to make the current user directory be that subdirectory which contains the desired material, say `book/chapt3/sect4`. Such a change is perfectly possible; Unix permits any directory whatever to be the current working directory. The home directory is privileged or special only in the sense that it is made the working directory at login time.

Changing to another directory as the working directory is accomplished by the **cd** command, in the form

```
$ cd book/chapt3/sect4
```

which makes the named directory into the current directory. From this point on, all file references will be sought in the new current directory, so that file `book/chapt3/sect4/subsec2` is referred to simply as `subsec2`.

Changing directories downward in the hierarchy is easy, since only the subdirectory names need to be specified. Changing upward requires knowing the full pathname of the desired directory. It can be determined using the **pwd** command, which produces the full pathname of the working directory. This command allows no parameters or arguments and returns the name of the current directory in the fullest form possible:

```
$ pwd
/usr/bftsplk/book/chapt3/sect4
```

The **cd** command may then be used to change to a different directory as the working directory:

```
$ cd /usr/bftsplk/book/chapt2/sect1
$ pwd
/usr/bftsplk/book/chapt2/sect1
```

If issued without any argument at all, **cd** returns the user to his home directory, the directory automatically assigned when logging in. In most cases, the home directory of every user is a subdirectory of `/usr`:

```
$ cd
$ pwd
/usr/bftsplk
```

File hierarchies can become quite intricate. As a result, **cd** and **pwd** are among the most frequently used Unix commands of all.

File Access Permissions

Not all users need to have access to all Unix files, nor is it desirable that they should. On many occasions, a user may wish to keep some files strictly private, as for example in commercial data processing. Others must therefore be denied access to those files. An even more important reason for denying access is that there are ways in which a small mistake can result in disastrous damage. For example, destruction of the root directory of a file system can easily make the entire file system useless. To prevent such damage, users must be forbidden to delete certain protected files, which surely must include the root directory. For reasons of both privacy and security, all Unix systems therefore include a formal scheme of file access permissions. Except as otherwise arranged, users have full access to their own files, restricted access to selected system files, and no access at all to files belonging to others.

Under the Unix file access permission scheme, an ordinary file can be accorded three forms of permission: *read*, *write*, and *execute*. Any given user may be granted any desired combination of these; the three permissions are entirely independent and none presupposes any other. Permission to write means permission to alter the file contents, including destruction of the file. Most often, users have writing permission to their own files, but at times they may wish even their own files to be denied writing permission, to guard against inadvertent alteration or removal of valuable material. Permission to read really means permission to copy. Since Unix does not differentiate between files and devices, listing a file at the terminal is regarded as copying it to the special file which represents the terminal. Hence, no distinction can be drawn between reading and copying; reading permission therefore does have significance even for a binary file which is unreadable in the ordinary sense. Execute permission means that the file may be used as a running process; it does not presuppose permission to read, for the user does not need to copy a file to execute it. Typically, users have execute permission for a large number of system facilities—editors, compilers, linkers, and so on—but they very likely do not have permission to read or write into those files.

It is worth noting that permission to write into a file and permission to erase items from the file are not distinguished. This arrangement is generally satisfactory for scientific computing, but it may complicate matters a little in some types of administrative or financial data processing. In an accounting department, for example, it may be convenient to allow many account clerks to write transactions into the same journal, but it is not at all desirable to allow any account clerk to delete transactions!

Directories are assigned the same three categories of permission as ordinary files: read, write, and execute. Directory files are stored in a binary format, not as text files, so that simple reading produces apparently random garbage on the terminal screen; they are displayed by the **ls** command, which processes the binary representation into legible form. Reading permission is therefore interpreted to mean listing permission, while writing permission constitutes the right to attach new files to the directory or to delete files. Having execute permission for a directory means that the files in the directory can be accessed (provided the appropriate permissions exist for the files themselves) or searched. For example, if a user has reading permission but not execute permission for file `/usr/spool`, he can list this directory and discover that it contains a subdirectory `/usr/spool/at`. However, he cannot access `/usr/spool/at` itself, because he lacks execute permission for `/usr/spool`.

Access permissions are granted to a user in three categories: personally, as a member of a user group, or as a member of the general public. When first authorized by the system manager, every user is assigned a personal login name and membership of a group. Classification of users by groups is a convenience, particularly in large installations. For example, a new experimental Fortran compiler might well be made executable by all members of the compiler development group, so as to permit testing by group members; but execute permission will probably be denied to other members of the general public until the compiler has been certified to work properly. In small installations, groups may be insignificant or trivial; the group may well consist of a single user, or all authorized users may belong to a single group. Even if they are not really used, groups are always defined for purposes of defining access privileges.

When a file is newly created, it is assigned a set of access permissions by default. A common arrangement would be to grant full permissions to the file owner, read and execute permissions to other members of the same group, and execute permission only to the general public. But default settings differ from installation to installation, indeed from user to user. If the default settings locally used appear inconvenient for some user, the system manager should be consulted, for it is a simple matter to reset the default values.

Keeping Track of Directories

At any one time, every user has some directory serving as his working directory. The operations he must be able to carry out, so as not to get lost in the system, include at least the following:

1. changing to another directory as the working directory,
2. determining which directory is the working directory,
3. listing the contents of a directory,
4. creating new subdirectories, and
5. removing an existing directory.

There are five commands corresponding to these five operations: **cd**, **pwd**, **ls**, **mkdir** and **rmdir**. The **cd** and **pwd** commands have been dealt with above; the remainder will be described briefly in the following.

Making new directories and removing old ones are almost as easy as changing them. A new directory is made by the **mkdir** command. For example, the command conversation

```
$ pwd
/usr/johnson
$ mkdir book
```

creates a new directory /usr/johnson/book. The current directory, however, is not changed. The newly created directory is automatically made to be a subdirectory of the current directory, unless a full pathname is given in the **mkdir** command so as to create it somewhere else. Naturally, a new directory can only be created in an existing directory where the user has write permission.

Removal of a directory, if desired, is accomplished by the **rmdir** command, which is analogous to (but not the same as) the **rm** command:

```
$ rmdir manuscr
```

Removal of a directory should not be attempted unless the directory is empty, i.e., unless it contains no subdirectories and no ordinary files. Disaster may otherwise befall the files listed in the directory to be removed! Whether the directory is empty or contains any file names can be verified by asking for a listing of the directory contents, using the **ls** command. This command simply lists the file names at the terminal, in alphabetical order:

```
$ ls /usr/johnson
book
grub
prog
```

The listing may produce one name per line, or it may string out the names across the screen (a better idea) in various versions of the Unix operating system. In any case, it is not absolutely necessary to give the directory name in the **ls** command; if none is shown, the current directory is assumed. The **ls** command is necessary, simple printout of a directory file will not do, because directories are stored in a special, compacted, binary format. Attempts to display them in the same way as ordinary text files (e.g., using **cat**) will produce what appears to be gibberish.

Directory Listings

A file can be attached to a directory in various ways. It may be attached to that directory only, ever since its creation; or it may be linked to it at some later date. Furthermore, it may be attached with various user access permissions.

The access permissions, number of directory links, indeed almost every conceivable form of information about a file may be determined by using the **ls** command. In its simplest form, **ls** merely lists the names of all files in a directory. But there are options for asking **ls** to sort the listing by the time of last file access, time of last modification, time of last permission alteration, or alphabetically—or any of these in reverse order. There are options also to list not only names but to give much more extensive information (file sizes, i-numbers), as well as to include both the directory itself and its parent directory. Some of the more commonly employed options include **-l** (long form), **-a** (all entries), **-t** (sort by time of last modification), and **-r** (reversed order). For example,

```
$ ls -al
total 24
drwxrwxr-x   6  johnson   friends    678 Feb 28 17:32   .
drwxrwxr-x   9  johnson   friends    212 Jan 12 10:02   ..
drwxrwxr-x   1  johnson   friends    143 Mar 11 15:50   book
-rwxr-x---   2  johnson   friends   8822 Feb 14 12:09   grub
drwx------   1  johnson   friends    657 Feb 22 19:33   prog
```

In this listing, the first line shows how many file blocks are occupied by the files listed. Blocks are 512 characters each in most older Unix systems, 1024 characters in some of the newer ones (such as System V). The remaining lines of the listing give the actual directory entries, beginning with the directory itself (.), then continuing with its parent directory (..), and finally giving the other files (`grub`, `book`, `prog`). Their order is alphabetic (i.e., in order of ASCII character sequence). It bears no particular relationship to sequence of creation, time of last access, or file content.

In the line given for each file, the first character indicates whether the file is a directory (d), special file (b or c), or ordinary file (-). The next nine characters constitute three groups of three and describe the access permissions granted to the owner of the file (first three characters), other members of the same group (next three characters), and the general public (last three). The letters `r`, w, x are used to denote read, write, and execute permissions, always listed in that order. If the relevant letter appears, permission exists; if it has been replaced by a minus sign, the indicated permission is denied. For example, grub is identified as an ordinary file by the absence of a leading d. The file owner *johnson* has full access privileges to grub. Members of user group *friends* may read the file or execute it but may not write into it. The general public is denied all access to grub.

The long-form listing above also shows, following the permissions, the number of directories in which the file appears (the number of *links*, in Unix jargon), the owner's name, the owner's group name, the number of characters in the file, and the time the file was last modified.

A subtle point about **ls** is that the file name given in the command line could be the name of a directory or the name of a non-directory file. If it is the latter and such a file is resident in the current directory, information will be given about that file only:

```
$ ls -l grub
-rwxr-x---   2  johnson   friends  8822 Feb 14 12:09  grub
```

This feature is useful if a directory contains many files and full information is only required about one.

Altering Access Permissions

From time to time it becomes necessary to make files accessible to other users or to deny previously existing access privileges. To alter the permissions on a file, the **chmod** (change mode) command is used. In this command, it is necessary to specify

1. whose permissions are to be set,
2. what the settings are to be, and
3. which file.

Thus, the **chmod** command must have three arguments, leading to the form

$ chmod *who settings filename*

The characters u (user = login owner), g (group), o (others), or a (all) may be used to indicate whose permissions are to be set. The settings are given in the form of a sign (+ - or =) followed by one of the characters r, w, x. For example,

```
$ chmod u-w precious
```

says that the user wishes to deny (minus sign) himself (u) write permission (w) on file *precious*, presumably to guard against accidents. The minus sign - removes permission, the plus sign + grants it, and the = assigns permissions absolutely (without reference to what they may have been previously). The command

```
$ chmod a=rx precious
```

sets the permissions to `r-xr-xr-x`, allowing everybody to have read and execute permission and nobody to have write permission.

chmod can be used equally well for ordinary files or for directories, with exactly the same results. It should be noted that, unlike most commands, **chmod** insists that no blanks be placed between the who-identifier, the signs, and the `r`, `w`, `x` characters. Blanks placed there will usually result in error messages, because the next character following a blank will be assumed to be a file name.

It is probably redundant to point out that the alteration of permissions is a privilege available to the owner of a file but not to others. Were it not so, the accident protection aspects of the permissions system might still be workable. Privacy, on the other hand, cannot be safeguarded by locked doors if everybody has a key!

Moving and Removing Files

Files attached to a particular directory may be moved to another quite easily. The command **mv**, issued in the form

```
$ mv filename directoryname
```

moves a file to another directory. The moving is accomplished by rewriting the links (directory entries) that form the directory tree, not by actually copying the file. Thus the "moving" really is just a matter of moving the file name; the name is removed from one directory, inserted in another. Nothing is left behind in the old directory.

Variations on **mv** are obtained by moving a file to another file or a directory to another directory. These operations amount to simple renamings, since once again the moves are done by rewriting names and links (indexing pointers), not by actually copying files. An exception arises when a request is made to move a file from one physical device to another, say from disk file to magnetic tape. To remain consistent in usage, **mv** in this case does really copy the file; the old copy is destroyed and all directory entries are rewritten to point to the new copy.

Removing a file by the **rm** command amounts to deletion. The removal is effected by destroying the specified directory entry, then checking whether the file has any entries left in any other directory. If no entries are left, the file has become inaccessible and has ceased to exist so far as any user is concerned. The physical storage space occupied by the file is therefore cleared and released for other use. Removing is a potentially dangerous activity, particularly if wild-card constructions are used; for example,

```
$ rm * .old
```

(with a blank following the asterisk) will destroy all files in the current directory!

It is possible for an ordinary file to be listed in two or more different directories, just as a single physical telephone may be listed in several telephone books. Any number of listings is permitted, all with different names if desired. A new directory entry may be created for an existing file by the **ln** (link) command, which has the form

```
$ ln oldname newname
```

The names `oldname` and `newname` are given in the usual form of file names—either as full pathnames or as partial pathnames from the working directory downward. Creation of multiple links is particularly convenient if, for example, several users need to have access to a common data file. However, it should be noted that under the general system rules, directory structures must always be strictly hierarchical. Therefore, it is possible to create a duplicate listing for an ordinary file, but not for a directory.

It should be emphasized that creating a new link with the **ln** command does not create a new copy of any file; it merely lists the same physical file in another directory, exactly as a telephone might be listed in several telephone directories. Any alteration made to the file will be made in the file as seen by every user, a point to keep in mind if several users have permission to write into the file.

File Location and Identification

The hierarchical directory layout used by Unix systems is powerful and flexible. But it does make it easy for users to lose themselves in the intricate nooks and crannies of the directory structure. There is probably no experienced user who has not at some time remembered with absolute certainty that a particular file was called `trig`—but without recalling the precise directory and subdirectory path. In such circumstances, the **find** command is invaluable. It permits searching an entire tree structure, from a specified directory on downward, to find all files that answer a particular description. **find** is in general used in the form

$ find *pathname conditions*

where *pathname* identifies the root directory for the search (all its subdirectories, sub-subdirectories, etc. will be searched) and *conditions* is a set of qualifiers which tell what characteristics are to be sought. Conventionally, the pathname of the current working directory may be given as `.` and the pathname of its parent directory as `..` if it is not desired to specify full pathnames.

A simple application of **find** occurs when the name of a file is known, but its full pathname is not. The command

```
$ find . -name trig -print
```

will begin searching at the current working directory (signified by `.`) and continue through all subdirectories, for all ordinary files named `trig`. Whenever one is located, its full pathname will be displayed at the terminal, as a result of the `-print` qualifier. In a more or less similar fashion, one can search for files whose names contain specified character strings, files of a particular size, files belonging to particular owners,. . ., indeed almost all specifiable characteristics of a file. These descriptions can be joined in logical combinations using logical union, intersection, and negation operators. The complexity of combinations is limited only by the imagination of the user. For example, it is possible to issue a command (despite its appearance, it is not gibberish!) like

```
$ find /usr/joe -name trig -mtime -6 -atime -2 -print
```

to find and display full pathnames for all files named `trig`, which were modified less than six days ago and most recently accessed over two days ago. The search will start at directory `/usr/joe`.

The great flexibility of **find** arises from the way in which the string of specifiable conditions is handled. While getting the conditions right is sometimes not easy at all, the principle is simple: the character string denoted by *conditions* is considered to be a logical expression and is evaluated for every file in turn. In point of fact, **find** does nothing other than evaluate the logical expression; it does not even produce any output. To produce output, the logical function `-print` is included in the logical expression as its final member. This function always has the value *true*, but evaluating it has the side effect of sending the name of the file currently being examined to the standard output. The trick here is that evaluation of the logical expression is continued only until the expression is known to be *false*, so `-print` is not evaluated (and therefore nothing is sent to the standard output) if the logical predicates ahead of `-print` are found to guarantee that the entire conditions predicate is false. The evaluation sequence is important: the command

```
$ find . -name trig -print
```

will cause display of all files named `trig` in the current directory and its subdirectories, but the command

```
$ find . -print -name trig
```

will evaluate the `-print` function (hence send the file name to the output) before it examines the file name, so it will display the names of all files!

The **find** command can locate files, but it does not examine their contents. Although **ls** does indicate the general type of a file (ordinary, special, or directory), it does not identify what kind of material the file might contain. Thus, there is need for some command which will permit identifying file contents without necessarily printing them out. The **file** command attempts to do so by not only examining the identification bits attached to each file but also by looking at the file content itself. It has a form as simple as one might hope for,

```
$ file filename
```

which contrasts pleasantly with the complexities of **find.** Several file names, or file names with wild cards, may be specified. **file** then responds by producing an informed guess of the contents of each file named. For example, in one version of Unix

```
$ file /etc/*
```

produces a long list which includes (among many others) the lines

```
/etc/accton:      separate executable
/etc/checklist:   ascii text
/etc/ddate:       empty
/etc/default:     directory
/etc/lpinit:      commands text
/etc/mnttab:      data
/etc/ttytype:     English text
```

If the file is identified as ASCII character text, **file** usually tries to guess further. If the text looks like a recognizable programming language, it also takes a stab at identifying the language. Unfortunately, **file** does not always guess right. To see why, a somewhat contrived little example might suffice. The set of lines

```
call johnny
stop
end
```

constitutes a correct and valid Fortran program. It is also a syntactically correct shell command file. It might well be intended as input for the **nroff** text formatter and would be valid as such. It might even be thought to constitute English text. The correct answer can never be known by examining the file itself, only by asking its owner what was intended!

Archives and Libraries

A special form of object file called a library or archive is available under all Unix systems. Such files differ from other object files in having internal directories which the **ld** (loader) program can scan. Like most operating systems, Unix provides ready-made libraries of mathematical functions, commonly used input-output routines, and much else.

Any user can create and maintain archives or libraries, using the **ar** archive maintainer program. Users with many small subprograms of frequent application are wise to do so.

In using and creating libraries, it should be borne in mind that searches performed through libraries are done strictly in one direction. When loading programs, users should therefore always specify file names in a sequence that will make searches successful. If program A calls B as a subprogram, which in turn calls C, loading will be successful if files present the program modules to **ld** in the order A, B, C; but it will be unsuccessful in the order C, A, B because (searching one way only) C cannot be found when it is required by B. The **ar** program permits the user to arrange the order of modules in a library, so that at least within each archive such problems can be avoided.

Removable File Volumes

One great convenience that results from setting up directories hierarchically is that whole new file volumes can be attached to the existing file structure easily. Such volumes may take various physical forms such as magnetic tapes, disk cartridges, or floppy disks. Floppy disks in particular are assuming increasing significance as the computer user community comes to recognize the inherent merits of a cheap machine-readable medium which conveniently fits into a standard filing folder. But having removable media means that the operating system has to be informed, whenever appropriate, that the disk or tape on a given storage device has been changed. Appropriate commands for this purpose are provided; they are described in this section.

Extending the File Structure

To use a removable (demountable) volume, it must first be mounted (i.e., attached to the Unix system). The physical act of mounting, for example, placing a floppy disk in a disk drive and closing its gate, is necessary but not sufficient. In addition to making the new volume physically available, the system must be told of its existence and its place in the file hierarchy by means of an appropriate command. To be compatible with directory management rules, every physical file volume is made to contain a directory structure of its own. The directory structure of a volume is hierarchical as always, and it begins at a root directory which has no name. All files on the volume can be made available simultaneously by making the root directory of the removable volume be a subdirectory of the user's working directory. To do so, the user requests the system to substitute the root directory of the newly mounted volume for an existing (but empty) directory in all file references.

Like many things, the principle of mounting removable volumes may appear complicated, but it isn't really. Suppose user *joe* possesses a floppy disk containing the manuscript of a report, structured as shown in Figure 3.3(a). On first logging in, the working directory is automatically made `/usr/joe`. To access the files on floppy disk, *joe* first makes a new directory `report`, a subdirectory of one of his existing directories. The new directory of course is part of the already existing file structure in the system, as indicated in Figure 3.3(b). Incorporation of the file structure on floppy disk only requires the empty subdirectory `report` and the root directory of the floppy disk to be made the same, as in Figure 3.3(c). Once the two directories have been identified as being the same, the file structure on the floppy disk has become in every way a part of the entire Unix file

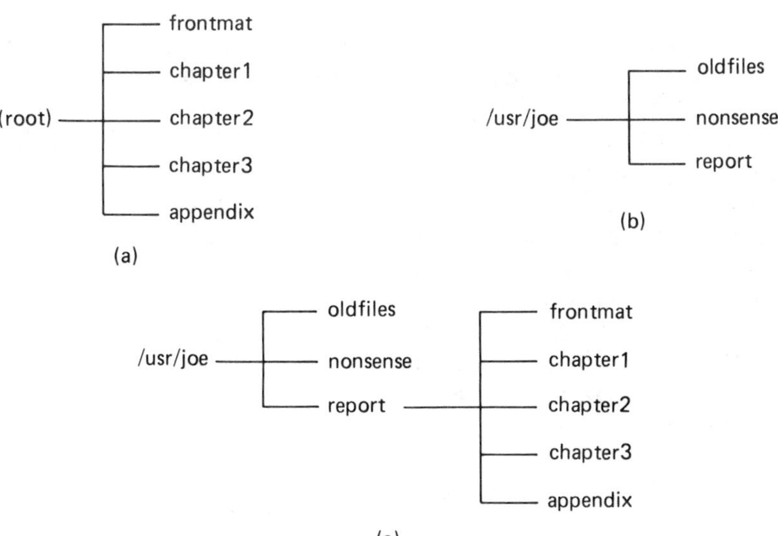

FIGURE 3.3. (a) Directory structure on a floppy disk. (b) An empty directory *report* is added to the user's file structure. (c) The floppy disk directory is identified with *report*.

structure. The file reference /usr/joe/report/chapter3, for example, is understood by the system immediately.

The **mount** and **umount** Commands

The user with a volume to attach generally first performs the physical act of mounting the tape or inserting the diskette in its slot, then tells the system about it by using the **mount** command. Typically,

```
mount /dev/fd0 /usr/joe/report
```

achieves the desired result: the root directory of floppy disk drive *fd0* (accessed through the device special file /dev/fd0) becomes identical with the already defined but empty directory /usr/joe/report. Aside from the time delays occasioned by the need to access files on such slow devices as cartridge tapes, the user will not even be aware that the file storage is split between several devices.

Under most Unix systems, a volume is generally mounted with a command in the form

```
$ mount /dev/xxx directoryname
```

or

```
$ /etc/mount /dev/xxx directoryname
```

where /dev/xxx is the name of the special file that handles the physical device in question and directoryname is the name of the directory file for which the root directory of the removable volume will be substituted. Both the device special file and the directory be taken over by the root directory must exist when the **mount** command is issued. The directory to be taken over must be empty at the time it is taken over. It should be noted that the mount command itself resides in /etc, a directory normally reserved to the system manager. In several versions of Unix the **mount** command requires the full pathname to be given for directoryname; names relative to the current directory are not accepted.

When the time has come to unmount the removable volume, the same steps are retraced in reverse. The command for doing so is **umount** (not "unmount"):

```
$ /etc/umount /dev/xxx
```

This command has only one argument, the name of the special file /dev/xxx associated with the physical device on which the volume resides. The directory file to which the volume root directory was attached is released after the **umount** and appears as a healthy, normal, but empty directory. The **umount** command, like **mount**, resides in directory /etc.

If the physical volume (disk or tape) mounted by the **mount** command does not contain a Unix file structure (if there is no directory on it), the system will attempt to read and to mount it all the same. The most usual result is a system crash. This disaster potential probably explains why the Version 7 Unix system reserved the **mount** command to the system manager. It might be presumed that the system manager, of all people, should know better!

The **mount** and **umount** commands are among the least consistent and least standardized Unix commands. Options differ considerably between system versions and so do the access permissions. Although the principles remain much the same, details differ sufficiently to make it essential to consult the full system manuals on these two commands.

Mounting and unmounting a volume is also possible by way of system calls, which may be accessed from C, Fortran, assembler, or other programs. This fact allows mounting and unmounting data sets under program control, while a program is actually executing. However, only advanced users and system programmers are likely to be interested in this possibility.

Making New File Structures

When a removable volume is mounted on some physical device, the logical task of mounting is performed by substituting the root directory of the demountable volume in place of an existing directory. As detailed above, the procedure is to substitute the volume root directory for one of the leaves of the Unix directory tree. The substituted directory must initially be empty, precisely to guarantee that it really is a leaf of the tree. Such a substitution is clearly impossible unless a directory structure exists on the removable volume before any attempt is made to mount it. A brand new magnetic tape, for example, cannot be mounted because it does not contain any directory.

To create a directory structure on a new magnetic medium, the **mkfs** command is used. This command first cleans the volume, irretrievably destroying all records on it. It then creates a single brand new (empty) directory on it, unnamed because it is the root directory for that volume. The volume can then be mounted in the usual fashion. The **mkfs** command is commonly used in the form

$ /etc/mkfs *specialfile filesize*

where *specialfile* is the name of the special file which serves to access the physical device in question, and *filesize* is the size of the file structure in blocks, a decimal number. The file size will usually (but not necessarily) be equal to the full size of the physical volume. It is perfectly possible, though not very often of practical interest, to make two or more file structures on the same tape or disk.

Like **mount** and **umount**, the **mkfs** command resides in directory `/etc`. In larger Unix systems, it is therefore available only to the system manager. This arrangement is not altogether unreasonable, since unrestricted access to **mkfs** makes it possible for any user to destroy entire diskfuls of files simply by mistyping the name of a special file!

Working with Floppy Disks

Floppy disks are a popular file medium in small Unix systems. The design of Unix in its early versions (including Versions 6 and 7) did not cater particularly well to removable media under user control and it certainly could not consider floppy disks, for floppy disks were just being invented! Procedures appropriate to using floppies exist under System V, however. To what extent they exist (and to what extent they are available) depends on the system size and the nature of the user community, for almost anything that can be done with removable volumes exposes all users to some risk. Small scientific installations, for example, can usually afford to take liberties quite unthinkable in large systems that maintain commercial data bases.

Floppy disks are used under Unix in two ways: as block-structured devices with random access to data (resembling a hard disk) or as sequential devices (resembling a magnetic tape). Either way, a floppy disk is unusable until it has been formatted, that is, until it has had sector marks written on it that will subsequently allow the system to locate places on the disk. This operation is perhaps analogous to drawing a grid on a map, making it possible to identify precise locations and to return to them at will. Many Unix systems do so by means of the **format** command; the floppy disk is placed in drive 0 (in most small computers, the upper or left-hand drive) and the command

```
$ format /dev/fd0
```

is issued. In System V derivatives, it is usually not even necessary to specify the device name; `/dev/fd0` is understood by default. Some system versions will not even allow formatting of any device except `/dev/fd0`, presumably to avoid the horrible consequences of some user accidentally reformatting the hard disk on which the system resides!

Once a floppy disk has been formatted, a file structure may be made on it with the **mkfs** command. In some systems, that operation is not even necessary; **format** automatically invokes **mkfs** as well. In others, the user needs to run **mkfs** explicitly. How large a file system can be accommodated on a floppy disk depends on all the usual factors that surround the peculiar world of floppy disks: how many tracks per inch, how many sectors, single or double sided. Floppy disks house half a megabyte, give or take a factor of two or three; it is essential to consult the system manuals for local details.

A useful feature of the **mkfs** command of particular benefit to the floppy disk user is its ability not only to accept a file structure size but to create a file structure identical to a prototype specification given in a named prototype file. In plain English, this means that a user can have available a version of **mkfs** that says effectively "make a file structure for a double-sided floppy" without worrying about the details.

Restrictions on Removable Volumes

Once a removable volume has been mounted, the directory structure does not show, indeed it makes it difficult to find out, on what physical device the files reside. However, there are a few subtle difficulties which may arise in the use of removable media. These are resolved by placing some restrictions, fortunately gentle ones, on the directory structure.

Suppose a magnetic tape contains a root directory, with a single subdirectory `math` which in turn contains ordinary files `algb` and `trig`. Suppose user *joe* mounts the tape on a tape drive and attaches its root directory to a previously empty directory whose pathname is `/usr/joe/tape`. To user *joe* it then becomes irrelevant whether the ordinary files reside on tape or elsewhere, since reference to `/usr/joe/tape/math/trig` serves to access the ordinary file `trig`, just as if it had resided on the system disk files. The user directory structure is then (in part) as shown in Figure 3.4.

The file-naming rules in general insist that directories must be related to each other in tree structures. On the other hand, ordinary files may be listed in any number of directories. In other words, the insistence on hierarchical structuring applies to directories only, not to ordinary files. Indeed, the **ln** command exists precisely so that ordinary files can conveniently be listed in two or more directories. However, a problem may arise when ordinary files resident on removable volumes are cross-listed in several directories. For example, file `/usr/joe/tape/math/trig`

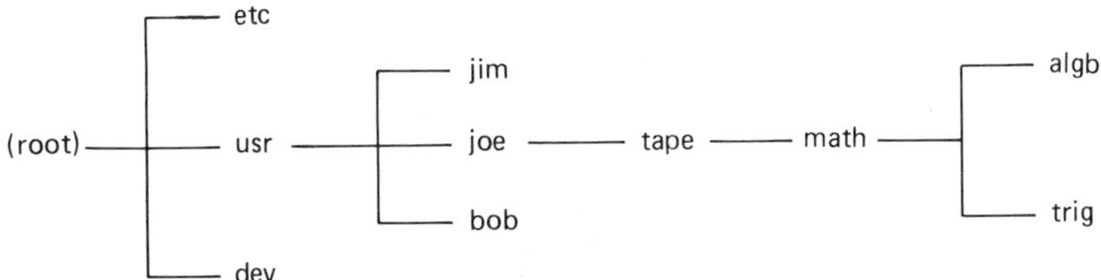

FIGURE 3.4. Directory structure resulting from the mounting of a tape.

may also interest user *bob*, who may therefore wish to attach it to his directory. In principle, it is perfectly acceptable to provide a second listing for the same file, as `/usr/bob/trig`. But the directory `/usr/bob` is resident on a physical device (typically, the system disk) different from the device where file `/usr/joe/tape/math/trig` is located (the magnetic tape unit). If user *joe* unmounts the tape file structure from directory `/usr/joe/tape` and then removes the physical tape, file `/usr/bob/trig` suddenly becomes inaccessible to user *bob*!

To avoid problems of the sort described, ordinary files on removable-medium devices may not be cross-listed to directories on other devices. Linking file `trig` to directory `/usr/bob` as above is therefore forbidden. This rule is imposed to keep system management simple; if the rule did not exist, the procedure of unmounting any volume would become very difficult. For example, what should the system do if user *joe* wished to unmount the tape while user *bob* was not even logged in? This prohibition on cross-listings is not really so draconian as it may seem, for it does not prevent any user from having access to files, merely from listing them in directories in a particular way. If user *bob* really wishes to have a copy of `math/trig`, he must request it by means of the **mv** command which will actually copy the file across devices. Alternatively, a copy of it may be made using **cp**.

Backup Files

Few computer users have not experienced a total feeling of frustrated defeat as the realization gradually dawns that a whole day's work has just evaporated, the result of accidental file erasure. Once burnt twice shy, goes the saying—one learns to keep backup files. Keeping backup copies is more of an issue with Unix than with many other operating systems, for Unix is miserly with disk space; it does not keep copies of previous versions of modified files.

Backup copies are necessary not only because hardware and operating systems sometimes malfunction but also to protect against the user's own blunders. Blunder protection is not hard to arrange if one adopts systematic working habits. For example, suppose user *joe* is working on a report, kept in a directory structure like that of Figure 3.3(c). To provide blunder protection, another directory is created, say `/usr/joe/report.bak`, into which to copy a backup version. To do so, user *joe* need only request

```
$ cp report/* report.bak
```

every now and then. While working on the report, making a new backup copy every half an hour or so probably suffices; the loss is limited to whatever has been done since the last backup copy. Unix even allows for forgetful people, by permitting regularly timed processes (so-called *at-processes*) to do the backup creation automatically at specified intervals.

Protection against externally caused disasters clearly requires that a storage medium not part of the computer system be used to house the backup copy. For moderate-sized file structures that will fit on a single floppy disk, a procedure similar to the above is used, with the difference that the floppy disk must first be mounted and must be unmounted afterward:

```
$ mount /dev/fd0/usr/joe/report.bak
$ cp report/* report.bak
$ umount /dev/fd0
```

A system crash may of course occur while this backup procedure goes on. In that case, user *joe* is left high and dry in spite of the most sensible precautions, because no backup copy exists at all during the moment when the old backup copy is being replaced by the new one. Very careful users therefore keep two copies on floppy disk, not merely one.

Where floppy disks and removable disk-packs are inconvenient—because they do not exist or because the files to be backed up are too extensive—Unix provides an alternative in the standard command **tar**. Its name is an abbreviation for *tape archiver*; its operation runs accordingly. The general format is

```
$ tar options directories
```

where `directories` is the name of a directory, or of several directories, whose contents are to be archived. The archiving is recursive, in the sense that the directory structure is followed through all subdirectory levels down to the ordinary files. Options available under **tar** are numerous and for the most part obvious: **tar** will either write to tape or extract files from an existing tape. It can be told to write to a new tape, or else to an existing tape in an update mode, replacing only those files which differ from their earlier versions. For backup creation,

```
$ tar u report
```

is the right choice; it tells tar to update the tape contents, comparing with the contents of directory report. The word *tape* may of course mean other physical media used in a sequential fashion, as if they were tape; diskettes (floppy disks) are often used this way in small systems.

The file format used by **tar** has changed little between Unix versions and does not vary between implementations. Tapes or diskettes in **tar** format are therefore the favored distribution medium for Unix files; they come as near to universal readability as anything can. On the other hand, a file in **tar** format really is archivally stored; it is inaccessible until it has been copied into its place in the system file structure. File-structured volumes are thus more convenient, provided the files are small and transport to another computer is not envisaged.

The distinction between **tar** formatted media and file-structured media is important; the two are different and cannot be mixed. Here is another source of potential blunders. Because a diskette may contain files in either format, users must remember to label them to identify not only the content but also the format in which it is written —and must remember to change the label when different contents in a different format are placed onto the same disk.

Chapter 4

Unix Command Shells

The Unix operating system contains many software components. Two hold particularly privileged positions: the kernel and the shell. The kernel is the operating system in the narrowest sense of that word, the supervisory program which schedules all processes and executes them in the proper way at the right time. Which programs to execute, how to run them, what to do with the output, and similar matters are communicated to the kernel through the Unix command decoder program, the shell. In this chapter, the external appearance of the shell is described in sufficient detail to allow reasonably complete use of its main facilities. However, the shell is a complex program and many of its more esoteric features can only be hinted at here.

To be precise, Unix does not have a shell; it has several. The most common is known as the Bourne shell after its originator; there is probably no Unix system where the Bourne shell is not available. The next most common is the C shell (pronounced *sea shell*). Both are general-purpose programs. Various special-purpose shells, not discussed in this chapter, also exist. For reasons now lost in history, the usual shell prompt character is $ for the Bourne shell and % for the C shell; wherever it is necessary to distinguish between them in this chapter, the $ and % characters will be used.

Issuing Commands

The shells are the Unix command decoder programs; they request commands from the user, decode them, and communicate the user's wishes to the kernel. As the name shell suggests, the shell envelops the kernel, in the sense indicated by Figure 4.1. All communication between the kernel and the terminal user must pass through the shell.

Basic Shell Action

Whenever a user logs in, a Unix shell is automatically invoked and started running, a separate and personal copy for each user. Once started, the shell displays the $ prompt on the screen, signalling its readiness to accept a command. When the user issues a command, the shell institutes a search for a program with the same name as the command. If such a program is found, the shell instructs the kernel to execute it. When execution is complete, the shell tells the user and requests another command, by displaying the $ prompt again. In other words, the shell alternately requests commands and executes them, in the following cycle:

issue shell prompt;
wait for keyboard input;
decode command line and search for program;
instruct kernel to execute program and wait;
accept kernel reply, then go back to issue a prompt;

This cycle continues until the shell encounters a control-D character in the keyboard input. This character is used consistently throughout the system to denote end of transmission. From the shell's point of view, the string of keyboard characters coming from the user is very much like a file, so the shell interprets control-D to mean "end of keyboard input", that is, to signify that the user does not intend to send any further commands. The shell therefore instructs the kernel to log out the user.

Command verbs in the Unix system are invariably names of executable programs, so that execution of a command really means execution of the program with the same name. Indeed, any user can define more commands at will, simply by creating programs and using their names as command verbs.

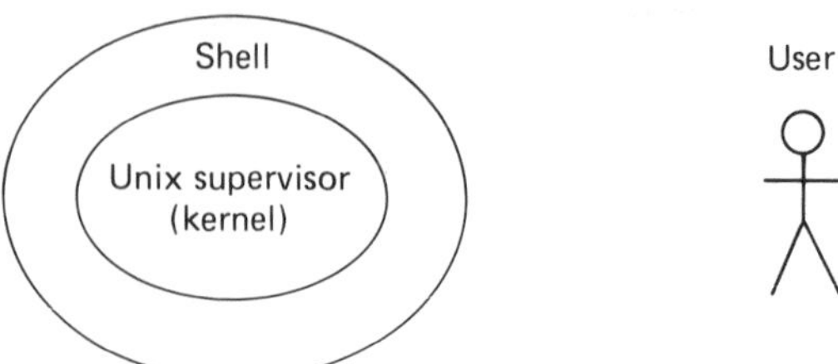

FIGURE 4.1. The user at the terminal is isolated from the system kernel by the command decoding shell.

Form of Shell Commands

All commands understood by the shell, and therefore all commands the kernel can act upon, have the same general form. This fact should not be surprising since they are all processed by the same decoder. The form is

command-verb [argument] [argument] [argument]

The *command-verb* is always required, but *arguments* are optional; they may or may not be needed. Because the command verb is understood by the shell to denote the name of a program, it will institute a search of the system file directories for a name to match the command verb, usually in the following sequence:

1. user's current directory; if not found,
2. directory `/bin`; if not found,
3. directory `/usr/bin`; if not found,
4. message issued, search terminated.

The command must appear in one of these directories as the name of an ordinary file for which the user has execute permission. Because the searching sequence is defined in advance, the shell does not expect full pathnames for files which can be located unambiguously by the above order of searching. For example, the Fortran compiler is always invoked by the command

```
$ f77 arguments
```

There is no need to specify it by its full pathname as

```
$ /bin/f77 arguments
```

but there is nothing wrong with doing so. An exceptional case occurs if a file name in the user's own directory duplicates the name of a system-provided command. If, for example, the user creates a brand new file called `f77`, it will be found in the very first step of the search; but it will not be the Fortran compiler! To override the default search sequence, the full pathname will be required in such cases.

Most of the system-provided general utilities reside in directory `/bin`, some in `/usr/bin`. A few are elsewhere. The users' own contributions of course may reside anywhere their creators care to (or can!) put them.

Arguments in the system-provided commands are of two principal forms: adverbs (modal arguments) and direct objects (file names). Adverbs are usually called *options* in the *Unix Programmer's Manual* as well as in other descriptive literature. For example, to compare two files `file1` and `file2`, one may use the command

```
$ diff -e file1 file2
```

The argument **-e** is an option; when used with **diff**, it indicates that an editor script is to be produced so that the standard Unix editor **ex** can recreate `file1` from `file2` and the differences that form the output of **diff**. The option must be preceded by a hyphen (a minus sign) in this command, and indeed in practically all the system-provided commands, to show the shell that **-e** is not a file name.

Like most of Unix, the command syntax lacks a formally defined standard. It is probable that one will be defined before long; for the moment, however, some informally proposed standards do exist. By common agreement, all command verbs are at least two and not more than nine characters long, always composed of lowercase letters and possibly numerals. Options are ordinarily one character long, preceded by a minus sign. Some options take additional option arguments; these, if there are any, follow the option letter. Sadly, these simple rules are broken by some common commands—occasionally because there is a good reason, more often because it just happened that way and nobody has got around to repairing the damage.

Options naturally differ from command to command. Nevertheless, most standard commands use the same letters to signify similar actions (though exceptions do exist). For example, **-l** often denotes "long form", whatever that may mean in the context of a particular command. Some commands allow few or no options; some admit more than ten, which may be specified in almost any sensible combination. For example,

```
$ ls -l -r -t
```

requests that the current directory contents be listed, giving all entries in long form (**l**), sorted in reverse (**r**) order by time (**t**) of last modification. Multiple single-character options are normally combined into a single adverb clause by concatenating all the option letters and prefixing them with a single hyphen, as in

```
$ ls -lrt
```

Blanks or commas must not be inserted between option letters in an adverb clause, for if a blank is inserted, the shell will assume that the next character belongs to a file name, not an option.

When file names are specified as command arguments, the standard conventions for file naming are used. In other words, pathnames beginning with / denote paths starting at the root directory and pathnames beginning without the / character begin at the current directory. However, the search sequence applicable to commands does not apply to files named as direct objects; if a named file is not found exactly where specified, no other directories are searched for it.

Multitasking and Waiting

In the ordinary course of events, the shell initiates execution of a command and does nothing until the appropriate process has entirely run its course. Typically, the user requests a process to be run, the output appears on the terminal screen, and the shell comes back with the $ prompt when ready for the next command. For example, anyone wishing to know who is currently logged on the system may use the **who** command:

```
$  who
michael   tty01   Feb 10 14:32
nora      tty02   Feb 10 14:19
boss      tty03   Feb 10 09:29
cleo      tty05   Feb 10 15:15
wurzel    ttyh4   Feb 10 16:06
adler     ttyh8   Feb 10 15:21
$
```

who checks the system tables to see which user is logged in at what terminal and since what time. The answers are presented on the terminal screen, while the shell simply waits for **who** to finish. On completion of **who**, the shell prompt reappears, indicating that the shell has regained control.

Sometimes it is desirable to set a program running but to go on doing something else at the terminal while the job runs. For instance, running a spelling check to find typographic errors in a long document may be a time-consuming job, but it requires no intervention at the keyboard. The user may therefore simply wish to set it going and to get on with editing some other files with the **vi** editor while the spelling check runs. Unix is fortunately a multiprocessing operating system, one which permits a user to have multiple processes running concurrently. To make the programs **spell** and **vi** run at the same time, the user instructs the shell to run **spell** but not to wait for its completion. Not waiting is implied by the & (ampersand) character when used as a command suffix:

```
$ spell longdocument > mistakes &
21
$ vi
```

Here **spell** is told to use `longdocument` as its input file and to redirect any suspect words (which would normally be sent to the terminal screen) into file `mistakes`, but to do so without waiting for completion. In response to the command, the shell requests the kernel to set the spelling task running and returns to the user a process identification number, 21 in the above example. Because the ampersand sign & was included in the command line, the shell does not wait for the kernel to signal that the spelling job is complete; instead, it immediately issues the $ prompt, showing that it is prepared to accept another command. The user replies by asking for **vi** to be run. From that moment on, two processes are running for the same user, **spell** and **vi**. (In fact there are more, probably at least half a dozen.) The latter is interactive and will eventually be terminated by the user; the former will keep going until its job is complete. Noninteractive processes set running in this fashion are sometimes known as *background* processes, because they run invisibly while the user is engaged in doing something else at a higher priority.

Background processes are known to the system only by their process identification numbers. When a time-consuming process is set running in the background, it may be useful to note down its process identification number so the system can be given instructions about it later on. At other times, the user may realize, a moment after pressing RETURN, that the background process just launched was the wrong one (perhaps **smell** instead of **spell**) or that the wrong input file was specified. In that case, the background process can be stopped by the **kill** command. The instruction

```
$ kill 21
```

will stop **spell** in the above example, provided of course it has not yet terminated its run.

The status of background processes may be enquired into with the **ps** (process status) command. This command produces a screen display showing from which terminal the job was started, by what command, and how long it has been running; whether it is still running; for which user it is running; and a host of other (for the most part less interesting) things.

Standard Files

Every user process is automatically assigned a standard input stream and a standard output stream when it is started. In ordinary cases, these will be connected to the terminal keyboard and screen by default. Most commands that produce output, produce it on the standard output device; correspondingly, they expect input from the standard input device. Under this scheme, the user frequently does not need to bother specifying where output should be directed. For example, to list directory contents it suffices to give the command

```
$ ls
```

without any indication that the listing should be presented on the terminal screen. That is precisely where the listing will appear, unless the standard output assigned by default was altered.

If the user prefers to have input and output directed to devices other than the predefined standard, data can always be redirected elsewhere by reassigning the input or output streams to some other device or file. In the normal course of events, redirection is desired only for the duration of one particular command. Such temporary reassignment is achieved by the characters **>** or **>>** as in

```
$ ls -l > file1
```

or

```
$ ls -l >> file1
```

commands which cause the current directory contents to be listed (in long form, as specified by **-l**) to a file. The single right-arrow character **>** causes the contents of `file1` to be replaced by the listing, without presenting the listing on the terminal screen. The double right-arrow **>>** causes the listing to be appended to the existing contents of `file1`, without affecting previous file contents. If there was no `file1` in the first place, one is created. In a similar fashion, the left-arrow character **<** may be used to reassign input temporarily.

Many commands permit file names to be given as arguments but will assume that standard input or output is intended if file names are omitted. For example, the command **cat** (an ugly abbreviation for *concatenate*) copies one or more named files to its standard output:

```
$ cat file1 file2
```

It can be used to concatenate two files or simply to list one on the terminal screen, as in

```
$ cat myfile
```

If no file name is given, **cat** uses its standard input. Thus

```
$ cat
```

performs the (not always useful) task of merely echoing on the screen whatever is typed at the keyboard. If the standard input is reassigned,

```
$cat < myfile
```

file `myfile` is again displayed on the screen; the commands

```
$ cat myfile
$ cat < myfile
```

are thus equivalent. Redirection can even be used to make **cat** copy a file:

```
$ cat file1 > file2
```

There is a third standard data stream, the standard error output; it handles error messages and other supplementary communications. Redirection of the standard output does not affect the standard error output. This separation of streams is deliberate and convenient. When the standard output is redirected, complaints about missing files, wrong access permissions, and the like do not mess up the output file but appear on the screen instead.

Pipes and Pipelines

The Unix shell permits establishing *interprocess pipes*. Pipes are data channels that funnel output from one program directly to another without creating any intermediate files. A pipe appears like an output file to one program and an input file to another. It is created by routing the standard output of one program directly into the standard input of the other, however, without the creation of any intermediate entity. The vertical rule character | represents a pipe in shell commands. For example,

```
$ who | lp
```

requests execution of two programs, **who** and **lp** (a program that copies its input file to the line printer); the standard data streams are redirected so that the output of **who** is piped directly to **lp** as its input. Together, this command pair will list who is currently logged on the system, but on the line printer instead of at the terminal. The apparent effect is precisely the same as would be achieved by the command sequence

```
$ who > temporaryfile
$ lp < temporaryfile
$ rm temporaryfile
```

But no file space is needed for `temporaryfile`, because no such file is ever created.

When a pipe is specified, the kernel starts both processes running immediately, just as if they were background tasks. In the above pipeline, **who** starts producing output right away and **lp** proceeds to do the housekeeping necessary to prepare for printing. The output of **who** is handed over to **lp** as rapidly as it is produced, without waiting for **who** to terminate. By way of contrast, if the job is done by a sequence of three separate commands the **lp** program is only launched after completion of **who**. In the pipeline, **who** and **lp** will execute synchronously, forced into synchronism by their interlocking needs for input and output. In fact, for all practical purposes the two may be regarded as a single compound process.

The notation for pipes differs from the notation used for redirection: it lists commands whereas redirection lists files. The command line

```
$ who > lp
```

is syntactically quite correct. However, it sends the output of **who** to a user file called `lp`, not to the line printer; the redirection symbol > informs the system that `lp` is a file name, not a command name.

A pipeline may contain as many processes as desired. The individual processes in it are always executed from left to right, with the output of one process chained to the next as input. To illustrate, the above example may be extended to include alphabetic sorting, using the sort utility:

```
$ who | sort | lp
```

This pipeline works as follows. The **who** program will produce the identifiers for all users currently logged in and hand over this output to **sort** as it is produced. In its turn, **sort** will place them in alphabetical order. Finally, **lp** will send the output to the line printer, which will eventually yield

```
adler    ttyh8   Feb 10 15:21
boss     tty03   Feb 10 09:29
cleo     tty05   Feb 10 15:15
michael  tty01   Feb 10 14:32
nora     tty02   Feb 10 14:19
wurzel   ttyh4   Feb 10 16:06
```

All processes in a long pipeline are set running simultaneously and their running is synchronized by the need of each to wait until it receives input from the process preceding it. The effect is that of a bucket brigade moving information from hand to hand as soon as it becomes available, never waiting for more information to accumulate than is actually required for the next step.

In plumbing, fittings are needed in addition to straight pipe runs. Unix provides one standard fitting, the **tee**; it copies its standard input to its standard output and makes an additional copy to another file besides. If a record is wanted of who is logged in on the system,

```
$ who | sort | tee whofile | lp
```

will pass the output of **sort** to **lp** and write a file `whofile` at the same time. If desired, **tee** can be used to copy to several files at once, or to append to them rather than overwrite, by specifying the **-a** option.

Input Handling by the Shell

User interaction with the Unix shell takes place through the keyboard and screen. Commands are received by the shell through the keyboard handler, a program for collecting the keystrokes as they arrive and organizing them into lines the shell can interpret. The shell proper deals with input lines rather than characters; it tries to parse lines and to decode them to make sense as commands. An understanding of shell operation simplifies effective use of the Unix system; it is therefore worth examining the rules of shell input in some detail.

Input Buffering

All keyboard characters are received by the keyboard handler which echoes them to the screen and immediately places them in its text buffer, a reserved memory area used to store the characters until they are needed. Whatever is typed at the keyboard is not immediately processed by the shell; it is stored in the buffer until the shell develops an appetite for input and at least one input line is complete. Only at that time is the input line actually handed over to the shell for decoding. On the other hand, the keyboard handler may accept from the keyboard, and store in the buffer, two or more lines. If the shell is not ready to accept the extra lines, they are simply left to wait in the buffer.

The buffer area used for keyboard input is of a fixed size, usually 256 characters. In normal use, the shell displays the $ prompt on the screen and the user replies by typing a command, terminated by a RETURN keystroke. The command line is then handed on to the waiting decoder and processed. When it is ready for more, the decoder prompts for more. But if the user continues to type at the keyboard without waiting for the prompt to reappear, no harm is done. The keyboard handler only stores the characters as they are typed; they will be transmitted from the keyboard buffer to the decoder program whenever the latter is ready for more input. A difficulty only arises if the user attempts to type too many extra characters, thereby overflowing the buffer. In that case, the surplus characters are discarded without any prior warning. However, problems rarely arise in practice, since 256 characters represents over a dozen average commands.

Experienced users turn the keyboard buffer capacity to good profit by typing ahead the commands they know they will wish to issue next, especially if the execution times of some are known to be a bit long. The screen display can then become truly confusing. The keyboard handler echoes characters on the screen as they are typed; but the shell prompt and any program responses only come when the commands are executed. The screen display therefore will not reflect the actual sequence of operations, but will show all the commands as they are typed, then a sequence of shell prompts and program outputs as they are produced. The order of input lines on the screen will be a faithful image of their typing sequence, not of the order they were received and decoded by the shell.

Errors and Error Correction

Even the most expert computer user occasionally issues a wrong command or strikes the wrong key. The way keyboard input is buffered means that no action is ever taken in response to keystrokes until the RETURN key has been pressed at the terminal, so errors can be remedied at least until that moment.

Incorrect characters typed at the keyboard may be corrected by erasing them. Erasure of a single character is achieved by the erase character, which is usually the BACKSPACE key. Each time the BACKSPACE key is struck, one character is erased in the input buffer and the screen cursor is moved back one character. Many display terminals, however, only move the cursor, they do not erase the incorrect characters on the screen. Since backspacing is usually followed by overwriting, the correct characters appear on the screen in the end; however, the screen appearance may temporarily be wrong. For example, a user may type the command **passwd** incorrectly, discover the error, and backspace four times,

```
$ paxxwd
```

ending up with the screen cursor at the first x. The text buffer will now contain the characters pa, the four characters xxwd having been deleted. Typing sswd yields the screen display

```
$ passwd
```

again a faithful reflection of the buffer contents.

When using a printing terminal, backspacing and overstriking are not possible. Instead of BACKSPACE, the # key is then used. Each time # is struck, one character is erased in the buffer but # is printed at the terminal. The resulting printout can be a bit messy, with

```
$ paxxwd####sswd
```

understood to mean **passwd** despite its curious appearance.

If an error occurs near the beginning of a long command line, a great many characters may have to be erased and retyped. Starting the line over, without individually erasing every character, may be easier; typing the kill character expunges everything typed so far. The kill character is usually @, sometimes control-X.

The erase and kill characters are both resettable. In other words, they are not permanently fixed as BACKSPACE and @ respectively but can be altered by the user. A table of terminal characteristics is maintained to describe every terminal connected to the system and these two characters are part of the terminal description. The user can alter any of the information in the terminal description table through the **stty** command, which is described more fully below. The most common default settings are those described here. But if the default settings should prove inconvenient, a user may indeed define some other erase and kill characters, for example % and <.

The BACKSPACE key on any normal terminal generates the control-H character. If a terminal does not have a BACKSPACE key, no matter; control-H will always do precisely the same job.

Characters Given Special Treatment

The shell does not consider all characters to mean what they say; quite a few have special meanings. Peculiar uses of the characters & < > | have already been encountered above. Several other so-called metacharacters have special meanings to the shell. These will be considered briefly in the following.

The semicolon ; is treated as equivalent to RETURN, provided the keyboard buffer contains at least one full line terminated by RETURN. To restate this bit of gobbledygook in plain words: several shell commands may be typed on a single line with semicolons between commands. When the time comes for command decoding, semicolons will be replaced by RETURNS, so that the individual commands will be decoded as individual lines. The shell does not act any differently, but the screen display looks different. For example,

```
$ who > temporaryfile; lp < temporaryfile; rm temporaryfile
```

This feature is particularly useful when long shell script files are built up. Since many shell commands are quite short, long command sequences form narrow ribbons of typing along the left edge of the terminal screen. They can be made to occupy fewer but longer lines, and thereby become easier to read, if semicolons are used judiciously.

In many commands, it may be desirable to name a whole range of file names. As an example, a particular project may have involved creating a whole family of files `project.f`, `project.o`, `project.a`,. . . and it may be desired to remove all the files at the completion of the project. Rather than typing out the names individually, the shell decoder permits using so-called wild-card characters, which are considered equivalent to any and all others. The asterisk * and question mark ? are used for this purpose; the asterisk is taken to represent any string of characters (of any length, including no characters at all), the question mark to stand for any one character. Consequently,

```
$ rm project*
```

will remove all files whose names begin with the character string project and continue with any (or no) characters. On the other hand,

```
$ rm project.?
```

will remove all files whose names begin with the eight-character string project. and contain exactly one additional character.

Sometimes it is necessary to identify groups of characters more finely, e.g., "any lowercase letter from a to k" or "any one of the numerals 3, 5, 8". For such purposes, wild cards to match only within specified sets may be defined. A range of characters, or a list of characters, encased in square brackets is taken as a match for exactly one character in the set. For example,

```
$ rm project.[a-k][358]
```

will cause removal of all files whose names begin with the eight- character string project., contain a lowercase letter in the range a–k next, and end with one of the numerals 3, 5, or 8, for example project.b3. As indicated in this example, the square brackets may contain either a range of naturally ordered characters (e.g., alphabetics or numerals) or a list of individually identified characters. Where ranges of characters are shown, they are assumed to be listed in their ASCII character sequence, with all numerals, special characters, alphabetics, and even unprintables having their proper order. Thus, the range specification [7-C] is equivalent to the list [789:;<=>?@ABC] because part of the set of punctuation marks appears between the numerals and the uppercase alphabet in the ASCII character definition.

Protection of Special Characters

Shell operation often involves special characters to delimit commands, to denote wild cards in file names, and indeed for other purposes yet to be discussed. It is not generally a good idea to use special characters in file names, because confusion may arise. For example, star*wars is a legitimate Unix file name, but one best avoided because the asterisk character may be misunderstood as a wild card. If such difficulties are encountered, all is not yet lost. Special characters can be stripped of their special nature by use of still more special characters: reverse slants (backslashes) and quotation marks.

The reverse slant character \ can be used in shell commands to force any character to have its literal (rather than special) meaning. The two commands

```
$ rm star*wars
$ rm star\*wars
```

are not the same. The first removes all files whose names begin `star` and end `wars`, no matter what characters may occur between these two strings; the asterisk is taken to stand for any string of zero or more characters. The second, however, treats the asterisk as a literal asterisk character, not as a symbol standing for some other string; it removes the file named `star*wars` and no others. In cases of doubt, giving a character its literal value with the reverse slant is always a safe course, for if an ordinary character had no special meaning in the first place, preceding it with a reverse slant endows it with no new meaning. The super-cautious user might therefore like to type file names in the form `\s\t\a\r\*\w\a\r\s` to be safe! Even the reverse slant character itself can be protected by another reverse slant. Perverse souls may wish to use reverse slants in file names, as `file\name`; but it will be necessary to ask the shell to deal with `file\\name`. Reasonable people for the most part choose to stick with lowercase alphabetics and numerals, with an occasional period (dot) thrown in for good measure.

Reverse slants protect single characters, not character strings. Protection for character strings is obtained by enclosing them in quotation marks. Two sorts of quotation mark are used, double and single. (Single quotes ' are of the apostrophe variety, ASCII octal 047—not ` which is called the grave accent or the back-quote). Double quotation marks cause all characters between them to be considered a single character string, thus solving the problem (among others) of how to include the blank character in a string. Single quotes play a similar role to double ones in keyboard work, but having two kinds of quotation marks solves another perennial problem—how to place a quotation mark inside a quoted string!

Argument Echoing

Because the shell command decoder may understand wild cards or other special characters in a way not intended by the user, a utility command **echo** is provided for previewing the effect of any particular command line. The **echo** command actually does nothing except display on the terminal screen the arguments entered with the command; but it displays them in fully expanded explicit form. For example, a user may feel diffident about a file name such as `project.*`, particularly in a destructive command like `rm`. Just what would be removed can be determined by first issuing the command:

```
$ echo project.*
project.c project.f project.o
```

The response lists all the currently possible values of the **echo** argument, i.e., all the file names in the current directory which match the wild-card construction given. Similarly, a user may feel uncertain about a character string like `star\\\*wars` (how many and which reverse slants are going to be taken literally?). The shell's understanding of the character string may be checked by

```
$ echo star\\\*wars
star\*wars
```

The echo again shows exactly what the character string, as finally decoded by the shell, will look like. **echo** is of course not a part of the shell, but a system utility just like **ls** or **cat**.

Resetting Terminal Parameters

Experienced users at times find it desirable to alter the erase and kill characters associated with their terminals or to reset other terminal characteristics. To do so, the **stty** program may be used. Like **echo**, the **stty** program is not really a part of the shell at all, but it does affect the operation of the shell.

Resetting the erase and kill characters is easily accomplished. The new characters are given in the command as arguments; for example,

```
$ stty erase % kill +
```

will make % the erase character and + the kill character, until the system is otherwise instructed by another **stty** command.

Terminals vary widely in their operating characteristics. The basic machine, on which nearly all later computer terminals were patterned, was designed and built by Teletype Corporation a long time before the computer era. Standard terminals are therefore widely termed "teletypes" in computer jargon, and the name is echoed in such abbreviations and mnemonics as **stty**. Modern terminals generally are equipped with either a cathode-ray tube (television type) display screen or a paper printing mechanism. The latter is slower than a display screen, because mechanical motions are required to make it run. At line-ends, they need extra idle time to allow the printing head or carriage to return to the start of a new line. They generally also require slower character transmission than display terminals. The speed settings, tab settings, in fact all the characteristics of the terminal can be reset through **stty**. Of course, resetting these merely tells the system what the terminal characteristics are; it does not alter the terminal itself. A slow mechanical printer will still run at its natural speed regardless of what the system might expect. Most of the facilities of **stty** are therefore used when changing the real terminal characteristics, such as the transmission speed or character parity. To find out the current settings of a terminal (as the system terminal communication software imagines them to be, not necessarily as they really are!), the **stty** command is issued without any arguments. For a fairly ordinary screen terminal, the result might be

```
$ stty
speed 9600 baud; evenp hupcl
brkint -inpck icrnl onlcr ff1
echo echoe echok
```

The first phrase in this output shows that the communication speed is 9600 baud (960 characters per second); the remainder have the following significance:

`evenp`	transmission is done with even character parity
`hupcl`	hang up the phone connection after last close
`brkint`	signal interruptions on all breaks
`-inpck`	no parity checking is done on the input
`icrnl`	input carriage returns are made into newlines
`onlcr`	output newlines are made into carriage returns
`ff1`	delay one time unit after a form feed
`echo`	echo every character typed at the keyboard
`echoe`	echo erasures so erased character disappears
`echok`	echo a newline after each kill character

The form of display varies considerably from one Unix system to the next and the various system versions keep track of different sets of terminal characteristics; the sets seem to keep growing as time goes on. Most of the settings are of a yes/no variety—characters either are echoed or they are not—and show a minus sign where the negative choice is made (as for `-inpck` above).

In System V, **stty** allows about fifty or sixty different options; the Seventh Edition manuals listed only half that many. Options may be combined in any way the user likes even though many combinations are senseless. No checking is done by **stty** to find out whether the options a user specifies are reasonable. It is therefore possible to become deeply mired in nonsense, but escape is available through

```
$ stty sane
```

The `sane` option resets all terminal parameters to be pedestrian but sensible.

The Shell Programming Language

In describing shell commands, it has been assumed so far that all commands are issued by the user at the keyboard and are executed immediately. In other words, the shell command language has been regarded as a control language that enables the user to specify each action as and when it is to be carried out. But there is an alternative possibility: shell commands can be used as a programming language. Sequences of shell commands actually constitute programs, for they prescribe sequences of actions. Such sequences, called shell procedures or shell scripts in Unix jargon, may be stored away in files just like Fortran or Pascal programs, to be executed when required.

Shell Programs

The key to understanding how shell scripts are written and used lies in recognizing that the shell itself is just another utility program. In point of fact, several different shells are available in most Unix installations, the most popular being the Bourne shell and the C shell (pronounced *sea shell*). The Bourne shell, named after its designer Stephen Bourne, is called **sh**; the C shell goes by the name of **csh** and is so called because much of its command syntax resembles that of the C programming language. There are also several other shells, which are much more rarely encountered. Many of the elementary commands used by the Bourne and C shells are identical, so that a beginning Unix user may not even know which one is in use. When writing shell scripts, however, the divergences begin to make themselves felt. In the following, both shells will be dealt with and their differences noted.

The shell differs from all the other system utilities in one important particular: it is automatically set running when the user logs in. However, being just another program, another copy of the shell can be started up at any time by the **sh** command. **sh** reads its input (which could be the keyboard or a file) and interprets the file contents as shell commands. For example, suppose the file `status` contains

```
date
ps -f
```

and that it is handed to a copy of the shell as input:

```
$ sh < status
Tue Jun  3 18:49:44 EDT 1986
    UID   PID  PPID  C    STIME TTY  TIME COMMAND
  peter    37     1  0 09:26:51 02   0:39 -csh
  peter   388    37  0 18:49:40 02   0:01 sh status
  peter   391   388  6 18:49:46 02   0:12 ps -f
```

The processor status report given by **ps** shows that user *peter* had three processes concurrently running at the moment the date stamp was placed in the output. One was a copy of the C shell, launched at login time; one a copy of the Bourne shell **sh**; the third the processor status enquiry **ps**. While the **ps** program was actually running, **sh** was waiting for **ps** to finish; **csh** was waiting for **sh** to finish.

Because the default input file to **sh** is the terminal keyboard, simply issuing the command

```
$ sh
```

causes a copy of the shell to run, taking its input from the keyboard. This is precisely the manner in which Unix and its many cousins normally operate, the first copy of the shell being started for the user by the system itself at login. It remains to note—as might be obvious from the above—that the shell uses the standard input mechanism so that

```
$ sh < status
$ sh status
```

are equivalent in their action though slightly different in the internal mechanisms. Since the shell thus launched is just another program as far as Unix is concerned, it could be made a background process,

```
$ sh status > record &
```

Output is directed to a file so the process is able to run without bothering the user at the terminal.

Because the shell can accept input from files, users can create processes not ordinarily provided in the Unix system, simply by putting together pipelines of existing utility programs. To illustrate, suppose it is desired to know which users are logged in on terminals of type *ttyh*, ignoring users logged in at any other type of terminal. The **who** command gives a full listing of users, containing not only the desired information but a lot of superfluous items as well. A file can be weeded by the **grep** command, which extracts those lines containing a predetermined character pattern, in this case *ttyh*. They can be pipelined with **sort**, to form a file called *whottyh* containing just a single command line:

```
who | grep ttyh | sort
```

Whenever it is desired to determine what users are logged in on terminals of the *ttyh* type, one issues the command

```
$ sh whottyh
```

and the above short pipeline is executed. An earlier illustrative example produced the screen display

```
$ who
michael   tty01   Feb 10 14:32
nora      tty02   Feb 10 14:19
boss      tty03   Feb 10 09:29
cleo      tty05   Feb 10 15:15
wurzel    ttyh4   Feb 10 16:06
adler     ttyh8   Feb 10 15:21
$
```

but now there will only result

```
$ sh whottyh
adler     ttyh8   Feb 10 15:21
wurzel    ttyh4   Feb 10 16:06
$
```

Four more users are shown in the output of **who**, because they are logged in; but they are filtered out by **grep**, because their corresponding output lines from **who** do not contain the string *ttyh*.

Shell Scripts

Files containing shell command strings can be executed by causing another copy of the shell to run, taking its input from the file, by either of

```
$ sh commandfile
$ sh < commandfile
```

Both forms are acceptable. A neater and more elegant way of dealing with command files, however, is to turn them into commands in their own right. This conversion is extremely simple: it is only necessary to turn the command file into an executable file, by attaching the correct permissions to it. For example,

```
$ chmod a+x commandfile
```

gives everybody permission to execute **commandfile**, which has now become a command! Consequently,

```
$ commandfile
```

will be executed just as if it were a system-provided command.

Conversion of shell command files into commands, or shell scripts, is feasible because the kernel and shell coordinate their interpretations of what is executable. When **commandfile** is issued as a command, the kernel finds it unacceptable because its contents do not make up an executable object file in the proper form. It is therefore handed back to the shell for interpretation. To state the matter briefly: executable files which do not contain machine language code are assumed to contain shell scripts.

Parameter Passing

Shell scripts may contain symbolic parameters which are given real values only when the commands are interpreted and executed. Symbolic parameters are handed to shell scripts in an extremely simple manner. Up to nine special symbols `$1`, `$2`, . . ., `$9`, each consisting of a dollar sign and a numeral, may be used in place of character strings in the file containing the shell script. When the script is invoked as a command, the corresponding number of file names, numeric values, or other actual arguments must be provided, as strings of characters. These are then substituted in place of the symbolic parameters by the shell, the first one in place of `$1`, the second in place of `$2`, and so on.

To illustrate, suppose once again that a listing of all users logged in at a particular type of terminal is desired. Procedure `whottyh` as described above works for one particular terminal type, but not for any other type, because the character string `ttyh` is permanently embedded in it. The `whottyh` procedure can be generalized, creating a procedure file **whoterm** containing just the one command line

```
who | grep $1 | sort
```

This procedure contains one symbolic parameter, so when it is invoked, one parameter value must be supplied. Since **grep** expects a character string to use in pattern matching, the actual parameter must be a character string also. Thus,

```
$ whoterm ttyh
adler    ttyh8   Feb 10 15:21
wurzel   ttyh4   Feb 10 16:06
$
```

produces exactly the same result as `whottyh` because the character string `ttyh` is substituted for `$1` before execution. But parameter passing makes for flexibility:

```
$ whoterm tty0
boss     tty03   Feb 10 09:29
cleo     tty05   Feb 10 15:15
```

```
michael   tty01    Feb 10 14:32
nora      tty02    Feb 10 14:19
$
```

Here the same script **whoterm** was used unchanged, but with a different parameter substituted for `$1`.

Conditional Execution

The command language understood by the shell has an interesting and somewhat unusual feature: when executed, every command has an attribute called *exit status*. The exit status is merely a logical flag which indicates success (or failure) in executing the command. For example, suppose the **rm** command is issued to remove a file. If the specified file cannot be found, it cannot be removed and the attempt to execute **rm** is regarded as unsuccessful. The exit status is therefore returned as false. Its value can be tested by the shell and used to decide whether to take some other action. It is thus possible to give the shell such conditional commands as "remove file `qtty.c`, and if successful, remove file `qtty.f` as well".

The basic mechanism by which conditional commands are made to run will be familiar, at least in principle, to Pascal and Fortran programmers. Just as in those high-level languages, ordinary command statements can be qualified by an *if* clause. In the shell language, *if* exists in two forms: *if . . . then* and *if . . . then . . . else* . . .. A simple illustration will serve:

```
$ cat rmqtty
if rm qtty.c
then echo "Removed qtty.c and qtty.f"; rm qtty.f
else echo "No qtty.c found"
fi
$ ls -m q*
qtty.a, qtty.c, qtty.f, qtty.x
$ rmqtty
Removed qtty.c and qtty.f
$ ls -m q*
qtty.a, qtty.x
```

The first three or four lines of this example show the contents of file **rmqtty**. It attempts to remove file `qtty.c`; if successful, it removes `qtty.f` as well and echoes a message to that effect; otherwise, it sends a message declaring its failure. Note the terminator *fi* used to identify the end of the conditional clauses; it is essential because the shell would not otherwise know how far the conditional command list extends. Next in the example, the **ls** command is run to see that files `qtty.c` and `qtty.f` do exist.

Executing **rmqtty** produces the expected message, and a second **ls** clearly shows that the files were indeed removed.

The shell script shown above has a flaw, quickly evident when it is executed a second time:

```
$ rmqtty
rm: qtty.c non-existent
No qtty.c found
$
```

The first message comes from the system, the second from the shell script. If the messages are not desired, the second one is easily suppressed by altering the shell script, but the first one cannot be reached quite so readily. To prevent messages from Heaven-knows-where popping up when shell scripts are run as background jobs, the command **test** is provided. It examines files, character strings, or integers and yields an exit status but performs no other activity. It can be used, for example, to determine whether a file exists and is writable, by

```
test -w filename
```

The key to message suppression is to test first and take action thereafter. The same example, done a bit better, then reads as follows:

```
$ cat rmqtty
if test -w qtty.c
then echo "Removed qtty.c and qtty.f"
rm qtty.c; rm qtty.f
else echo "No qtty.c found"
fi
$ls -m q*
qtty.a, qtty.c, qtty.f, qtty.x
$ rmqtty
Removed qtty.c and qtty.f
$ rmqtty
No qtty.c found
```

This time the absence of `qtty.c` causes no protest messages, for an attempt to remove this file is made only if it exists and if the user has write permission for it.

The keywords *if, then, else, fi* (as well as numerous others used in shell scripts to provide control of command execution) are only taken to denote a control construct if they appear as the first word of a line (or, what is equivalent, the first word following a semicolon). On the other hand, there is no restriction on the number of commands in an *if* clause; it may contain one single command (probably the most usual case), or there may be a set of several. However, only the success of the last command to be executed is tested, for there is only one exit status flag and that one is set or reset after each command.

Testing for Exit Status

The **test** function is the key to decision-making in shell scripts so a few lines devoted to its operation will be well invested. **test** actually evaluates the logical expression which follows it and sets the exit status accordingly. The arguments of admissible logical expressions may be file names, character strings, or integers.

Tests for file names are almost always of the form already encountered above: an option letter indicating what to test for, followed by the file name. There are over a dozen possibilities, of which the following might be the most important:

-r`file`	`file` has read permission
-w`file`	`file` has write permission
-x`file`	`file` has execute permission
-f`file`	`file` is an ordinary file
-d`file`	`file` is a directory
-s`file`	`file` size is greater than zero

The exit status is returned as true if the file meets the given description; if it does not, or if the file does not exist, the exit status is false.

Some of the tests available on strings and integers are

`string1 = string2`	the two strings are identical
`string`	string exists (is not the null string)
`integ1 -eq integ2`	the two integers are numerically equal

In the integer comparison, various comparison operators may be used, abbreviated in Fortran style as `-gt` (greater than), `-ge` (greater than or equal to), and so on. The exit status is in each case returned as true if the relevant condition is met.

The test expressions used with **test** are logical expressions, not options in the usual Unix command style; they cannot be combined in adverb clauses simply by stringing them together. However, they can be combined with logical operators `!` (not), `-a` (and), and `-o` (or). They can be grouped with parentheses as required. For example,

```
test -f file -a -w file
```

determines whether file is an ordinary file with write permission.

The arguments that enter into logical expressions need not be explicit; symbolic parameters or variables are perfectly acceptable. To illustrate this point, consider the shell script **vib**. Its object is to run the **vi** editor but to keep a backup copy of the file being edited. **vib** is invoked with a file name, as in

```
$ vib file
```

`file` is then opened for editing and a backup copy `file.b` is preserved. The shell script runs as follows:

```
if   test $1
then if   test -w $1 -a -f $1
     then cp $1 $1.b
     fi
     vi $1
else echo "Must name file!"
fi
```

The first line checks that the command was accompanied by a character string argument; if not, **vib** issues a protest message and exits. If a name is given, the file is checked to determine that it is a writable ordinary file. If it passes that test, a copy is made with the **cp** command; the name of the copy is the same as the name of the file, with a `.b` suffix appended. (Note that `$1` stands for the character string, so `$1.b` is the same string with the `.b` suffix.)

One criticism often heard of the Unix editors is that they always overwrite the original file; they do not keep backup versions. The script **vib** shows why: if users wish to have backup copies (or several levels of backup copies!) they certainly should have them. After all, it only takes a simple shell script. The general Unix philosophy is to provide a selection of simple working tools, supplemented by shell programming facilities to permit a high degree of customization.

The command verb **test** is frequently left out of shell scripts, for the Unix shells are willing to accept an alternate form. Instead of writing the word **test**, the test condition may be encased in square brackets insulated from it with blanks, as in

```
    #        vib: vi editor with backup
    # ____________________________________________
if  [ $1 ]                           # Was file name specified?
then if   [ -w $1 -a -f $1 ]         # if so, writable ordinary?
then cp $1 $1.b                      # Make a backup copy first,
fi
vi $1                                # then edit the file.
else echo "Must name file!"          # If no file name, protest!
fi
```

Comments have also been added here, to improve the legibility of the script and to make it comprehensible even a few days after its creation. Any occurrence of the # character at the beginning of a word (i.e., preceded by a blank or other whitespace) is taken to introduce a comment. In this form, the shell script begins to look just like a program written in Pascal, Fortran, or C. Indeed, a large part of the difference between the Bourne shell **sh** and the C shell **csh** lies in the niceties of language; where the two differ, the syntactic conventions of the C shell are close to those of C, so experienced C programmers find it easy to write shell scripts.

Repeated Program Loops

The *if . . . then . . . else . . . fi* construction is the fundamental form of program flow control in shell scripts. However, there are others with which Pascal or C programmers will immediately feel at home. For example, there is a *case* or *switch* statement, a generalization of the *if* construct to choose between several courses of action, not just two. There is a *for . . . do* loop similar to that of Pascal, useful for actions to be repeated for some denumerable class of cases. Repetitive looping, continued forever provided a specified condition remains true, is available with the *while . . . do . . . done* construct, which may also be regarded as a generalization of *if . . . then . . . fi*: *if . . . then* only carries out its action once, *while . . . do* does it again and again.

While the actions performed by the Bourne and C shells are similar, the command syntax differs, the Bourne shell resembling the Pascal language while the C shell hews a little closer to C. For the casual user, however, the distinctions are not too important because most constructs valid for the Bourne shell are accepted by the C shell as well. Again proceeding by example, here is a shell script to notify the user when another logs in:

```
    #                         await                               #
    #_____________________________________________________________#
while test ` who |grep $1 | wc -l ` -eq 0          # test if there
do     sleep 120;   done                           # if not, wait;
echo \^G\^G\^G\^G\^G\^G\^G\^G\^G                   # on login,
echo "$1 is now logged in."                        # squawk.
```

The structure of this script is really very simple; it just contains a single *while . . . do . . .* done construct. It is set running by a request such as

```
$ await joe &
```

It will check whether the specified user is logged in and return a message if so. If not, it will wait for two minutes (the **sleep** command does nothing but wait for the specified number of seconds) and then check again—and again, and again, until *joe* does log in.

Several points of detail in the **await** script merit attention. The first concerns methodology. The **who** command produces a list of everybody currently logged in; **grep** extracts the lines that contain the name `joe`. The word count program **wc**, with the **-l** (lines only) option, is then applied to count lines. The result is a single numeric string whose value equals the number of terminals on which *joe* is logged in. A second point, perhaps marginal to the issue of shell programming, concerns the output messages. The character string \ ^G (reverse slant followed by control-G) is echoed as a single control-G, a nonprintable character which rings the terminal bell. The two echoes shown therefore send both visual and aural notification of *joe*'s arrival!

The most important point requiring explanation is unfortunately a little more complicated. The pipeline preceding `-eq` is placed in back-quotes. These cause their enclosed pipeline to be executed and the standard output of its last member to be substituted for the character string that defines the pipeline, so that the `-eq` comparison examines the line count output by **wc**. Were the quotes not there, **test** would check the exit status of **who**, then feed its null output (for **test** produces nothing) to **grep**, which would of course find no match, . . . with no useful result at the end. Ordinary single or double quotes would not do the trick:

```
$ echo `who | grep joe | wc -l`
1
$ echo "who | grep joe | wc -l"
who | grep joe | wc -l
$ echo 'who | grep joe | wc -l'
who |grep joe | wc -l
```

In the first case, the output of **echo** is the number of lines counted by **wc** (i.e., the number of terminals on which *joe* is logged in). In the second and third, the argument of **echo** is the literal character string that makes up the pipeline definition. These characters are not numerals so they cannot be compared arithmetically to zero; and even if they could, the answer would not be what is wanted.

Simple shell scripts like **await** are quickly written and handy but often not robust enough for use by other people. The request

```
$ await
```

will produce a diagnostic message because **grep** does not like to search for null strings; after that, it will go to sleep for 120 seconds, then produce the diagnostic again and again and again. This sort of failure is usually tolerated by the author—"I made a stupid mistake in not specifying a name, there is nothing wrong with my program!"—but it is unacceptable if others are to have access to it. Good software practice requires not only documentation of better quality than shown above, but also a set of validity checks. If no name was furnished, either a default value should be used or, better still, the program should ask the user to specify a name.

The form of *while* loop discussed above applies to the Bourne shell. In the C shell, a directly comparable looping structure exists. However, its syntax is a little different.

Shell Variables

The shell language would certainly not be a true programming language were it not to allow symbolic variables to be defined and used. Variables are given names much like names in conventional programming languages; they may contain letters, numerals, and the underscore character, but no other special characters. A few variables do use special characters, but these are all predefined in the shell and users cannot redefine them. In programming the Bourne shell, it is conventional to use uppercase letters for variables. However, this practice is mere habit; the shell is quite as happy with lower case. Upper and lower case are considered distinct, so dAy, DAY, and Day are three different names. Bourne shell variables are assigned values by a simple assignment statement much like that familiar in Fortran:

```
$ DAY=Wednesday
$ WAM="Wolfgang Amadeus Mozart"
```

In the second case, quotes are used to make the blank characters part of the character string. Were they not there, the shell would assign WAM the value *Wolfgang* and would then be confused what to do with all the leftover characters on the same line. There are no blanks before or after the equal signs; the Bourne shell dislikes them because it cannot make up its mind whether they are part of the character strings or not.

To find out the values of shell variables, the **echo** command may be used:

```
$ echo DAY WAM
DAY WAM
```

but this does not work, because **echo** does exactly what it has been told to do: it echoes the character strings DAY and WAM. To replace the variable names by their values, the names are encased in braces and prefixed with a dollar sign:

```
$ echo ${DAY} ${WAM}
Wednesday Wolfgang Amadeus Mozart
```

Wherever no confusion can arise, the braces can be dropped:

```
$ echo $DAY $WAM
Wednesday Wolfgang Amadeus Mozart
```

The need for braces is illustrated by

```
$ echo ${DAY}s we always meet for lunch
Wednesdays we always meet for lunch
$ echo $DAYs we always meet for lunch
we always meet for lunch
```

When the braces are dropped, the shell tries to find the variable DAYs, which does not exist; it therefore substitutes the null string. With the braces in place, however, exactly the desired result is obtained.

To assign values to variables in the C shell requires use of the set command; simple mention of the variable name is not enough. On the other hand, the C shell is more tolerant of spaces:

```
% set day = Tuesday
% echo $day
Tuesday
```

In keeping with the traditions of the C language, C shell programmers generally stick to lowercase letters in variable names. As with the Bourne shell, this preference is purely a matter of usage; the shell is equally happy either way.

A sticky little problem of Unix file structures can be solved elegantly by defining new variables. The **ln** command permits ordinary files to be cross-listed in several directories. Unfortunately, a whole lot of files cannot be cross-listed automatically by linking the directory in which they reside, because directories may not be linked into others under any circumstances. This seeming shortcoming is easily circumvented by defining a variable name to stand for the directory name. For example, suppose user *bob* needs access to all the files in directory usr/joe/lispint/artin/source which belongs to user *joe*. Provided all the files have the necessary permissions, user *bob* defines a new variable joes as a synonym for the directory name, and the job is done:

```
joes=/usr/joe/lispint/artin/source
$ echo ${joes}/main
/usr/joe/lispint/artin/source/main
```

The only immediately visible difference between linking and defining a synonymous name is the need to type an extra dollar sign and braces, a small price to pay for not having to bother with the otherwise insufferably long pathnames!

Aside from variables defined by the user, the shells recognize a dozen or more others which are permanently defined. These can be accessed in shell scripts just like any user-defined variables. The most important are

HOME	name of the home (login) directory
PATH	search path (directory path) for commands
PS1	shell prompt, dollar sign $ by default
#	number of positional parameters (decimal number)
$	process identification number of this shell
!	process number of the last background process

The value $HOME figures prominently in many system-provided shell scripts. The convenience of knowing how many arguments (positional parameters) were presented to a shell script in the command line is probably obvious.

for . . . do Loops

Wherever an action needs to be carried out for every member of a set of objects, the *for . . . do* loop provides a natural control mechanism. For example, the following shell script finds out how much disk space is used by each of a selection of files:

```
$ cat space
for i in /usr/joe/indx /usr/joe/sourc /usr/joe/objct
do du $i
done
$ space
2         /usr/joe/indx
1368      /usr/joe/sourc
1788      /usr/joe/objct
```

The loop is executed by making the variable i—which is a true shell variable—assume every value in the list of three directory names. For every one, the **du** command is executed; it reports the number of 512-byte slices of disk space occupied by each directory and gives its name. The keywords *for*, *do*, and *done* must be the first words following a newline or a semicolon, just as they did in the *while* and *if* control constructs.

Many shell scripts are run with parameter values following the script name. To generalize the disk space reporting script shown above, the list of variables can be made to be the string of positional parameters appended to the command line, so that different names can be typed in at different times:

```
$ cd /usr/joe
$ space indx sourc objct
2         indx
```

```
1368    sourc
1788    objct
```

This use of *for* loops is extremely common, so much so that a special form of the *for* construct exists.

```
$ cat space
for i
do du $i ; done
```

Omitting the list altogether is taken to mean that the variable `i` is to range over all the positional parameters given with the shell script invocation; there is no need to list them as `$1 $2 $3 . . . .`

The C shell, as one might well expect, also provides a looping construct of similar effect but differently expressed:

```
foreach i /usr/joe/indx /usr/joe/sourc /usr/joe/objct
repeat du $i
end
```

As before, the choice of shells is more a matter of taste than science.

Running the Unix Shells

If at least two shells are available on most Unix systems, which one is the best? Many people feel that the C shell offers more to the interactive user at the terminal, while the programming constructs of the Bourne shell are a bit more powerful. For most users, therefore, the C shell is "the shell" when it comes to keyboard work, while shell scripts are often written using the Bourne shell. Taste certainly plays an important role in this choice; it is hard to defend any position firmly.

Customizing the Bourne Shell

After an initial try at running Unix, most serious users grow to wish the shell acted a little differently from how it really does. The Bourne shell permits considerable latitude in user tastes, for many of the decisions made by the shell are alterable by the user.

Every time a Bourne shell is started two files are executed as shell scripts: **/etc/profile** and **$HOME/.profile**, the latter being located in the user's home directory. The former is normally not modifiable by users, but the latter can be edited as desired. So far as user wishes can be accommodated through setting variables or executing shell scripts, **.profile** is the place and time to take care of them. Typically, this file will contain a set of commands like the following:

```
PATH=:/bin:/usr/bin              # directory search path
MAIL=/usr/spool/mail/joe         # mailbox
PS1="$HOME $ "                   # shell prompt
umask 022                        # file creation mask
export PATH MAIL                 # available to others
```

Users with unconventional needs or tastes often have much more complicated **.profile** files. For example, anyone who often logs in from a particular maverick terminal type is wise to include in **.profile** one or more **stty** commands.

The PATH definition in **.profile** consists of the names of directories to be searched for commands, in the order of searching. Directory names are separated by colons and the first directory to be searched must follow immediately after the equal sign. A null string is taken to denote the current directory. This strange convention implies that the PATH given above searches

1. (current directory)
2. /bin
3. /usr/bin

The mailbox location is more or less standard, though some users keen on privacy hide their mail somewhere else. Prompt strings are something else, though; users and user groups delight in making up interesting prompts. From a practical point of view,

```
PS1="peter $ "
PS1="$HOME $ "
PS1=`pwd` $ "
```

are good choices because they do something useful. The first displays the user login name, a useful identifying mark; the second shows the home directory name. The third identifies the working directory at the time the shell was started (note the back-quotes!); because the variable is set once and left at that value, the prompt will not change when the working directory is changed. All three prompts include a dollar sign $, a reminder that they are Bourne shell prompts.

The **umask** command specifies what access permissions shall be denied any newly created file. Its numeric argument is coded in the same way as in the **chmod** command. However, the action here is one of masking (i.e., denial); the permissions attached to the file will be the standard ones, less anything held back by **umask**.

History and the C Shell

The C shell includes a selection of features not present in the Bourne shell but particularly well liked for interactive terminal use. The most striking is undoubtedly historical recall, the ability of **csh** to remember what it was doing some time ago. To see what commands were decoded by the shell recently, all one needs to do is ask:

```
122 % history
   112 pwd
   113 rm tempry
   114 vi annrep
   115 nroff annrep | more
   116 vi annrep
   117 nroff annrep | more
   118 spell annrep | lp
   119 vi annrep
   120 nroff annrep | more
   121 nroff annrep > text
   122 history
123 %
```

In response to the **history** command, the C shell exhibits the last few commands and the **history** command itself. The numbers shown in the left column are called event numbers. Every command received by the C shell is assigned an event number and many systems show the current event number in the command prompt, as illustrated in the prompts above.

Commands can be repeated without having to retype them at the keyboard, by saying which previous event is to be repeated. For example, to verify the current directory name, it suffices to request that historical event 112 be repeated:

```
123 % !112
pwd
/usr/bob/repts
```

The C shell retrieves the appropriate command from its historical record, echoes it to show what it remembers, then immediately executes it. The exclamation mark `!` is a predefined C shell variable and stands for the event number, so `!112` is event 112. The historical recall ability of the shell is limited to the commands shown in the historical display; there is no point in attempting to go back further.

Historical events can be recalled precisely by their numbers, but it is also possible to recall them in more general terms. In the above example, a repetition of the spelling check could be requested in the following ways:

```
!118     the command of event 118
!-5      the fifth last command
!s       the last command beginning with s
!spe     the last command beginning with spe
!?lp     the last command to contain the string lp.
```

Repeating the last command requires typing `!-1`. Because this request is a frequent one, the special form `!!` is accepted as a synonym for `!-1`.

Repetition of commands usually involves some alteration, since the most frequent reason for repetition is that some slight change or improvement is wanted. The historical recall mechanism of the C shell makes extensive—probably much too extensive—provision for selecting and editing within a command line before it is repeated. Individual words within a command can be selected by following the command description with a colon and the word number (beginning the count with 0!), while word ranges can be described by giving beginning and ending numbers:

```
123 % echo !120:0-1
echo nroff annrep
nroff annrep
124 %
```

The first response shows what the C shell thinks the command consists of; the second response is that obtained when the **echo** command is executed. The selection mechanism used in this way allows various changes, for example, the inclusion of a forgotten option:

```
123 % !120:0 -o1-5 !120:1-3
nroff -o1-5 annrep | more
```

Here `!120:0` refers to the zeroth word of event 120, `!120:1-3` to the first through third words. The insertion of `-o1-5` instructs **nroff** to produce only the first five pages of the text document. To substitute one character string for another (e.g., to have the output called `annrep.tx` instead of `text`), a simpler construction would be

```
123 % !120:s/text/annrep.tx
nroff annrep > annrep.tx
```

There are nearly a dozen ways of selecting a word out of a historically known command, and nearly a dozen ways of modifying it. For most users, however, simple selection and substitution will probably suffice; commands are only single lines so it is often less trouble to retype a line than to figure out clever ways of editing it.

Aliases and Commands

The command repertoire of any Unix system can be extended by defining new shell scripts and making them into executable commands. Many such scripts only amount to a line or two, however, and will be entirely personal; maintaining lists of scripts may seem like unnecessary fuss. Some users, for example, rarely wish any directory listings except full ones and prefer them in reversed order of time and date. Having to type the command with its full list of options, as

```
% ls -otr
```

can be avoided by using a mechanism called *aliasing*, which the C shell provides. One declares

```
alias lst ls -otr
```

and thereby creates a new command **lst**, synonymous to **ls -otr**:

```
% lst
total 10
-rwxr-xr-x    1 peter        406 Jun  4 10:30 agchr
-rw-r--r--    1 peter        129 Jun 10 09:50 outtext
drwxr-xr-x    1 peter         29 Jun 10 09:52 stuff
```

This newly defined alias behaves exactly like a command. Admittedly, an equivalent effect could be achieved in either the Bourne or C shell by defining a variable name `lst`; however, invoking it as a command then requires typing a dollar sign (and possibly curly brackets) to force evaluation—not much trouble, but less tidy and one more thing to remember. More than one command can be placed in an alias,

```
% alias info "date; ls | sort; pwd"
```

but quotation marks are then essential to clarify that the first semicolon separates commands within the **alias** and does not terminate the **alias** command itself. The **alias** command, without any arguments at all, displays the list of currently recognized aliases; the **unalias** command removes a named alias from the list.

Aliases are stored as character strings but they are not merely another form of shell variable; they cannot be used for any purpose other than commands. They are treated as commands rather than as character strings in every respect including their listing in the history file where the single command **info** will appear, not the commands or pipelines that define it. As far as the shell is concerned, the input command is **info**. This arrangement makes it possible to introduce parameters into the middle of an alias string. For example,

```
150 % alias info "date; ls \!* | sort; pwd"
151 % info subdir
Tue Jun 10 12:23:40 EDT 1986
alice
budget
textpr
/usr/joe/direc
```

uses the parameter *subdir* given with the current event (i.e., with the **info** command) as the argument for **ls**. Note that the current event number symbol is protected by a reverse slant, for it must survive translation by the alias mechanism so as to reach the shell for execution.

There is no interference between aliases, shell commands, executable files, and shell variables. For example, there exists an internal command in the C shell called **history** and there is also a shell variable called `history`. There is nothing much wrong with creating an alias called **history**, but the built-in **history** command then becomes unreachable because the C shell looks for aliases first, built-in commands thereafter, and executable files last. If the same name has been used for all three, the alias will be executed. There is a way of reaching executable files, however: the full pathname can be given so there is no confusion. Files in the current working directory or near it can be made accessible by using abbreviated pathnames such as **./history** instead of simply **history**.

Customizing the C Shell

The C shell, more even than the Bourne shell, can be tailored to suit the tastes of individual users. While the Bourne shell seeks and executes files called **.profile** when it starts up, the C shell looks for three different files, two on starting and one when it exits. The startup file **.login** is executed as a shell script when the user logs in to a C shell; the login shell and any further C shell initiated for the same user look for and execute another file called **.cshrc**. When the user logs out, the login shell executes the shell script **.logout**. All three are sought in the user's home directory; if one or more are not present, they are simply ignored.

The startup and shutdown files of the C shell can be used to set up shell variables, define aliases, set the shell prompt, indeed to do anything that can be done by a shell script. A **.login** file typically contains statements like the following:

```
setenv  SHELL /bin/csh            # identify shell
set ignoreeof                     # no logout with ^D
set path = (. /bin /usr/bin)      # command search path
```

Typically, it will also contain statements that describe the terminal on which the user habitually logs in. The path variable setting is much like its opposite number in the Bourne shell, except for notation; the `setenv` command (equivalent to the Bourne shell `export` statement) makes the login shell identification available to other processes. The `ignoreeof` variable prevents logging out with a control-D and makes **csh** demand the word *logout* instead.

Other user-definable settings may occur in the **.cshrc** file, which is executed every time a new shell is spawned. It may contain commands such as

```
set history=10        # save 10 commands
set prompt=\!\ %\     # establish prompt
alias dir ls -lrt     # directory listing
```

The history variable is set to the number of commands retained in the recall file. The choice of prompt is subject to much the same considerations as for the Bourne shell, with one exception: the event number is often included in C shell prompts, as an aid to users who make extensive use of historical substitutions and repetitions.

The **.logout** file on occasion allows the local system programming staff to have its bit of fun. It is widely agreed that the control-D form of logging out is not convenient, although it is logically consistent and accepted in the Bourne shell. The standard defeat mechanism in the C shell is to set the variable `ignoreeof`, so that the word *logout* must be typed; but there are other, more interesting, possibilities. For example, the C shell script

```
#      .logout        #
tonintr -                           # Ignore all interrupts,
unset ignoreeof                     # defeat "logout".
set bye                             # Create bye
while ( $bye != adieu )             # check if it's "adieu";
echo "Use \"adieu\" to log out\!"   # remind with message,
set bye = `line`                    # request keyboard input.
end
```

asks the user to type the word *adieu* in order to log out, then sets the variable bye to the word received from the terminal keyboard (via the command line). It repeats this action until the word *adieu* is finally recognized. More serious uses of the `.logout` file include tidying-up operations such as reminding the user to remove any magnetic tapes and floppy disks or displaying an accounting log of the computer resources used during the terminal session.

Choosing the Right Shell

Received wisdom in the Unix community holds that the C shell is preferable for interactive work, the Bourne shell for writing shell scripts. Choosing the C shell for terminal work is probably a good idea. The Bourne shell has several unpleasant habits (as does the C shell); logging out users when the shell receives a control-D must rank high among them. While the Bourne shell can be customized to make it more agreeable, there is little doubt that the C shell allows more custom alterations and therefore can come closer to the user's individual wishes. However, extensive alterations take knowledge, patience, and time; most beginning users lack at least one of these.

A good reason for choosing the C shell as the normal interactive shell is that the C shell can deal with Bourne shell scripts, but the converse is not true. The following example will illustrate why and how:

```
% cat cshsrc
# C shell script
echo "SHELL = $SHELL, shell = $shell"; ps
% cat shsrc
 # Bourne shell script
echo "SHELL = $SHELL, shell = $shell"; ps
% cshsrc
SHELL = /bin/csh, shell = /bin/csh
   PID TTY TIME COMMAND
    38 03  0:33 csh
   204 03  0:04 csh
   205 03  0:12 ps
% shsrc
SHELL = /bin/csh, shell =
   PID TTY TIME COMMAND
    38 03  0:33 csh
   206 03  0:01 sh
   208 03  0:11 ps
```

Here two short shell scripts are run: both ask the system to identify the currently active shell and to display the status of every process associated with the user terminal. The scripts are identical except for their comment lines. These differ in one major respect: the comment character # is the first character in the file in **cshscr**, while a blank precedes it in **shscr**. The C shell uses this first character as an identifier. It treats the file as a C shell script if # is present, as a Bourne shell script if not. (Conventionally, Bourne shell scripts are begun with the colon : to identify them.) To execute either kind of script, the user's C shell process (38 in the example) launches a new shell, either **csh** or **sh** as required. This action is evident in the example: when executing **cshscr** the active shell (process 204) is identified as **csh**, but when executing **shscr** it is **sh** (process 206).

The Bourne shell is the "senior" shell, so it does not recognize most things peculiar to the C shell. However, the C shell does understand many Bourne shell conventions. For example, the requests to echo $SHELL and `$shell` above are understood by **csh**, but only $SHELL is echoed by **sh**. Similarly, repeating the above experiment with **sh** as the login shell will lead to **sh** being used for both scripts; the Bourne shell does not spot the # character at the head of the file as anything special.

The Bourne shell is available under virtually any Unix system; the C shell under most but not all. The *System V Interface Definition*, for example, does not mention the C shell. To be sure that shell scripts can be run anywhere by anybody, it is probably wise to write them using the Bourne shell conventions. On the other hand, the slightly less universal availability of the C shell is no disadvantage when working at the terminal, while its greater flexibility can be an asset.

Chapter 5

The System Kernel

The kernel is that part of a Unix operating system which actually controls the allocation of machine time, memory space, and communication channels to the various tasks that users may have running at any particular moment. It consists of a central supervisory program flanked by service routines to take care of such essentials as fetching characters from a keyboard, writing to memory, and looking at the system clock.

A great many data processing activities are relegated to separate, essentially autonomous, programs under the Unix system. Most, though not all, such programs are directly visible to the user: they are stored in separate files whose names the shell considers to be commands. Since most users communicate only with the shell, not directly with the kernel, a knowledge of what the kernel contains and how it operates is not really necessary to most people. This chapter is directed primarily to those who wish to know a little more about the inner structure of the system, as well as to others who may occasionally need access to some of its internals and wish to consult a brief overview before tackling the much more complete system manuals.

Nature of the Kernel

By its external appearance, the Unix operating system seems to be made up of two parts: a large set of programs, each one corresponding to a command, and the shell, which manages user commands and coordinates the running of programs. In an analogous fashion, the inner part of Unix may be divided into two portions: a large set of service routines, to perform functions actually related to hardware and software tasks, and the kernel, which takes care of their interplay with currently running processes. The service routines are invoked as needed, while much of the supervisor code is permanently resident in memory. It provides the basic software environment for practically everything that happens. This part occupies only a small amount of computer memory, leaving as much as possible to user processes.

Functions of the Kernel

Most computer users are not deeply interested in the machine hardware employed to solve their problems, nor in the details of the operating system software. The Unix system caters to this common user preference by interposing the shell between user and machine so that the user communicates with a virtual Unix machine whose appearance is entirely that of the shell.

The Unix kernel has an analogous role, but one level below the shell: it hides the physical machine from those programs and also from those sophisticated users who may from time to time request access to the lower-level system services. The kernel does so by creating a virtual machine whose characteristics closely resemble those of a broad class of physical machines. Real computers are then made to look like the virtual machine by interposing a program of a few thousand lines between machine and user. Rarely does the physical machine hidden beneath the shell become visible. This structure is the key to creating portable operating systems. Since the shell addresses itself to the virtual machine, it can be mounted on a new computer by rewriting only the machine-level programs that convert the real machine into the virtual machine.

The virtual machine created by the kernel has three primary functions: (1) it schedules, coordinates, and manages process execution; (2) it provides system services such as input/output and file management; and (3) it handles all other machine dependent operations. All three functions are related to the details of computer hardware structure.

Kernel Structure

The overall size of a Unix kernel is around 10000 lines of program code, but this figure varies widely with the Unix version as well as the type of machine. As a fraction of total Unix program code (shell, utilities, kernel, and all else), it may range from under 5% to over 10%. The proportion of total code in the kernel is variable not only because kernel size varies from one machine to another, but also because Unix installations differ in the number of utility programs provided.

A substantial part of the kernel deals with memory management, including user scheduling and process scheduling. This part also keeps track of stack contents, machine register contents, and the various other environmental details, as processes are swapped into memory. Furthermore, it responds to processor traps which may arise, for example, from hardware memory faults. This major portion of the kernel, perhaps 70-90% of the whole, is written in the C language. It deals almost entirely with the virtual machine and is therefore portable to any machine for which a C compiler can be found. A large part of the kernel code is consequently the same in systems and system versions intended for broadly similar kinds of computer.

Scheduling, memory management, and control of process execution are matters requiring fast response. They are therefore initiated and controlled by the permanently resident part of the kernel. On the other hand, the service routines are numerous and more extensive, so they are loaded into memory only as needed.

Device drivers, the programs that actually address the data registers in peripheral devices, form another substantial part of the kernel. They handle interrupts raised by peripheral devices and effect error recovery. Device drivers are entirely hardware dependent; after all, the whole object of a device driver is to move data into particular hardware device registers. Most Unix device drivers are also written in the C language. The device driver code in minimal Unix systems may be around 1000 source lines, but it is sure to rise much higher in systems with many peripheral devices.

The third important part of the kernel, the only one that must be written in assembler language, is a set of machine primitives. These are the true creators of the virtual machine. They place characters in the line printer data register, enable or disable machine interrupts, read the disk drives, and so on. These may amount to 1000 or more lines of assembler-language code. This number too is highly variable, depending on the complexity of the real computer and how closely it resembles the virtual machine.

System Calls

The shell and large parts of the Unix kernel are written in high-level languages. These programs, as well as many others that users create from time to time, require access to various facilities for which high level languages provide no standard commands. Such actions include

initiating a new process,
opening a file for reading,
writing on a file,

getting the system clock time,
terminating a running process, and
changing read/write/execute permissions.

Most such machine-dependent actions are intrinsically simple and those of the virtual machine created by the kernel are among the simplest.They are accessible through system calls, programs that fetch information, write words into a machine register, or consult the relevant tables. System calls are the instructions that the virtual machine carries out—indeed, it could well be said that the set of system calls *is* the virtual machine.

System calls are commands issued to the kernel, just as ordinary Unix commands are instructions given to the shell. They are accessible to programs written in C, exactly as if they were ordinary C functions. They are available to Fortran 77 and Pascal programmers through function calls because the conventional Unix language processor structure handles Fortran 77 and Berkeley Pascal through the second pass of the C compiler. The entire repertoire of system calls extends to a hundred or more, a long list of individually simple things. Compared to the list of system-provided commands, the set of system calls has grown slowly as updates and new versions of Unix derivatives have come along.

Some system call actions are also available as shell commands. The shell command then usually consists of a short program which does little more than rephrase the user's request and pass it on to the kernel as a system call. Obvious examples include **chdir**, **kill**, **mount**, **sleep**, and **umask**, all requests for some simple action to be performed on directories, process tables, peripheral devices, or the system clock.

A few commonly employed system calls are briefly described in this chapter. They represent only the smallest tip of a very large iceberg, but most of the iceberg is of interest only to true Unix cognoscenti. For more information on what system calls are available and how to use them, a serious session with the full *Unix Programmer's Manual* is recommended. Volume 2 in particular defines the actions performed by each system call and gives details of how they are accessed from both assembler language and C.

System Standards

The relative portability of Unix systems derives largely from the ability of C programs to issue system calls. Both the applications programmer and the systems programmer can do their work almost entirely in high-level languages, allowing machine dependence to be localized in the C compiler and the system primitives. As indicated in the chapter on language compilers, C is a language well suited to writing operating systems, for it is able to deal with entities at the machine word level. However, even the best C programs cannot be portable unless the virtual machine is standardized—in other words, if the same system calls are available on all computers that support Unix.

Until about 1983 or 1984 the Unix system—the Seventh Edition or the Berkeley 4.2 BSD release—was largely used and maintained by academic institutions or commercial firms. No standard prescribed what system calls were to be available; worse, many versions of the system incorporated improvements or modifications. These no doubt made the system run better but also prevented software from being moved between Unix systems. In 1984, /usr/group, an independent society of Unix users, published a proposed system standard comprising two parts: about three dozen system calls and equally many C functions, intended to constitute the fundamental library of utilities for the C programmer. About the same time, the AT&T organization appears to have realized that random unchecked growth would hurt rather than help the Unix cause; to clarify and standardize, the *System V Interface Definition* was published in 1986. This book is descriptive rather than normative—it says exactly what System V actually does rather than what any Unix-style operating system ought to do. The Institute of Electrical and Electronics Engineers, Inc. (IEEE), an organization active in various facets of computer standards, also in 1986, drew up its *Standard for Portable Operating System for Computer Environments*. (Of course, Unix does not enter the name—it is a trade mark, after all.) Although there are differences, the IEEE document and the AT&T definition come remarkably close to each other. There is reasonable hope, therefore, that something very much like the IEEE definition (or System V) will be adopted as an ISO as well as ANSI standard within a few years.

One important point needs to be observed: the IEEE standard, as well as its precursor the /usr/group document, only deals with kernel-level standardization. Standardization of shell commands will likely follow, but in the near future it will still be a matter of every man for himself in the shell jungle.

Process Coordination and Management

Under a multiuser operating system, many user programs can be running at the same time. Of course, there is only one central processing unit in the computer so only one program can really be running at a given instant; the phrase "at the same time" means that the several programs are interleaved in time, with the central processor allocated briefly to each one in turn. But although only one user program may be actually running, several could be resident in memory at the same time if the memory is large enough. The kernel must keep track of how programs use processor time and memory space; in other words, it is responsible for process scheduling and memory management. The latter includes not only sharing out the available slices of memory but also deciding whether and when to swap a process from memory to disk and back again.

Process Initiation

A process under Unix is distinguished from a program: a process is a program executing in a specified environment. The word *environment* here means which files are open, what access permissions are attached to files, the values assigned to shell variables, the identity of the user, and all the other things the system must know to run a program but which are not part of the program itself. A process is said to be *active* if the kernel knows about it and intends to do something about it. In other words, a process is considered active even though its program may be waiting its turn for time and memory.

A process is initiated under the Unix operating system through the action of another process: processes start up other processes. When a user first logs in, the kernel sets a copy of the shell running for him; if the user then issues some command, say **who**, the shell finds and initiates **who**. In fact, there is no way for the user to initiate a process, except to have it done for him by some other (already active) process! The natural result is a hierarchical structure of processes. This hierarchy is created by means of a mechanism called a *fork* (after the system call which requests the mechanism). To fork, the kernel replaces an existing process by two, as in Figure 5.1(a): itself and another, newly initiated, process. The original process is called the *parent* process; the newly added one is called its *child*. The child generally shares all files with the parent process. Once forked, both processes run as if they were independent, unless a specific request is made for the parent to wait until completion of the child. Of course, the child process (process 2) may need to initiate yet another process. It can do so, by forking again.The result is shown in Figure 5.1(b), three processes active concurrently. The new process (process 3) is regarded as a child of process 2. It will have access to files opened by the previous two processes, though they may not have access to files it has opened. The general rule is that files are always made accessible to processes lower down in the hierarchy.

When a user first logs in, the kernel initiates a copy of the shell to run as a process for him. Process 1 is created when the user issues some command to the shell. As a result, process 3 would be executed concurrently with the shell as well as processes 1 and 2. In fact, the shell could well fork again (e.g., if 1, 2, and 3 were background processes), thereby creating process 4. The result is sketched in Figure 5.1(c). Intricate process hierarchies can be created easily and rapidly in this way.

When new processes are initiated by the shell, the forking is normally so arranged that the shell waits for the process to complete. In other words, the normal procedure is for all processes to wait until the most recent one has finished work. If it is desired to run some process in the background,

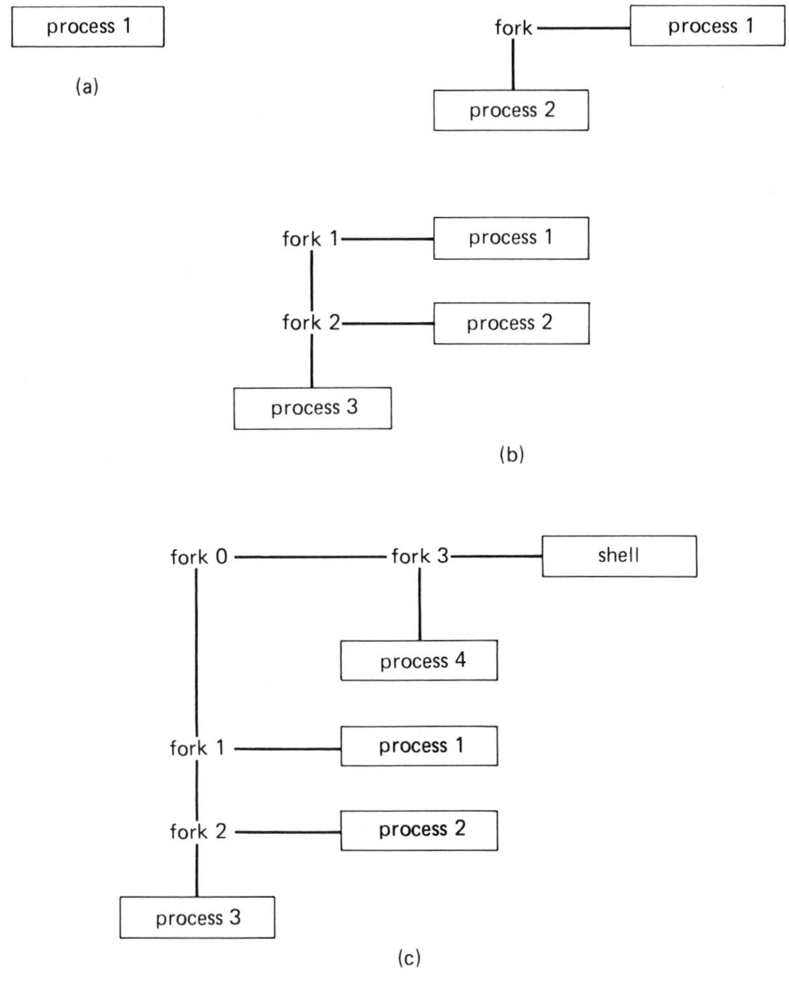

FIGURE 5.1. Forking of processes. (a) A single process is replaced by itself and its child process. (b) If the child process forks, multiple concurrent processes are created. (c) Repeated forking creates a process hierarchy.

say process 1, the user can so request (by appending an ampersand & to the shell command). The shell prompt is then issued as soon as the child process has been initiated. More detail on forking and waiting will be found below.

A Process Hierarchy

To see the process hierarchy as it exists at a particular moment, the **ps** command may be used. With the appropriate options selected, this command can show practically every kind of known information about the processes currently known to the system. On a particular Unix system, with three users logged on, the output (slightly edited to eliminate superfluous information) shown in Figure 5.2 is obtained. This display shows the status S associated with each process (*sleeping* or *running*); the user identification number UID; the process identification number PID and the number PPID of its parent process; the priority number PRI of the process and the size SZ of its program (blocks); the terminal number TTY with which the process is associated; the TIME the process has consumed to date; and the command CMD which caused the process to be initiated. System-initiated processes have no terminal numbers associated with them, hence the question marks in the TTY column.

The number of concurrent processes may seem large at first glance, and it may seem strange that some are not associated with any terminal at all. These processes belong to the system itself; they reside at the root of the process hierarchy as it were. A better overview of the process structure may be obtained by drawing a graph of the parent-child interdependences of processes, as in Figure 5.3. The processes at the left and top of the graph, with process numbers below 30 and process 34, are initiated by the system; those further to the right and downward are caused by the users. The initial provisions made by the system are for initialization and swapping of processes and updating of system information. The programs **lpsched** and **cron** are, respectively, the line printer scheduler and the clock daemon, who watches for timings and initiates all actions dependent on clock time. There is a fourth terminal on the system, idle at the time shown; the **getty** program checks from time to time whether anyone is trying to log in on it.

S	UID	PID	PPID	PRI	SZ	TTY	TIME	CMD
S	0	0	0	0	2	?	0:02	swapper
S	0	1	0	30	15	?	0:02	init
S	201	31	1	30	23	co	0:26	csh
S	202	32	1	28	20	02	0:13	sh
S	0	18	1	40	12	?	0:24	update
S	14	23	1	26	26	?	0:02	lpsched
S	0	27	1	26	26	?	0:12	cron
S	0	33	1	30	20	03	0:16	sh
S	0	34	1	28	15	04	0:04	getty
S	201	175	31	28	46	co	5:55	vi
S	202	217	32	30	20	02	0:02	sh
S	202	219	217	30	22	02	0:00	sh
S	202	220	217	26	7	02	0:02	tee
S	202	221	219	26	35	02	0:13	sed
S	202	222	220	26	14	02	0:13	deroff
R	202	223	220	54	66	02	0:10	sort
S	202	224	220	26	18	02	0:01	spellpro
S	202	225	220	26	65	02	0:02	spellpro
S	202	226	220	26	6	02	0:01	comm
R	0	227	33	54	26	03	0:14	ps

FIGURE 5.2. Status report on all processes running in a four-user system with three terminals active and one dormant.

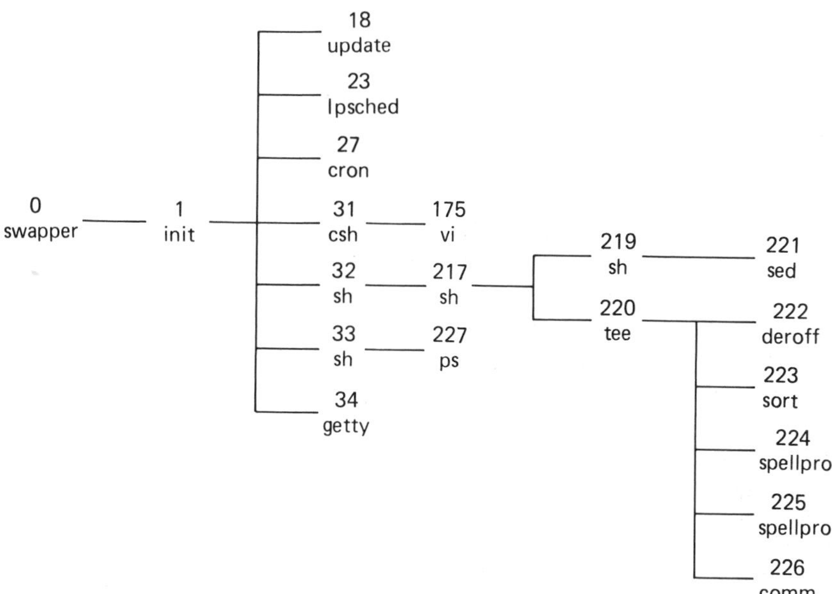

FIGURE 5.3. Process structure in a four-terminal system, with one user editing, one running a spelling check, and one terminal idle.

When the process status shown in Figure 5.3 was taken, one user (on the console) was editing with the **vi** editor and one (terminal 2) had just recently launched a spelling checker job. The **spell** program invokes several other processes, so process 32 has a whole subgraph of further processes attached to it, including two more copies of the shell itself. All these processes, however, are seen to be sleeping, except for the **sort** program (process 223) which presumably is sorting words at this time. Terminal 03 has another copy of the shell attached; it is currently running the process status enquiry command **ps**.

Process identification numbers are on occasion needed by users, for processes (unlike their associated programs) have no names. To kill an existing process is easy enough if the process is running at the terminal—interrupting with a DELETE keystroke suffices. Background processes, on the other hand, can only be killed with the **kill** command which requires specifying the process number.

Memory Allocation

Unix is both a multitasking and a multiprogramming operating system. That is to say, it not only keeps track of many concurrent processes but also maintains control over all the programs resident in main memory at the same time. In normal operation, each program is loaded into a different area of main memory. Time-sharing operation can then proceed without swapping the memory content onto disk. Each program can be made to run for its allocated slice of time in turn, remaining quiescent in memory when it is not running. Only the machine registers themselves are shared between programs, so that swapping programs really only amounts to swapping register contents. The system kernel is responsible for keeping track of which processes are considered active at any given time and which one is actually executing, deciding whether and when to swap and determining where in memory to load newly initiated programs. When a process terminates, the kernel decides whether termination was normal (successful) and sets the exit status variable accordingly. This status can be examined and used by the shell.

Unix programs can be set up in two different ways, reentrant or not. Reentrant code has all program instructions occupy a group of memory locations separate from any modifiable data and all writable data locations separate from the program code. Nonreentrant code mixes the two. While running, processes whose programs are reentrant are allocated three distinct portions of machine memory: a text segment, a data segment, and a stack segment. The text segment contains pure code and is write-protected. The data segment contains all user-defined data, values of variables, and so on. The stack segment contains system information, required to keep the process intact when it is swapped in and out. Nonreentrant programs of course cannot separate stack and data from program.

Making the program code and data separate achieves two useful goals. First, it reduces the quantity of information to be swapped, by swapping the text segment one way only. Since the text segment is never modified, it must always be an exact image of the user program initially available on disk, so there is no need to write it to disk when swapping the process out. Second, some programs such as the **vi** editor are used often; in larger installations several users may need it at the same time. The shell, in fact, must exist in at least as many copies as there are users logged in, for a new shell is started for every user when he arrives. If two or more users need the same program text, there is no need to create duplicate copies of the text segment, for text is guaranteed to be and remain identical in all copies. It suffices to create, and swap when needed, one writable data segment and one stack segment for each user. The writable segments are rarely large compared to the executable code of a complicated program like the shell.

Time and Resource Sharing

In multitasking operating systems, individual processes are not ordinarily allowed to run to completion but are granted slices of processor time on a modified round-robin basis. It is not usual to grant them equal time slices in turn, because the needs of different processes may differ considerably.

The time slices granted to individual processes depend on several factors, among them process importance, availability of required input data, and availability of output devices. Some can be decided and acted upon entirely by examining the process itself. Others may be altered by the needs of other processes (e.g., if input data are awaited from some other program) or the computer hardware (e.g., printer presently busy). Unix, like most operating systems, therefore allocates time slices to individual processes so as to maximize the use of hardware resources while giving due precedence to critical tasks.

The Unix kernel allocates time to competing processes in accordance with process priorities. Priorities are expressed numerically, with the largest numbers signifying the least important tasks. (In other words, a high priority under Unix is a low priority!) Priority ratings can be examined with the **ps** command; they are updated periodically, typically at intervals of a few seconds. At every updating interval, jobs with a high ratio of processor time to terminal time are downgraded, while those requiring relatively less computing are upgraded. In this way, users with a great deal of interactive work (e.g., typing at the keyboard) have high priority and therefore should have nearly instant terminal response. Tasks with large amounts of computing, it is argued, are quite likely to keep someone waiting anyway, so there is no harm in making them wait a little longer. For similar reasons, system-initiated tasks always have higher priority than user-initiated tasks. Because priorities are regularly updated, processes which change character will have the wrong priority for only a short time. For example, a computation-intensive task initially launched with high priority will soon enough have its priority number increased. Conversely, a process with initially low priority will tend to move into the foreground if it requires little processing but a good deal of terminal input and output.

Priority numbers of Unix processes run backwards, with high numbers denoting low priority. Numbers typically lie between 0 (for the vitally important kernel processes) and perhaps 50 or higher. Users can influence the priority ratings of processes in two ways: by declaring them to be background jobs or by asking for the priority number (the nice number, in Unix programmer jargon) to be incremented. The command

```
$ nice -10 ls -lR $HOME > alldir &
```

is equivalent to

```
$ ls -lR $HOME > alldir &
```

but with the priority augmented by 10 so as to push the task further into the background. The command itself creates a file `alldir` containing a long-form listing of all the directories the user owns (the `-R` option forces recursive consultation of all subdirectories). Normal users can increment the nice number but not decrement it; that privilege is reserved to the system manager.

When the time allotted to a particular process has been used up and another takes a turn, the first program may need to be removed from main memory to make room for the second. Processes are swapped by writing into a disk file (the swap file) an image of each user process; when the user is swapped in again, the swap file is read and the state of the computer is restored exactly as it was when the user was swapped out. In this way, the user program can resume precisely where it left off, having merely been delayed. The process image maintained in the swap file includes the contents of the user writable parts of memory, the contents of the machine registers, the name of the directory currently in use, a list of open files, and a few other relevant items of information.

`fork`, `execl`, and `wait`

To clarify how the access permissions and priority ratings of Unix processes work, the forking procedure needs to be examined a little more closely. The `fork` system call creates a new process, with both *parent* and *child* active. The terms parent and child are apt in this context; the two processes are created alike. `fork` does actually make two processes exist but endows both with the same program and almost the same environment—almost, because one differs from the other by being listed in the system tables as the other's child. This procedure may seem a little curious, but it does have its own logic: since the two processes are identical, there is no need to swap any program code in or out, nor to copy anything but writable data areas. Execution of another program is requested by another system call, which specifies what program is desired. Half a dozen system calls, essentially alike but differing a little in the way their arguments are presented, serve this purpose. For example, forking can be requested from a C program by

```
i = fork();
```

and subsequent execution of the program `newprog` through

```
j = execl (newprog, arg1, arg2, . . ., argn, 0);
```

where `newprog`, `arg1`, . . ., `argn` are pointers to character strings that specify the program name and the names of its arguments. In response to `execl`, the kernel will cause the original program to be replaced (overwritten) by the new one. In other words, the sequence `fork-execl` first cheaply creates a copy of the parent process, then replaces the program text of the child with the program it is actually desired to run. Although it contains a new program and probably new data, the identity of the process (as contrasted with the program) is still the same.

In normal interactive work at the keyboard, processes are set running as soon as commands are issued and the requesting process (usually the shell) is asked to wait until the child process has exited. Simply forking will not do the trick here; to make the parent process wait, the system call `wait` is issued. It forces the parent process to hang until the kernel signals it that the child process has terminated.

Effective User Identification

The `fork-execl` system call sequence creates a new process which inherits the environment of its parent, then overlays the program with a new one. Except as deliberate changes are made, the environmental parameters remain those of the parent process: same owner, same terminal, same home directory. This arrangement works well in most cases but causes difficulty with access permissions occasionally. The problem and its solution merit brief examination.

Various programs resident in a Unix system are available publicly but require access to closely restricted files. The **passwd** program, for example, may be used by anyone; but the file of user passwords is available for writing only by the system manager. A conflict arises here, however: user *joe* can run the **passwd** program but that program cannot update the file of passwords, because the password file is writable only by its owner, not *joe*! Much the same problem arises in many commercial applications, where a data file may need to be updated by several account clerks but no account clerk can be allowed unlimited access to the whole file. The problem is solved by trickery. When the shell owned by user *joe* initiates the process containing the **passwd** command, the child process inherits *joe* as the process owner, so a conflict arises when needing access to files owned by the system itself. If the user identification of the child process is altered to *root* (i.e., the system itself) rather than *joe*, all necessary files will be available to the child. The child process, in other words, has an apparent owner different from the parent process. In Unix jargon, the user identification of the child process is called the *effective user identity*, as contrasted to the *real user identity* inherited from the parent. The effective user identification belongs to the environment of the child process, not of the parent; it therefore expires with the child.

Processes running for a user may appear to belong either to the same owner as the parent process or to the owner of the program file. When a new process is launched, the effective user identification is set to match the ownership of the file, provided a flag bit (called the SUID—*set-user-identity* bit) attached to the command file is set. If it is, the file is shown in directory listings not merely as executable but executable with SUID set, the permission letter shown being s rather than x:

```
-rws--x--x   1 sysinfo    12826   df
-rws--x--x   1 root        6898   mkdir
```

```
-rws--x--x   1 root       19168   passwd
-rws--x--x   1 sysinfo    25525   ps
-rws--x--x   1 root        7181   rmdir
```

Setting the effective ownership can cause some system security problems. If some program owned by *root* can fork to produce a new shell, that shell inherits the ownership of its parent and therefore has unlimited access to the entire system!

cron the Clock Daemon

Timed processes in the Unix system are governed by the system clock through the agency of **cron**, a process described by the manuals as the *clock daemon*. A daemon is a minor god of Greek mythology, not to be confused with a demon (an evil spirit); **cron** is thus the clock-god who ensures the correct timing of events.

When first launched, **cron** consults a set of tables to see when the first event needing the clock-god's attention is scheduled to occur. All such events are processes to be initiated at specified times. Having consulted the schedule, **cron** goes to sleep, awakening just in time to fork the first scheduled process. It starts that process, consults the tables for the next scheduled event, and goes to sleep again. System managers make extensive use of **cron** for administrative tasks, for **cron** does not forget, nor does it mind doing accounts in the wee hours of the morning when the computer is probably lightly loaded anyway.

Not only the system manager but ordinary users as well can ask **cron** to take care of processes. Processes to be launched periodically are conveniently copied from a file into the **cron** tables by the **crontab** command,

```
$ crontab filename
```

The same command, with appropriate options, also serves to remove table entries or to list the current ones. Events may be scheduled by giving a sequence of five integers corresponding to the minute, hour, date, month, and day of the week, stating what command is to be executed at that time. For example,

```
0,55 9-16 * 1-5,9-12 1-5 bell
```

might serve for the class bell in a school: it will execute the command **bell** at 0 and 55 minutes past the hour, for all hours from 0900 to 1600, on any date of the month (as signified by *) during January-May and September-December, Mondays through Fridays.

A pleasing feature of **cron** is that anything sent to the standard output file when the user is not logged in is automatically redirected to **mail;**

nothing need be lost. A displeasing feature is that if the computer is shut down at the time a process should be initiated, it is omitted forever, not caught up when the machine is restarted.

Input and Output Operations

To the shell, all input–output operations look like file operations; the shell does not recognize the existence of any peripheral devices. Indeed, this equivalence of files and devices is a key characteristic of the shell command structure. However, this viewpoint cannot be appropriate to work involving the kernel, for the kernel's job is precisely to hide the real physical devices behind the facade of apparent files.

Device Independence

Most present-day operating systems permit programs to access files on different physical volumes in a similar fashion, so that applications programs can read any files on any volume or device. Systems with this characteristic are said to exhibit a high degree of *device independence*. Device independence is achieved by creating a fictitious physical machine with the external appearance of a disk drive containing numerous files, then writing all programs to communicate with files stored in this virtual device. Every real physical device naturally does not have all the assumed characteristics of the virtual device. Each physical device is therefore endowed with a special program, called a *device driver*, which translates the required actions of the virtual device into those of the real one. User programs can then communicate with any new device added to the system, provided a device driver exists for it. The Unix system carries device independence to its logical conclusion, by making all physical devices on the system look to the user's programs as if they were simply files. Because these files are somewhat different from user files, they are referred to as *special files*. Reasonably enough, special files have read and write permissions attached to them, as indeed they must; after all, the line printer is a write-only device and all users must therefore be denied reading access.

First Level Interrupt Handling

Many events that occur in a multiuser computing system occur in real time and must be dealt with on the spot. Such events include, for example, a user pressing a key at the terminal keyboard. A keystroke may well be followed by another within a hundred milliseconds or so, and whatever action is to be taken in response to it must be taken within that length of time.

Events requiring immediate attention are signalled to the kernel through hardware. Such an event causes an interrupt condition to exist: whatever program is currently running is halted at the end of the current machine instruction cycle and control is transferred to another, usually very small, program called an *interrupt service routine*. The interrupt service routine determines the cause of the interrupt, does whatever is necessary in response, and thereafter returns control to the program that was executing previously. Servicing an interrupt is thus an action somewhat similar to executing a subroutine: the principal program is left waiting while some other activity is carried out. But unlike a subroutine, an interrupt service routine is initiated by hardware and executed asynchronously, in response to some external event.

Since a multiuser installation may contain many terminals and each terminal can send out several characters per second, the time available for dealing with interrupts is small. Keyboard input is therefore handled in a two-level fashion by almost all operating systems. The first level interrupt handler merely collects the newly arrived keyboard character, examines it to see whether it is one of the special characters requiring immediate response (e.g., DELETE), places it in a keyboard buffer area for later attention, and echoes it to the terminal. The time taken for these actions might amount to a few dozen or a few hundred microseconds, depending on the type of computer. The user can easily gain the impression that typed characters are merely stored at the terminal, so fast is the echo sent by the interrupt handler. Even several users typing along furiously will leave plenty of machine time for other processes to run.

If the first level interrupt handler finds that the character typed at the keyboard requires action, a second level of activity is called into play: the action required is identified and carried out. For example, if an end-of-line is received from a terminal, the input line is examined for kill and erase characters and any necessary editing is done. The processed text is then placed in another queue from which it is sent on to the program expecting input. This process is likely to take much longer than a simple storage of commands.

Special Files: Block and Character

Special files are of two generic varieties: block and character. Prototypes of these are disk files and terminals, respectively. In other words, two kinds of peripheral device are recognized: disk-like and terminal-like. Devices which are neither are made to look like one or the other to the system; and the system in turn strives to make all devices look like files to the user.

Block input-output is arranged through a pool of data buffers. Typically, a dozen or more buffers may be in use. In normal operation, none is permanently dedicated to any particular user, buffers are allocated as required. When a process requests input, the kernel searches the buffers for the desired data. If the text requested is resident in a buffer, it is communicated to the process without any data transfers between memory and disk having to take place. Correspondingly, a request to write is understood to mean writing into the buffer. The buffer content is actually transferred only at a later time when the buffer is needed for some other purpose or when an explicit request is made to flush buffers. Since the buffers are not earmarked for any particular user, output buffer contents are not transferred as soon as each buffer is full, but only when all buffers are full and more buffer space is requested by some process. The input buffers are kept filled by reading ahead a good deal; output operations may involve delayed writing. Input-output operations are thus asynchronous with the program, so programs rarely need to wait for data transfers.

Character-oriented input–output by Unix device drivers is of the classical mould: the driver deals with individual characters which it either passes on or else recognizes as having particular meanings. As a simple example, a *newline* character, which denotes the end of a line in a Unix file, must be recognized and transmitted to a terminal as a sequence of two characters, *carriage return* followed by a *line-feed*. Similarly, terminals unable to tab to a particular column must be sent an appropriate number of blank spaces; terminals unable to skip pages must be sent the right number of blank lines in place of a *form feed* character. These substitutions all take place in the device driver.

Block input–output devices require only simple device driver programs, for all operations are directed to buffers of a standard form. By contrast, character devices need more complex drivers but can make do with less sophistication in the buffer management software.

Unix input–output arrangements are generally transparent to the user, and appear to be program synchronous: input is read and output is produced in exactly the sequence one would expect from reading a listing of the program. Should the system malfunction, however, the complexities of the Unix buffering scheme can become annoying. For example, output may sometimes be delayed or lost because it is still resident in buffers and hence not printed, although completely terminated as far as the program is concerned.

Physical Structure of Files

Users rarely need be concerned about the physical structure of files because the Unix system makes every file appear to the user as a simple contiguous byte (or character) string. But there are some occasions when even a rudimentary knowledge of the physical file structure allows better applications programs to be written. Besides, some users are interested as a matter of simple curiosity.

Disk files under the Unix system are physically organized into blocks. Blocks were invariably 512 bytes long in the early versions of Unix; more recently, both 512 and 1024 byte blocks have come into use. Every file is allocated an integral number of blocks and every block begins at a multiple of 512 bytes from the beginning of the file. However, successive blocks of a file are not necessarily contiguous on the disk; they may reside anywhere at all. This file organization contrasts with some small computer operating systems, which allocate space in one single contiguous area of disk. The advantage gained is that no file compaction or "garbage collection" is ever needed. In fact, the speed advantages of contiguous space allocation remain largely valid for Unix files, since contiguous space is used when it is available. Fragmentation of disk space, with every file spreading all over the disk in little pieces, only occurs when the disk is nearly full. But it is hardly necessary to point out that the management of files scattered about in penny packets is trickier than constructing simple tables of contents for contiguous files.

Ordinary files and directory files may be classified into four different size classes, occupying at most 10, 138, 16522 and 2113674 blocks of file space (assuming 512-byte blocks). The reason for this curious classification is that space is provided for 13 block numbers used to access data. The method of access is described below.

Storage of small files is straightforward enough. If a file occupies ten blocks or fewer, the spaces provided in the system tables are used simply to house the actual block numbers. For example, a file that requires three blocks might have the thirteen block numbers given as 07526, 16201, 01004, 00000, 00000, 00000, . . ., 00000. The first three denote physical block addresses on the disk; zeros show unused space. Up to ten blocks are addressed in this way, the last three words being reserved. This scheme is beautifully simple but only allows small files. Ten file blocks is 5120 bytes, about two or three typewritten pages.

Larger files are handled by an indirect addressing scheme. The first ten of the 13 block address words are used to point to file blocks containing data, exactly as if a small file were being stored. The eleventh address points not to data but to a block containing the addresses of up to 128 further file blocks. The desired data are stored in those further blocks. Since there can be up to 128 further blocks, files up to (10 + 128) = 138 blocks, or 70656 bytes, can be stored in this way. In other words, the first 10 blocks are addressed directly and the next 128 are addressed indirectly via the thirteenth block. This chapter is about 70,000 bytes long.

To store still larger files, a second level of indirect addressing is employed. The first eleven addressing words are used exactly as described above; the twelfth points to a block containing the addresses of up to 128 blocks which in turn contain the addresses of up to 128 data blocks each.

The number of additional data blocks made in accessible this way is clearly 16384 (128^2), so the total accessible data space is 10 + 128 + 16384 = 16522 blocks, or roughly eight megabytes. This book corresponds to about a megabyte of text.

The largest files are arranged in a similar fashion, but with the thirteenth addressing word used in a triple-indirect addressing scheme. The amount of additional space made available in this way is 2097152 (128^3) blocks, so that the largest possible file is approximately one gigabyte in size.

Directories are treated in the same way as ordinary files, though it is unusual to find directories growing quite so large; most users tend to structure their files hierarchically, with successive subdirectories containing perhaps one or two dozen entries. It is usually convenient to keep directories to a size that can be displayed on the terminal screen at one time.

For special files, the first of the 13 block addresses has a different significance. The first half of this word is viewed as the identification of a physical device type (e.g., magnetic tape drive), the second as the identification of a subdevice number (e.g., tape drive number 7). Restricting special files to a megabyte is not a problem, for they rarely exceed a few kilobytes.

Sequential and Random Access

The Unix system treats all devices and media alike as containing files composed of strings of characters. However, various physical file media differ in their characteristics so that some distinction must be made in practice between different kinds of file access. For example, a magnetic disk is an inherently random access device: it is as much work and takes as long to retrieve information from one place as another, so all characters on the disk are equally accessible. Writing or reading can take place in various sequences, including in one place several times. It is then necessary to keep track of where the next character is to be transmitted to (or from). A very simple mechanism is employed for doing so: a pointer is initially set to the beginning or end of a file and repositioned as reading and writing are done. Because the system always reads from the location pointed at, random access is achieved by repositioning the file pointer.

Certain media—for example, input keyboards and line printers—are strictly sequential. Characters once sent to a printer cannot be read back and reading is possible only in the sequence ordained by the input–output device. Unix achieves uniform treatment of all peripheral devices by pretending they too are files and equips them with a file pointer. Of course, movement of the file pointer associated with a sequential device is strictly unidirectional.

Media of an intermediate character, such as magnetic tapes, are viewed as logically indistinguishable from disk files. The only differences arise in their physical response, for operation of magnetic tapes as random access devices can require frequent rewinding and thus result in excruciatingly slow operation.

In addition to being strictly sequential, keyboards and line printers are also read-only and write-only devices. This physical fact presents no structural problem, since Unix software works with a system of read-write-execute permissions. A physical device which cannot be read is logically indistinguishable from a file without read permission. Thus, the existence of read-only and write-only devices fits naturally into the general system structure.

The Unix operating system provides random access to files in high-level languages such as Fortran and C, so that the average user never needs to worry about how the internal operation is carried out.

Input–Output Buffering

As far as the ordinary user can tell, file reading and writing operations appear to be synchronized to programs. In other words, all Fortran read or write statements, or equivalent commands of other languages, appear to be executed exactly when and where they appear in the program. They appear to be unbuffered: every read or write operation appears to fetch or send exactly the required number of characters, without reference to the file block size.

Since the files are physically organized in blocks, and the blocks do not necessarily occupy adjacent locations on the physical medium, such a synchronous and unbuffered appearance is only achievable by actually reading and writing files in a buffered fashion. While the details of the buffering are complicated, the principle is simple. A read instruction, for example, causes an entire block to be read from disk into a buffer area in memory. But only the required number of characters is transferred from the buffer to the program area. Similarly, writing is actually done by moving characters from the program area into a writing buffer; only when the buffer is full does physical transfer to disk take place. For example, suppose that a user program reads successive 64-character records via Fortran read statements. An actual disk transfer of data is required only once for every eight read requests, provided they ask for sequentially arranged data. On the other hand, reading randomly arranged 64-character records may require one disk access per read, if a different file block has to be fetched for each one.

Because most user programs tend to read or write to sequential locations, Unix uses a relatively complicated buffering scheme in which the next file block is preread ahead of time. Most input requests therefore find the necessary data already resident in buffers and do not need to wait for physical movement of disk heads or magnetic tapes. This speedup of operation is particularly valuable with large files, where multiple levels of indirect indexing may be needed to locate and retrieve the next sequential file block.

Data are always stored in file blocks of 1024 or 512 bytes. Input–output intensive programs theoretically should run a little faster if reading and writing are done in multiples or submultiples of the block size. However, the Unix input–output buffering scheme removes a substantial part of the speed advantage and most users do not find it worthwhile to concern themselves with this level of detail except where truly random file accesses are involved.

Buffering of output to and from special files is carried out in different ways for block and character files. Block files, i.e., special files that correspond to block-structured devices, are handled in much the same way as ordinary files. Character-structured special files naturally must work on a single-character basis. Their buffering scheme is quite simple and straightforward by comparison, without the many clever ideas incorporated in block buffering.

Mechanisms for File Access

Before a program can read or write to a file, the file must be opened or, if it did not previously exist, created. Similarly, a file must be closed before exiting a program that opened it. Files are opened and closed by the system calls `open` and `close`. In C programs, these calls can appear as function invocations, for example,

```
fillds = open (name, mode)
```

where `name` is a pointer to the file name and `mode` indicates whether the file is to be opened for reading, writing, or both. The function value `filds` returned by open is an integer called the file descriptor. All further system calls dealing with the file refer to it by this number. For example, the file is closed by

```
j = close (filds)
```

and `nchar` characters are read from it by

```
j = read (filds, buffer, nchar)
```

Two basic system calls, `read` and `write`, transfer characters from a file (which could be a special file, such as a peripheral device driver) to a specified memory buffer area. The function value returned by either call is the number of characters transferred; it might well be smaller than nchar if the file contained fewer characters than requested. File descriptors are numbers associated with processes; in fact, they are the linking numbers which tie together processes with files.

Certain file descriptors are allocated to processes automatically. File 0 refers to the standard input file, which is the terminal keyboard by default. File 1, the standard output file, is the terminal screen by default. File 2 is the standard error file, normally attached to the terminal screen also. It serves for handling system messages and diagnostics. Having this file separate from the standard output permits system messages to appear on the terminal screen even if the standard output has been diverted to a disk file or printer. The default file assignments can be changed by the user. Since the normal rules on forking apply to the shell, any files opened by the shell are accessible to any process spawned by the shell—therefore also to all its children, their children, and so on. The standard file assignments of the parent process are therefore carried through to all its descendants. The standard files are of course reassignable so input and output can be diverted from anywhere to anywhere else.

A Unix file is simply a string of bytes of known length. An open call opens a file and sets a pointer to point to its first byte; a read call reads bytes and moves the pointer the number of bytes read. Any subsequent read begins reading wherever the pointer last came to rest and moves it on by the number of bytes read. Writing operations move the pointer in a similar fashion. Files thus have the logical appearance of being sequential. Nonsequential access is provided by resetting the pointer to an appropriate place, for any subsequent reading or writing operations will then proceed from the new pointer position. Repositioning to `newplace` is done by the `lseek` system call,

```
newplace = lseek (filds, where, how)
```

Here `filds` is the file descriptor and `where` is the desired pointer position, expressed either relative to the old position or absolutely, as indicated by how.

File Identification

Directory entries in Unix directories only identify files by giving an index number (called the *i-number* in Unix system programming jargon) for each file. The index numbers for any given physical volume (disk, tape, etc.) are actually pointers to another table, called the *i-list*, which resides on the same device.

The i-list of a given device contains a set of entries called *i-nodes*; for this reason, the i-list is sometimes referred to as the *inode table*. An i-node is a set of data that contains the following information regarding each file:

1. The identifying number of the user who created the file.
2. The protection status of the file (read-only, open, etc.).
3. Thirteen words showing device blocks occupied by the file.
4. The size of the file.
5. The time the file was last modified.
6. The number of times the file is referred to in directories.
7. Bits to identify directories, special files, and large files.

Keeping track of how many times the file is listed in directories is important, because a non-directory file may appear in the directories of several users. If one of them wishes to remove the file from his own directory, only the directory entry (not the file itself) should be removed if there are any other directories in which the file still appears. On the other hand, the actual file itself should be purged (the file space should be released for other use) if the last user of the file removes it.

There are some occasions on which users may wish to inspect the i-numbers associated with files, usually because information regarding disk space is needed. The i-numbers are available through the **ls** command, invoked with the **-i** option. This option provides the listing that would normally be expected from **ls**, augmented by the i-number corresponding to each file name. These name-to-number correspondences are called *links* and serve as the main file identification and management tool. In principle, the **mv** command moves a link, **rm** removes one, and **ln** creates a new one. This fact may explain the curious command names employed for file deletion, renaming, and synonym creation.

Chapter 6

Facilities and Utilities

The Unix operating system provides a large variety of utility routines for performing computations, communicating with other users, and handling files. Some are important enough to merit chapters of their own, like the shell programs; or to deserve at least a large part of a chapter, like **ed**. Others appear in context with the shell, language compilers, or files. However, there are still others of considerable value which do not naturally belong in another chapter of this book. They have been collected together here, as a miscellany of handy items.

Communications

Under the Unix system and other similar operating systems, facilities are provided for the system manager to communicate with users and for users to communicate with each other. Two forms of communication are provided: mail and immediate messages. In principle, these two are analogous to the post office and the telephone company. One leaves messages in a mailbox for later collection; the other communicates directly but risks that no one will answer the phone.

Mail Services

Every user is assigned a file called his *mailbox*, which is not part of his directory structure (it actually resides in the directory /usr/spool/mail in most systems) but which he can read using the **mail** command. The same command makes it possible to write into another user's mailbox, leaving messages for collection later.

If there is any fresh mail waiting, Unix informs the user about it when logging in, before the first shell prompt:

```
You have mail.
$
```

When the user reads the messages in his mailbox, the system notes that there no longer exists any unread mail. The *You have mail* message will then not appear at the next login, unless of course another new message has been placed in the mailbox in the meantime. The Unix mail system can also be set up to delete old mail once it has been read; it is then up to the user to save it if he prefers. Such automatic deletion is considered desirable in systems with many users but little disk space; it economizes space by leaving little unused trash on disk. Mail arriving while logged in at the terminal is simply placed in the mailbox; this postman does not ring to notify about the arrival of new mail.

The message regarding mail is sent out at the conclusion of the login procedure, before the shell is started running. Thus, the message will only appear once, preceding the first appearance of the shell prompt. Any further $ prompts will appear without the mail message, as usual.

To read what mail there is, the user enters the command **mail**. In response, **mail** fetches messages from his mailbox and displays them one at a time, the most recent one first. For example,

```
$ mail
From bftsplk Thu Feb 29 11:29:44 1984
check your files, I may have wrecked some by accident
```

Every piece of mail is stamped with its time and date of transmission, exactly like ordinary post office mail. The name of the sender is also affixed to each message.

When the addressee looks at his mail, only one message is displayed at a time; it is followed by an enquiry about how the message is to be disposed of. Its recipient may simply make a mental note of the message, or have it deleted, or ask for it to be saved. In fact, a wide range of choices is open to the user: the message may be saved with or without the header (postmark), may be mailed on to someone else, may be repeated (useful for long messages), or retained in the mailbox. The most usual response is to go on to the next message by simply striking the RETURN key.

The mail command permits a few options, of which the most useful are **-e** (suppress display) and **-r** (reverse order). The former is useful in shell scripts because it returns an exit status of *true* if there is any mail, *false* if not; it therefore permits testing without reading. The **-r** option displays the oldest mail first.

Sending Mail

Any user may send mail to another, again by means of the **mail** command. To do so, the addressee's name is appended to the command, as in the following message sent to user *bftsplk*:

```
$ mail bftsplk
Which files do you suspect?
All my directories look OK.
```

The **mail** command line is followed by the message to be sent. It is perfectly all right to send more than one line; the message is considered terminated whenever either a control-D character is sent or whenever a period (the . character) occurs on a line by itself. But it is usually wise to keep messages reasonably short. The entire message is displayed on the terminal screen at once when the recipient looks at his mail, so messages longer than a screenful can be difficult to read.

Mail may be sent to more than one recipient at once, by listing the names of all the recipients in the command line. It should be noted that all mail handling is done by user login name; obviously, it is not possible to send a message to anybody whose login name is not known. The login name thus plays the same role here as do name and address at the post office. If a nonexistent login name is given in the command, **mail** may reply with an error message or (in some systems) simply ignore the command. If a message is addressed to the wrong login name, it is delivered as addressed.

A user is permitted to address mail to himself. The procedure for doing so is precisely the same as for sending to any other system user. Many users like sending messages to themselves, as reminder notes to remove unneeded files or to take action in some other matter. However, there is a basic danger here: when greeted by the *you have mail* message, it is tempting to assume the mail consists of the reminder note and not to bother reading it. Real mail from other users may thus become lost, or at any rate ignored.

It may seem strange that the **mail** command is fully implemented even on single-user Unix systems on microcomputers. It needs to be, for much Unix mail is sent to users by the system itself or by processes launched on the user's behalf by **cron**. The line printer spooler **lp**, for example, can be asked to notify users by mail when print jobs have run to completion.

Immediate Messages

In addition to mail, which is deposited in a mailbox for later collection, system users may send messages directly to others using the **write** command. Such messages are not placed in the addressee's mailbox, they are immediately transmitted to his terminal instead. Naturally, such direct transmission is only possible if the addressee is logged in at the time. The **who** command may be used to determine who is, and at which terminal (or terminals). Attempts to write to nonexistent users, or to users not logged in, result in error messages and no communication. The **write** command works somewhat like sending mail:

```
$ write abner
Please check your files.
I may have corrupted some by mistake.
```

In contrast to the **mail** command which deals with whole messages, **write** transmits every keyboard line immediately when the RETURN key is pressed. The **write** command line itself produces at the receiving end a line identifying the sender, for example,

```
message from bftsplk tty6
Please check your files.
I may have corrupted some by mistake.
```

Transmission initiated by **write** overrides whatever else the addressee may have been doing, and each transmitted line is displayed at his terminal even if that puts it in the middle, say, of a directory listing he may have been trying to read.

Once the **write** program has been set running, any and all lines typed at the keyboard will be transmitted to the addressee. Transmission is turned off by sending a control-D. This control-D will not cause logout, merely an exit from **write**. Once the **write** program is running, it takes two successive control-D's to log out: one to exit from **write** to the shell and one more to exit from **sh**.

If a user is logged in at more than one terminal at the same time, it is possible to indicate in the command line to which terminal the messages are to be sent. For example,

```
$ write bftsplk tty6
```

will display the transmitted lines at *tty6*, but not at any other terminals where user *bftsplk* may also be logged in.

Two-Way Communication

When a message is received from another user, it is natural to reply immediately. But doing so is a little tricky, because only one user can be transmitting at a time. Two-way communication thus resembles CB radio rather more than the telephone, for it is important to let the recipient know when the other fellow is prepared to listen for an answer and when he intends to keep on talking. One widely used method is to employ the word *over*, usually abbreviated to `-o-`, to signify "I will now listen for a reply", the words *over and out* (`-oo-` for short) to mean "I have finished and will neither transmit nor listen". A conversation may then look (from one end) like

```
$ write abner
Please check your files.
I may have corrupted some by mistake. -o-
message from bftsplktty6
Which files do you suspect?
All my directories look OK. -o-
Glad all is well, thanks for checking! -oo-
```

The words *message from . . .* signify that the other user has also started up a copy of **write**. They will only occur once at the startup of that program, not between every pair of messages.

At times when a critical job is running, no messages may be wanted from anyone. Some sensitive processes (e. g., the **nroff** text formatter) disable the message facilities automatically whenever they are initiated. But users may block the message passing channel at any time by means of the **mesg** command, as in

```
$ mesg n
```

where the **n** indicates "no". To turn messages on again, the same command is issued with a **y** (for "yes") argument replacing **n**. Blocked messages are not saved for later presentation to the intended recipient; they are simply discarded.

Logging in Elsewhere

Many Unix users hold valid login names on several systems. For example, a small system may reside in the executive office, a bigger one in an administrative complex, a third one at a laboratory or production facility—and the same user may need services from all three. On many occasions, it is desirable to log in to two or more systems simultaneously, so processes running on one system can have access to data resident in another or, in the simplest case, to move text files between machines. Unix provides a simple communication facility called **cu** (short for *call Unix*) able to do so.

In the following, it will be supposed that a user *joe* of a local system wishes to use a second, remote, machine as well. To establish communication, the **cu** program is first called into action. If the local system has an automatic dialler, as it often will, telephone connection is established by

```
$ cu 3925397
```

where the digits are the telephone number of the remote machine (*without* spaces or dashes!). Alternatively, the system name may be given in place of the telephone number; if the name is known to the local system, it will look up and dial the telephone number itself. Direct-wired connections only require naming the direct line, usually (but not in all systems) preceded with **-l**:

```
$ cu -l dir
```

When the remote system is connected, it behaves for all the world as if the user had logged in at a terminal, without going through the local system: it will demand a login name and password, notify about any mail waiting at the remote location, and issue its system prompt. The local computer merely acts as a terminal to the remote one. A simple example is

```
login: joe
Password:
L$ cu remote
Connected
Welcome to BIGSYS. Please login: palooka
Password:
R$
```

Here user *joe* has logged in to the local system (whose prompt is `L$`), then immediately called *remote*. The login name used does not need to be the same, nor the password, because the systems are really independent; the remote system neither knows nor cares that another Unix system, not merely a dumb terminal, is doing the calling. Its login procedure may be different, and so may its system prompt. Once communication with the remote computer has been established, **cu** acts merely as a message passer; the user really only sees the remote machine.

The point of logging in to the remote system through **cu** is surely to allow messages to be passed between machines; if not, the local system is only being used as a rather expensive terminal. While passing messages along, **cu** therefore watches for keyboard lines beginning with the tilde (the ~ character) and interprets these as commands directed to **cu**, not intended for passing to the remote computer. The most important is undoubtedly ~. (tilde followed by a dot), which terminates the conversation. This one should normally be used only after logging out from the remote system. The ~! command causes **cu** to start up a local shell, with which the user can do whatever seems appropriate; it also exists in the shorter form ~! *<command>*, in which a single command is given to a shell. An interesting embellishment is provided by ~$*<command>* which works exactly like ~! *<command>* except that the standard output of *<command>* is piped to the remote system. Although this command set is small, it effectively taps all the resources of two Unix systems, since it allows execution of any command at either machine!

The general **cu** commands can be used to send files or messages between machines, but file transfer is so frequent a need that special commands are provided: `~%take` for importing from the remote system and `~%put` for exporting to it. They are used much like the **cp** command on a single system:

```
R$ ~%take rfile lfile
```

where `rfile` is the file name at the remote system and `lfile` at the local system. The second argument may be omitted if file names are to be the same.

Only text files can be transmitted with **cu** because the communication protocol between machines can otherwise be confused by some nonprintable characters. File transfers under **cu** are not checked for errors and lack convenience because they are done on the spot, locking up the communication line while the transfer proceeds. Thus, **cu** is convenient for moving small quantities of text, but for substantial files a more appropriate tool is **uucp**. The latter permits file transfers to take place at the systems' convenience, much like background jobs.

File Management

The Unix family of operating systems provides a rich selection of file management tools applicable to text files. In fact, the standard tool kit is so large that most simple operations on files require no programming; the user need only ask for them. For more complicated tasks, the programmability of the shell allows new and unexpected combinations to be created out of elementary operations—all without any programming other than writing a few shell scripts.

Copying Files

Making copies of files, one or several at a time, in disk file form or as printed copy, is an elementary operation of file management. There are various ways of doing so. The most useful commands for this simple kind of file management are

cat	which concatenates files
cp	which copies a file, or several files

cp is straightforward: if one issues the command

```
$ cp file1 file2
```

`file1` is copied, the copy being named `file2`. Full pathnames may of course be given, so that the two files need not be within the same directory. When making copies, it will pay to remember that **cp** will happily replace an old file named `file2` by overwriting. In fact, **cp** always destroys first and writes afterward; care should be taken not to make mistakes in file names!

To copy files from one directory to another, a variant form of the **cp** command is available, which avoids the necessity of typing full pathnames both times. In the variant form, it suffices to name the files to be copied and the directory to which they are to be copied. Copies in both directories will then have the same file name, though of course the full pathnames will differ.

It is important not to confuse **cp** with **mv** or **ln**. **cp** really makes a copy, so that after the operation there are two real copies of the file occupying physical space on the disk. **mv**, on the other hand, merely renames the existing copy; no data transfer takes place. **ln** establishes two or more synonymous names but retains only the original physical copy of the file. After an **ln** operation, there will be two or more directory entries for the file, though only a single file will really exist. Directory entries (links) are allowed only if both the directory and the file reside on the same physical device (e.g., the same magnetic tape) or if the device is permanently attached to the Unix system (e.g., the permanent system disk drives). But **cp**, which makes physical copies, can be used to copy across devices.

To avoid the irreparable loss of precious files that might occur in a power failure or other computer malfunction, it is a good idea to make backup copies of files from time to time. These should preferably reside on a removable medium such as floppy disk or magnetic tape, one that can be physically removed from the computer. After all, the building might burn one day!

The **cat** command sends a copy of one or more files to the standard output device. Thus a file is easily inspected by the simple command

```
$ cat file1
```

Naming several files in the **cat** command merely produces a concatenation of the files in the standard output. The files will be concatenated in the order in which they are named in the command. **cat** may be made to perform much of the work of **cp**, by suitably redirecting input and output. In fact, **cat** may be used to turn the whole Unix system into a giant electric typewriter, by taking its input from the keyboard and directing its output to the printer.

When files are displayed at the terminal, lines are ordinarily scrolled up from the bottom to the top of the screen, and the top line is discarded. When large files are displayed, the inconvenience of losing the top line may be avoided by stopping the display scrolling. A control-S character sent from the keyboard at any time will halt transmission of more lines to the terminal, thereby stopping scrolling; a control-Q will restart transmission.

Display and Examination

Displaying a file on the terminal screen is easy enough; the near-universal **cat** program does the necessary once again. And once again, does it not well enough to be acceptable as the only program for the purpose. Because **cat** simply copies input to output, a large file can flash past at incredible speed and even the stop/start facilities of pressing control-S and control-Q will not allow the desired part of the file to be positioned on the screen. Any Unix system therefore includes either or both of two programs designed for screen display: **more** and **pg**.

The **more** program is simple and easy to use. Like **cat**, it displays its standard input, but unlike **cat** it pauses after each screenful and waits for the user to signal before continuing. For most users of fast communication lines (say 120 characters/second or faster), feeding almost everything to the screen through **more** quickly becomes a habit.

A pleasing extension of **more**, available on many Unix systems, is calling the **vi** editor through **more**. Normally, the user advances through the file by pressing the space bar (to see the next screenful) or the d key (to scroll half a screenful). Pressing v causes **more** to fork a new process which runs the **vi** editor, starting with the text positioned at the same place where **more** stopped. Because **vi** is entered through process forking, exiting from **vi** returns the user to precisely the erstwhile position in the **more** display. It is therefore possible to flip back and forth between file perusal and file editing, without exiting from either program.

The disappointing part of **more** is its inability to back up. It really does little more than **cat**, though that little represents a major advance in convenience. The **pg** program resembles **more**, but is cleverer to the extent of knowing how to page both ways, or to go to an altogether different part of the file. Pressing the space bar or the D key works exactly as with **more**; but prefixing either keystroke with a signed number causes display of a screenful either further on, or further back, in the file. Thus, typing -1SPACE goes back a screen, +3SPACE forward three screenfuls. The extremely frequent *1SPACE may have the *1 qualifier omitted. Like **more**, **pg** also knows how to start display at some intermediate point in the file, including points specified by giving a search pattern rather than a line number.

There is no v keystroke available in **pg**. However, **pg** recognizes ! as an instruction to pass information to the shell. Thus, `!vi filename` accomplishes more or less the same objective as the v keystroke in **more**: a copy of **vi** is launched to edit `filename`.

Often enough the last few lines or pages in a file are of major interest. The **tail** utility delivers the end of a file quickly and easily. It allows the amount of text to be specified, as in

```
$ tail -100 bigfile
```

meaning that the last 100 lines are wanted. However, requests for large chunks of file may go unheeded because **tail** works with a limited amount of buffer space.

The **pg**, **more**, **tail**, and **cat** utilities all work well with text files but prove useless with files containing non-ASCII characters or files which do not have a textual interpretation. There is one Unix facility guaranteed to yield up the secrets of any file, called **od** (octal dump). It displays the file content byte by byte (or, optionally, word by word —usually a word means a byte pair) in decimal, octal, hexadecimal, or character form. A directory, for example, is not a readable file; **od** delivers its contents as easily as anything else:

```
  o 001   . \0 \0 \0 \0 \0 \0 \0 \0 \0 \0 \0 \0 \0
  m 001   . \0 \0 \0 \0 \0 \0 \0 \0 \0 \0 \0 \0 \0
021 003   l  p  i  n  s  t  a  l \0 \0 \0 \0 \0 \0
035 004   z  u  s  e \0 \0 \0 \0 \0 \0 \0 \0 \0 \0
 \0  \0   f  r  a  s  e  r  .  t  x  t \0 \0 \0 \0
 \0  \0   f  r  a  s  e  r  .  o  l  d \0 \0 \0 \0
```

This display is in (nominally) ASCII character form. It shows the directory to contain six files: itself, its parent directory, and four ordinary files. The ordinary files have their names shown, padded out with null characters (echoed as \0). The leading two bytes are pointers to further information about the files. For the last two files in the directory, the pointers have been reset to nulls, to show that the files have been removed and no information can be obtained about them any more.

Printing Services

To print a file, the output of **cat** may be redirected to the line printer. But **cat** is rarely used in practice because it is not quite clever enough. Being a simple copying program, **cat** merely echoes the exact file content to its standard output, so attempting to copy a file to the printer special file, say `/dev/lp0`, entails the risk that some other user or system process might do likewise. The accepted way to do printing is therefore to use the line printer spooler process, which does more than just print: it queues files for printing so no interference can occur. This process is started up automatically when the system is started. The command

```
$ lp printfile
```

places `printfile` into the queue for printing when its turn comes and responds immediately by giving the user the print request identifying number. Printing will begin immediately if the printer is not busy, later if it has other work to do first. The user need not stay logged in to wait for the print job. The spooler and printer processes belong to the system; whether the owner of `printfile` is logged in at printing time is irrelevant.

Impatient or curious users can ask about the progress of their print jobs at any time, referring to them by their request numbers. So long as the printing has not yet been completed, print jobs may be cancelled. Cancelled requests are simply deleted from the queue if not yet started; if printing has begun, further transmission of data to the printer is stopped. Many modern printers, however, will keep on printing for a little while because they keep several lines (or several pages) of text in a local buffer memory within the printer. Although Unix can stop transmission of any more data, it cannot take back the characters already sent to the printer. Enquiries and cancellations use the commands **lpstat** and **cancel**. Their use is illustrated by the following:

```
$ lp wrongfile
request id is Lprt0-106 (1 file)
$ lp rightfile
request id is Lprt0-107 (1 file)
$ lpstat
Lprt0-106      peter       51923      Jun 12 10:27 on Lprt0
Lprt0-107      peter       79677      Jun 12 10:27
$ cancel Lprt0-106
request "Lprt0-106" cancelled
$
```

After placing two printing requests, the user realizes the first was erroneous. A status enquiry with **lpstat** shows two requests queued for *peter*, with the first already started printing on device `Lprt0`. The **cancel** command removes it from the queue and from the printer; how many pages will be printed despite cancellation depends on the printer speed, system response time, and the user's own dexterity.

When several users have printing requests pending, quite some time may elapse before any given request can be carried out. Repeated status inquiries are both irksome and distracting. Rather than to ask for status at frequent intervals, the **lp** command can be embellished with the **-w** option,

```
$ lp -w printfile
```

The print spooler will then write a message on the user's terminal when the job has finished; if the user has logged out in the meantime, it will send mail instead. If terminal messages are not desired, then **-m** will send mail in any case.

The printing request queue maintained by the spooler is effectively a directory of files maintained by the spooler for its own use. A file to be printed is not copied; instead, a link is established to the queue by a mechanism like the **ln** command. This means the files named in a print request must be ordinary files, otherwise the strict tree structure rule of Unix directories will be violated. All files in directory `/usr/bloggs` can be printed by requesting `/usr/bloggs/*` but not merely the directory name. Furthermore, what will be printed is the file content at the time the printing request is honored, not the file as it was when the request was placed. If there is any likelihood the file might be altered or removed before the printing task is completed, the **-c** option should be specified with **lp**. A temporary copy of the file will then be made immediately and any future changes in the file will not appear in the printed version.

Numerous Unix installations use an alternative command **lpr** for queueing print requests. This is an older version than **lp** and poorer in its range of options. For most ordinary purposes, however, the two differ in convenience features only; thus, **lpr** will send mail but will not write to the user's terminal.

Like **cat**, the **lp** and **lpr** programs do no text processing of any kind; they deliver a faithful image of their inputs to another place and time. For example, they know nothing about page lengths or page breaks. To obtain tidy file listings, it is usually more convenient to use **pr**, which breaks up large files neatly into numbered and dated pages. The output of **pr** is sent to its standard output device, so that **pr** is normally used in a pipeline to feed **lp**. Because **pr** knows how to print in two or more columns and is willing to truncate rather than fold long lines, it is particularly convenient for program listings written in assembler language or other languages (C included!) which tend to large numbers of short text lines.

File Sorting

One very comprehensive and flexible sorting program, called **sort**, is standard equipment in all Unix systems. **sort** expects input organized as lines of moderate length and sorts these lines into sequential order. The lines are not required to contain anything in particular, so **sort** can be applied to text files, numeric data, or even to nonprintable files containing anything at all. In its simplest form, one invokes **sort** by

```
$ sort inputfile > outputfile
```

and `inputfile` ends up sorted. Order is determined by the standard ASCII collating sequence, so that alphabetic characters are sorted into alphabetic order and numerics into ascending order. (A table of ASCII character codes appears in the Appendix). The ASCII character set includes not only the alphabetics and numerals, but punctuation marks and special characters, so these will be sorted too.

Sorting can be carried out according to a fabulous variety of criteria. First, characters may be sorted in different ways. It is possible to force "dictionary" sorting, i.e., to ignore all characters except alphabetics, numerals, and blanks. It is possible also to ignore the distinction between upper and lower case. White space (blanks and tab characters) can be ignored if desired. Duplicated lines can be eliminated and lines can be sorted into reversed as well as natural order. These possibilities are exercised through options specified in the **sort** command. For example,

```
$ sort -ubdfr inputfile > outputfile
```

will dictionary sort (**d** option) `inputfile` in reverse (**r**) order, ignoring blanks and tabs (**b**) while eliminating other than unique lines (**u**); upper and lower case will be considered equivalent (**f** option).

Sorting can be carried out using only parts of a line. In general, **sort** considers a line to be made up of a set of fields. A field is a string of characters, with a minimum width of one character. Fields are considered to be demarcated by a separator character, which is normally the blank but can be altered to be *<character>* by the **-t***<character>* option. **sort** can be instructed to skip one or more fields at the start of a line and to ignore all fields following some subsequent one. For example,

```
$ sort +2 -4 inputfile > outputfile
```

will begin sorting (**+**) after field 2 (i.e., with the third field) and will ignore (**-**) everything after the fourth field; in other words, only the third and fourth fields will be considered. Here is an immediate application:

```
$ ls -o annrept | sort +3 -4
total 174
-rw-r--r--    1 peter          68 May  4 10:19 tcont
-rwxr-xr-x    1 peter         749 Jun 12 09:16 savscrp
-rw-r--r--    1 peter         777 Jun 10 09:05 umacros
-rw-r--r--    1 peter        3891 Jun 12 09:14 appdx
-rw-r--r--    1 peter       14833 Jun 10 09:45 front
-rw-r--r--    2 peter       29980 May 13 12:40 chapt1
-rw-r--r--    1 peter       37156 Jun 10 09:14 chapt2
```

Sorting is keyed to the fourth column only; in other words, the directory listing is sorted by file size.

Even within a field, initial characters can be ignored to refine sorting still further. For example, in

```
$ ls -o annrept | sort +0.3 -0.4
-rw-r--r--    1    peter          68 May  4 10:19 tcont
-rw-r--r--    1    peter         777 Jun 10 09:05 umacros
-rw-r--r--    1    peter        3891 Jun 12 09:14 appdx
-rw-r--r--    1    peter       14833 Jun 10 09:45 front
-rw-r--r--    1    peter       38624 Jun 12 12:45 chapt2
-rw-r--r--    2    peter       29980 May 13 12:40 chapt1
total 1440
-rwxr-xr-x    1    peter         749 Jun 12 09:16 savscrp
```

the **sort** command says: "skip zero full fields and three characters of the next, also skip everything after the fourth character; sort on what lies between". In other words, the sorting is done on the fourth character in the first field. This example also shows why so few Unix utilities produce output with titles, header lines, or the like: unless filtered out beforehand, the header line ends up sorted with the rest.

Sorting can be carried out on a set of key fields, not merely a single one. Furthermore, each key field can have a string of options attached. For example,

```
$ ls -o annrept | sort -n +6 -7 -M +5 -6
total 174
-rw-r--r--    1 peter          68 May 4 10:19 tcont
-rw-r--r--    2 peter       29980 May 13 12:40 chapt1
-rw-r--r--    1 peter         777 Jun 10 09:05 umacros
-rw-r--r--    1 peter       14833 Jun 10 09:45 front
-rw-r--r--    1 peter       37156 Jun 10 09:14 chapt2
-rw-r--r--    1 peter        3891 Jun 12 09:14 appdx
-rwxr-xr-x    1 peter         749 Jun 12 09:16 savscrp
```

sorts by date: numeric sorting on field 6 first, sorting by month names (**M** option) on field 5 thereafter. Very complicated sorting procedures can be designed in this way.

The **sort** command can be employed to merge files if the **-m** option is specified. Together with the **-u** ("unique", i.e., eliminate duplications) option, it can be used for tasks such as merging mailing lists, indeed for updating them, since the entry retained is always the one first encountered. As the sorting options become more and more complicated, **sort** clearly ceases to have value as an interactive command at the terminal and becomes an important tool for writing shell scripts.

Comparing Files

Two distinct commands are available for comparing two files, **diff** and **cmp**. Interactive terminal users probably find **diff** to be the more useful because its output is richer and easy to read. The output of **cmp** is numeric and better suited to machine processing, so **cmp** finds ready application in the writing of shell scripts.

diff compares two files on a line-by-line basis, looking forward and backward in an attempt to spot where the common ground lies. It keeps two line counters, one for each file, and tells the user how the lines correspond. The correspondence is expressed in algorithmic terms, that is, **diff** tells the user what should be done to turn one file into the other. The command

```
$ diff file1 file2
```

will produce instructions on how to modify `file1` so as to make it identical to `file2`. The modifications are presented as two sets of line counter readings and a single-character instruction, which may be a (add), d (delete), or c (change).Each one is followed by the set of lines subject to modification, flagged by < if they belong to `file1` ("less than", meaning before any changes) or > if they belong to `file2`. For example, files `left` and `right` are obviously different, but related:

```
Interactive terminal users
probably find diff to be the
more useful because its
output is richer and easy to
read. The output of cmp is
numeric and better suited to
machine processing, so cmp
finds ready application in
the writing of shell scripts.
```

```
Interactive terminal users
new to Unix
probably find diff to be the
more useful because its
output is richer and easy to
read. The output of cmp is
numeric, so cmp
finds ready application in
the writing of shell scripts.
```

The difference program shows what must be done to make them the same:

```
$ diff left right
1a2
> new to Unix
6,7c7
< numeric and better suited to
< machine processing, so cmp
---
> numeric, so cmp
```

Two corrections are reported. The first is `1a2`, meaning "after line 1 of `left`, append line 2 of `right`". The line to be appended is then displayed. The second alteration is `6,7c7`, which might be read "lines 6 through 7 of `left` changed to read as line 7 of `right`" and shows a substitution of one line for two. The lines are again reproduced on the spot. To put the matter simply, **diff** produces the set of editing instructions which will allow the right file to be recreated from the left.

Producing editing scripts so people can read them is all very well—but if the editing steps are so clearcut, why should not a machine carry them out? In reply, **diff** allows two different forms of output. One, illustrated above, is readily comprehensible by people. The other is not quite so easy to read; it consists of instructions to the **ed** editor. It may be used to recreate `right` (by means of **ed** itself) from `left`:

```
$ diff -e left right > difrnc
$ cat difrnc
6,7c
numeric, so cmp
.
1a
new to Unix
.
```

This script only needs to be augmented with two further **ed** commands, to write the output file and to quit,

```
w right
q
```

to form a complete sequence of editor commands. File `right` can then be recreated from `left` and the augmented file `difrnc` by

```
$ ed left < difrnc
```

If `left` is large, the space required for saving `left` and the editing script `difrnc` will amount to only a little more than `left` itself. Even in this small example, the full editing script only contains 50 characters, as against 259 for `left`. Major economies can be effected in disk space by storing the original file and one or more editing scripts instead of several versions of the file. The saving is particularly great if the file versions do not differ greatly—for example, in program debugging where quite a few editing operations may be needed but each involves only a few lines. In effect, it becomes possible to save a whole sequence of intermediate versions of the program source code in little more disk space than required by the original version itself.

The **cmp** command also compares two files, but it does not yield an editing script. Instead, **cmp** shows exactly where (if anywhere) a difference was first found:

```
$ cmp left right
left right differ: char 29, line 2
```

cmp can be asked to produce all the differences, character by character; for files `left` and `right`, it produces no less than 195 lines of numeric output! On the other hand, cmp can be asked to keep quiet and say nothing at all, merely to make its exit status *true* if the files are alike. The latter form is attractive to shell programmers.

Filtering Files

As used in Unix literature, the term *filter* means a program which transforms its input in some simple way and copies it to its output. Many programs can be regarded as filters, depending on how far the notion of a simple transformation can be stretched. In this section, it will be understood more narrowly as transformation of character strings or extraction of specific lines from a file. Even then, there are five important filters to discuss: **prep**, **uniq**, **comm**, **tr**, and **grep**.

The **grep** command is the most powerful and flexible of the five filters examined here. It reads its standard input, one line at a time, finds the lines that contain a particular character string, and takes some action when such are found. Its basic action is to copy the line to its standard output, but variations are possible. The line may be counted toward a total and not displayed, or it may be counted and displayed. The action may be inverted, displaying or counting the lines that do *not* contain the required string.The power and complexity of **grep** lie largely in its ability to deal with wild-card constructions in the character strings, so the searches need not look merely for words like *grep* but could seek, for example, anything consisting of six alphabetic characters with the second letter *o* and the last two *at*. To do so, searching a Unix spelling dictionary (stored one word to a line) might be worth a try:

```
$ grep '[a-z]o[a-z][a-z]at' /usr/dict/words wordout
```

However, this won't do the job because it only looks for a six-character string of the appropriate description, without limiting the word length to six characters. It results in a very long file,

```
adsorbate
apostate
aristocrat
⋮
transportation
woolgather
```

The expressions **grep** can find are formed in exactly the same way as the searching patterns in the **ed** and **ex** editors. Thus, the period (dot `.`) can be used to match any single character, `[a-k]` the specified range of lowercase letters, `[13579]` any odd numeral. Character position in the line can also be specified; if **^** is placed at the beginning of a string or $ at its end, it is considered to match the beginning of a line or the end of a line, respectively. To locate the six-character word (permitting an uppercase initial letter just to be sure) is not hard:

```
$ grep '^[A-Za-z]o[a-z][a-z]at$' /usr/dict/words
bobcat
combat
format
```

If only **grep** could tell which output word also matches the description *marsupial herbivore*, solving crossword puzzles could become a matter of writing shell scripts—provided the dictionary is also improved to include *wombat*!

A complementary application of **grep** might also be illustrated briefly. The command

```
$ grep -v '^[Cc]' feprog.f > nocomment.f
```

strips all comment lines from the Fortran program `feprog.f`. The search string `^[Cc]` finds all lines containing either `C` or `c` in the first column position; the **-v** option discards them, keeping all the rest.

The **-l** option of **grep** throws away all lines but keeps track of the file names in which a pattern match is found. Because the input to **grep** may consist of a whole sequence of files—keeping in mind that wild card file names can cover large numbers of files—this option can be used to identify all documents containing a particular string. Such could include, for example, all Fortran programs containing a given variable or all letters signed by a particular person.

The character translation filter **tr** also searches for characters, but only single ones rather than strings. It accepts a table of character translation equivalences and replaces specified characters with others. For example, replacement of all uppercase letters with their lowercase equivalents is achieved by

```
tr '[A-Z]' '[a-z]' < fortprog.f > lowers.f
```

so that the old-fashioned (but standard) Fortran program written in upper case is translated to a form better liked by Unix programmers. The principle here is simple. **tr** is handed two character sets, each 26 characters long, and it replaces all occurrences of any character belonging to the first set `[A-Z]` with the corresponding character in the second set `[a-z]`. Options available include elimination of characters (mapping them into nothing at all) and squeezing multiple characters into single ones. While **tr** is easy to use in principle, it can become tricky because many translation tasks involve special characters. These must convey their intended meanings to **tr** but need to be protected against misinterpretation by the shell. Quotes and backslashes are used to shelter them temporarily.

Few programs could be simpler in principle than **prep**. It reduces a file to a list of words, one per line, by throwing out all nonalphabetic characters, lowering all uppercase letters and replacing all whitespace by line breaks. The remaining words, however, are in their original order, not sorted in any way. Superficially, the need for prep might be questioned, since the pipeline

```
tr '[A-Z]''[a-z]' < text | tr -cs '[a-z]' '[12*]' > words
```

does much the same thing. Explanation may be in order: after reducing all letters to lowercase, **tr** maps all nonletters (option **-c** complements the first character set) to *newline* characters (octal 012) and squeezes down multiple *newline* characters to single ones with the **-s** option. There cannot be any doubt, however, that typing

```
prep text > words
```

requires less by way of mental gymnastics. Furthermore, **prep** does a better job with hyphenated words and embedded apostrophes. **prep** or its derivatives are used in various Unix utilities (e.g., spelling checkers) for reducing text to a set of distinct words.

comm compares two files, both supposed to have been sorted into sequence with **sort** or some equivalent process, and looks for differences.

It could be regarded as a highly specialized version of **diff**, one that does not produce an editing script. Instead, it filters its input lines into three columns of output: those unique to file 1, those unique to file 2, and those contained in both files. In other words, if the files are regarded as sets of lines, **comm** locates the intersection of both (column 3) and the exclusions both ways (columns 1 and 2). When output is produced, any one or two columns may be suppressed. Suppressing all three columns is also possible, but then there will be no output at all!

In contrast to **comm**, **uniq** works on a single file. It compares successive pairs of lines and spots repeated lines. The output consists of the input file but with repetitions eliminated; or it can be made to contain only the lines repeated two or more times. To work fast, **uniq** only compares adjacent lines, so any files to be processed must be sorted with **sort** first. In a certain sense, **uniq** may be regarded as a highly specialized version of **sort**, for its comparison operations are similar. Like **sort**, it can be made to ignore leading blanks, to compare part of the line only, and to ignore segments of input lines. However, its searching arrangements are not quite so sophisticated as those of **sort**.

While there are applications in which these and other filters find individual use, they really come into their own when made to work together. To give another simple example, the pipeline

```
$ prep text | sort | uniq | grep '....*' > bigwords
```

produces an alphabetically sorted list of all words in file text, provided they are at least three characters long. (In the search string with **grep**, the dot . matches any one character and the combination .* matches zero or more characters.) Such a list is useful in assessing the lexical difficulty of written text because it permits critical examination detached from context.

Controlling File Size

File size is a measure of general interest. It may be measured in two distinct ways. For a text file, the numbers of lines, words, or characters may be of value as indices of its overall length. On the other hand, lines and words do not make much sense for a file containing data or executable programs. In such cases, the most important index of size is probably the amount of disk space occupied by the file. Commands exist for both forms of size assessment.

For readable files, the **wc** command may be used to produce a word count. **wc** also counts lines and characters and outputs the number of lines, words, and characters (in that order). Like most other Unix system utilities, it is able to accept input streams consisting of numerous files or indeed file specifications containing wild cards. Line and word counts can therefore be produced for numerous files by a single command. For example,

```
$ wc chapt*
    850    6227    32261 chapt1
    662    4591    20834 chapt2
   1512   10818    53095 total
```

yields the line, word, and character counts for all files in the current working directory beginning with the character string chapt. The totals for all files listed are also shown if there is more than one file.

When **nroff** files are processed by **wc**, some confusion may arise between word counts that include **nroff** commands and the true net word count. If the difference is likely to be significant, the net word count may be found by piping **nroff** output directly into **wc**. Of course, the processor time will be increased substantially, for **nroff** itself must process the text. A more elegant and equally accurate solution is to use **deroff**, a program that removes all **nroff**, **troff**, **eqn** and **tbl** requests but does not otherwise alter the text. It does less work and therefore runs faster than **nroff**.

The **size** command is useful with compiled object modules, for Unix object code traditionally comprises separate text, data, and stack sections. The command

```
$ size /bin/csh
44120 + 4268 + 3316 = 51704 = 0xc9f8
```

shows the sizes of the three sections (in decimal notation). This information is of particular interest to programmers using libraries or archives, for **size** applied to an archive shows the size of every member of the archive individually.

For files of any kind at all, readable or otherwise, the **du** command may be employed to determine the amount of disk space used. The space used is reported by **du** either in 512-byte units or in blocks (which may be 512 bytes or 1024, depending on the system). Reports may be requested either for files or for directories. If the block count is requested for a directory, the result is returned for that directory and for all its subdirectories as well. There does exist an option (**-a**) that also gives the block sizes for every file listed in the directory and its subdirectories.

The complementary question—how much disk space is there left—is of particular significance with removable file volumes, such as floppy disks. The **df** command permits enquiring after the space remaining on a particular device; again, the answer is reported in 512-byte units or in blocks as used by the system.

Other General Utilities

In addition to the file-handling utilities listed above, Unix systems incorporate various other convenient items. It is never easy to determine which will please most users by satisfying a real need and which might be regarded as luxuries. The following list therefore includes a few commands more likely to be necessary than frivolous.

Timed Requests

Because it is a time-sharing multitasking operating system, it is inconceivable that any Unix system could be run without a time clock. The user may access this clock in two ways: he can examine the clock, and he can ask the system to keep an eye on the clock for him.

The usual way of looking at the clock is through the **date** command, which causes the current day, date, and time to be displayed in the standard output. Time is given to the nearest second. In addition to serving a useful purpose for people who do not wear watches, **date** is often employed in shell scripts for date-stamping processes. By redirecting the output of **date** into a file along with other program outputs, the time and date of file creation can be recorded automatically.

One reason users are interested in clock times is to find out the execution speed of individual programs. It is not really convenient to determine execution times by asking for the clock time before and after; in fact, the answers are likely to be wrong, because **date** reports the clock time, not the processor time devoted to that particular program. With many users on the system, the difference could be extremely large! A tidier and more accurate procedure is to ask the system to do the timings with the **time** command. On requesting

```
$ time command
```

command will be executed and its execution time monitored. Unavoidably, the result may still be a bit inaccurate if there are many other users on the system and the process has to be swapped in and out several times.

The accuracy of the time given by the system clock, depends on the type of computer hardware used. Many small systems simply use the power line to generate clock pulses, so that the time accuracy is exactly that of an electric wall clock. A more critical point is that the system manager may well have just set the clock by a wristwatch when bringing up the system; the clock time is then as reliable as the system manager's watch.

Users can ask the kernel to keep an eye on the clock, and to do some specified thing at a specified future time. Since "clock" in this context includes "calendar", the delay times requested can be quite long. Examples might range from writing a message at the user terminal after a half-hour, as a reminder of the time, to the automatic removal of unused files at the end of the month. The **at** command is used for this purpose. Its general form is

```
$ at time < file
```

`file` will be used as input to the shell at *time*. In other words, `file` contains the sequence of shell commands to be executed at the specified time. The commands might include almost anything, even another **at** command to set up another timed process!

Execution of **at** commands does not actually take place at exactly the time specified. The kernel periodically looks for pending **at** commands and executes them if their time is due or overdue, and if they have not been executed yet. In other words, **at** processes are picked up on a specified schedule, each time taking those processes which are currently waiting, much as a bus picks up waiting passengers. The time specified in the **at** command is not the exact time of execution, but rather the time when the process is set waiting for the next scheduled time (the time of joining the bus queue, as it were, not the time the bus is scheduled to come). An **at** process may therefore execute at the set time or a bit later, depending on the frequency with which the local system handles such processes. Delays of minutes, even of a quarter or half an hour, may occur in some installations. If there is any reason for concern, the system manager should be consulted to find out how often waiting **at** processes are disposed of.

Timed processes are managed by **cron**, using event tables which it consults from time to time. Some system managers restrict access to **cron** drastically and may thereby make **at** processes unreachable. These access privilege denials, like others, may suggest passing an agreeable quarter-hour with the system manager, discussing the weather and other things.

System Documentation

Substantial sections of the *Unix Programmer's Manual*, the defining document for the Version 7 system release, have traditionally been furnished in machine-readable form, as an **nroff** text file. These sections may be consulted by invoking the **man** command. For example,

```
$ man date
```

will produce at the terminal the manual description of the **date** command. If required, this description can of course be redirected to the line printer, to yield a paper document. However, few users are likely to wish extensive printouts of command descriptions, because the same machine-readable documentation will still be there the next day.

By default, the **man** command searches that section of the manual which gives descriptions of the shell commands. The traditional organization of the Seventh Edition manual is in eight sections:

1. Shell commands
2. System calls (kernel access points)
3. Subroutine libraries
4. Input–output device driver descriptions
5. Include files and formats
6. Computer games
7. Special files
8. System procedures

The organization of the Berkeley 4.2 BSD manuals (and manuals of systems derived from it) is similar. Obviously, the contents of the sections are a bit different; but even then, many of the entries are virtually unchanged.

With System V, the manual organization appears to be shifting. The System V defining document views this system as having a layered structure:

1. Base System
2. Kernel Extension
3. Base Utilities Extension
4. Advanced Utilities Extension
5. Administered Systems Extension
6. Software Development Extension
7. Terminal Interface Extension

The Base System and the Kernel Extension provide a run-time environment for programs but include little that the casual user can easily appreciate. The bulk of frequently consulted manual material comes in layers 3–5. The Base Utilities are things of everyday need, like **ls** and **sh**; Advanced Utilities include **lp** and **vi**; Administered Systems administer **mkfs** and **mount** as well as accounting. The Software Development Extension concentrates largely on the C language, with a magnificent bundle of software development tools to go along with **cc**. Each layer, in effect, has a manual of its own within the System V Interface Definition. Systems delivered to customers by the various vendors generally have interfiled at least some of the manual pages, without regard to the layered structure.

Not every installation provides on-line access to all the manuals. In fact, the current trend is away from on-line manuals. Several vendors of Unix systems no longer provide any magnetically stored documentation, even though their printed books still show the **man** command and tell how to use it!

Chapter 7

Editing with **vi** and **ed**

Text editing is a fundamental activity under any operating system, for the excellent reason that every user must be able to create and modify files. Editors serve a variety of purposes ranging from program preparation to the writing of books, tasks which cannot all be best fulfilled by the same software package even though those provided under Unix come surprisingly close to being universal. Although many different editors run under the Unix system, the most common ones, capable of handling an incredibly wide range of tasks, are **vi** and **ed**. They are described in this chapter in some detail. Others of potential use to a wide circle of Unix users include **sed** and **awk**, batch-run programs capable of systematic alteration of text at a sophisticated level; these will not be discussed in this chapter.

The Unix operating system has been endowed with good editing facilities from the very start; indeed, the editing techniques initially developed for use with Unix have profoundly influenced text editing software ever since. Users acquainted with office word processors will be interested to discover within Unix the roots of many methods now considered conventional.

Text Editors

The most widely known and used Unix editor program is undoubtedly **vi**, a screen editor that displays text on the terminal screen and allows changes to be made by commands much like those of conventional word processors. In fact, early versions of **vi** formed the pattern on which many of the now common word processing programs were based. Fortunately, the **vi** control language is well structured and consistent in its grammar, so getting started is not difficult. Full mastery of **vi** and all its facilities, on the other hand, can take some time. A product of the Berkeley Unix project, **vi** only became part of "official" Unix at a relatively late date. However, it was commonly available even before being welcomed into the command repertoire formally. It has been distributed for quite a few years with the Berkeley system releases as well as with several commercially available systems based on the Seventh Edition.

Because **vi** permits a considerable amount of customization and tailoring of commands to user needs, learning to use **vi** well is at least partly a matter of learning to adapt **vi** to specific tasks. A better choice for book writing and document preparation than **ed**, **vi** is no less convenient for programming, especially in C, Pascal, Fortran, and Lisp.

The truly basic editing tool included in all versions since Unix time began is **ed**, an editor which this chapter also describes in some detail. Until **vi** came along, **ed** was the main editor in most Unix systems. Actually, **vi** is just the screen-oriented part of a larger editing system called **ex**, and **ex** in turn is an enlarged rewrite of **ed**. Being thus related, **vi** and **ed** have command sets similar in spirit. Of course, **ed** is not a screen editor so it is more difficult to use than **vi**. For text entry, **ed** has little to recommend it, except for a very high tolerance of varying terminal characteristics. Almost any terminal can be used with **ed**, whether of the printing or screen type, slow or fast, intelligent or dumb. Even terminals unable to handle lowercase characters can be pressed into service, though they are hardly to be recommended!

Both **vi** and **ed** are strongly line oriented, that is, they deal with material organized as individual text lines. This aspect makes them particularly attractive for the preparation of computer programs, though it can sometimes become a nuisance when dealing with manuscripts.

One reason **ed** has remained part of the Unix editor repertoire despite the appearance of **vi** is that **ed** can be used noninteractively: it is possible to write a script of **ed** commands and to have **ed** perform a set of editing operations on a large file, all automatically and without human intervention. In fact, some standard Unix utility programs can produce such **ed** scripts; it may not even be necessary for the user to write them. Such work, often called stream editing, can also be well done by a third member of the Unix editor family, called **sed**, which is totally noninteractive. It accepts commands broadly similar to those of **ed** and applies them to all or part of a file. Stream editors are useful for such brute-force jobs as replacing all occurrences of *Bell Laboratories* with *AT&T* in a large file.

Using the vi Text Editor

The basic text editor in the Unix system is **vi**. Its name is usually pronounced *vee-eye* and is supposed to stand for *visual interactive*, though not a few users refer to the program as *she* and pronounce the name as if it were the short form of *Violet*. **vi** is line oriented, that is, it regards a segment of text as being composed of individual lines. This feature makes it particularly convenient for preparation of computer programs. While organizing every text file as a set of lines is not natural for English text whose intrinsic unit is the sentence, it is at worst a minor nuisance most users are willing to live with.

In normal use, **vi** is asked to read a file, which is then modified; the modified text is subsequently written out to the same file. Unlike many office word processors, **vi** does not automatically save the old version as a sort of disaster insurance; backup copies must be created separately. The reading, writing, and intervening modification are all controlled by keyboard commands; so is the screen display. Quite a few different functions need to be controlled, hence there are many command sentences in the **vi** language. In the following, a subset of its many commands is discussed, one extensive enough to satisfy most ordinary editing needs yet small enough to avoid confusion.

Starting and Running vi

The operation of **vi** resembles that of many other editing programs or word processors. To edit a file, **vi** makes a copy of it in an area of computer memory called the *editing buffer* or *text buffer*. The user can examine the text in the buffer, correct it, rearrange it, and modify it in various ways. When alterations to the text are complete, the content of the editing buffer replaces the original file. If the file being edited is small, the editing buffer is entirely contained in the immediate-access memory of the computer. Otherwise, space is allocated for the buffer partly in memory, partly in a temporary disk file. The general pattern of organization is shown in Figure 7.1. Any text movement between memory and temporary file is handled automatically by **vi** so that the user normally does not know, indeed cannot

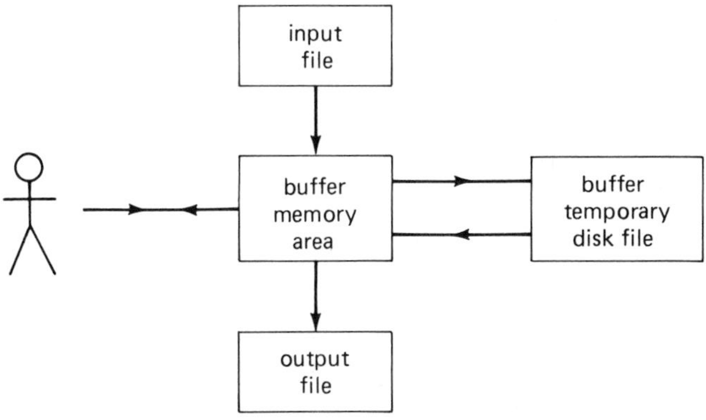

FIGURE 7.1. Text is automatically swapped between buffer areas in memory and on disk; the user is unaware of the swapping.

find out, whether the buffer is entirely housed in immediate-access memory or swapped into and out of it. So far as the user can tell, the buffer is extremely large, large enough to handle any file of any size.

Starting up **vi** is similar to starting up most other Unix utility programs. It is done in the obvious way,

```
$ vi filename
```

where `filename` is the name of the file to be edited. This command starts **vi** running, reads the file into the buffer, and displays the first screenful of lines.

As editing proceeds, **vi** automatically moves text from memory to disk and back again, making the buffer size appear enormous. Consequently, there is no size limitation on the files to be edited, other than the size of the disk itself. Because the use of disk and memory space is automatically taken care of, the user need never be concerned about where and how much space is available. Of course, operations that require swapping disk and memory contents may take perceptibly more time than operations that only involve the memory-resident buffer area, especially if there are many other processes running.

Exiting from **vi** is straightforward even though the command for doing so is not obvious:

```
ZZ
```

while **vi** is expecting commands. When **vi** ceases operation, the content of the editing buffer is written to the original file by ZZ. Before writing, however, **vi** checks to see whether any text modification has taken place.

If not, writing is considered unnecessary; it is therefore omitted and the buffer content is simply discarded.

The **vi** Screen Display

When **vi** is running, the terminal screen shows a portion of the text being edited. The screen can be thought of as a "window" through which a portion of the file (which might be huge) is made visible to the user. The principle is illustrated by Figure 7.2. The text is taken to be very long and to continue for a long distance in both directions; the window shows only the part currently of interest. If the text is too short to fill the screen, as it is certain to be when a new file is started, **vi** will show the tilde (the ~ character) at the left edge of every screen line that might otherwise contain text—saying, as it were, that the line is quite intentionally blank.

Because the screen window is small compared to most text files, **vi** permits the user to move the window relative to the text, so that different segments of the text housed in the editing buffer can be examined at different times. There is a group of **vi** commands which permit the window to be moved—or the text to be scrolled past the window, depending on the point of view. In the system manuals and in various descriptive literature on **vi**, the words *forward* and *down* are used to signify the direction of a movable window relative to fixed text, i.e., the direction of movement which results when a long text file is listed on a conventional screen-type

```
screen shows a portion of
the text being edited.  The screen can be thought
of as a "window" through
which a portion of the

file (which might be huge) is made visible to
the user.  The principle is illustrated
by Fig.  2.  The text
is taken to be very long, and to continue
for a long distance in both directions; the window
shows only the
part currently of interest.  If the text is
"textedit" [Modified] line 255 of 2080 -- 12%--

too short to fill the screen, as
it is certain to be when a new file is
started, vi will show the tilde (the ~ character) at
the left edge of every screen line which
might otherwise contain text --
```

FIGURE 7.2. The terminal screen shows part of the text file, with the cursor placed on one character. Note bottom line of window.

terminal. Correspondingly, *backward* and *up* signify that the window is moved to a position nearer the beginning of the text.

The bottom line of the screen display is reserved for messages sent by **vi**. This space is not used for text, but shows the size of the file currently being edited, displays error messages, identifies files, and takes care of other administrative details. The actual text area is therefore always slightly smaller than the full screen; but it could be a great deal smaller, for the window size is controllable by the user. The point of a smaller window is usually a gain in speed. To erase and rewrite a screen of ordinary size takes a second or less on a single-user workstation console, five or ten seconds if an ordinary serial line connection is used, or about 40 seconds over a slow dial-up telephone line at 300 baud. To cater for these widely different speeds, **vi** permits the window to be made smaller than the full screen. Although less text is then visible, screen updates are effected rapidly.

Working with text using **vi** resembles working with many popular word processing programs: the text being edited is shown on the screen with one character distinguished from the rest by a *cursor*. Depending on the terminal, the cursor may appear as a video inversion, blinking underscore, or some other distinguishing mark; but it is always attached to a single character. Practically all editing operations in **vi** are guided by the screen cursor, which serves as a pointing tool to identify position. For obvious reasons, **vi** possesses cursor positioning facilities which allow the cursor to be moved around from place to place within the display window. These are entirely distinct from the window control commands. They are extensive in scope and rich in variety; they will be dealt with at length further below.

Communicating with **vi**

The user generally needs to communicate two different forms of information to **vi**: commands that tell **vi** how to manage the editing buffer and text characters to be included in the buffer. For example, the instruction *insert here the word "horse"* contains the character string *horse*, which is intended for inclusion in the text. On the other hand, the character string *insert here the word* clearly should be understood and acted on as an instruction; it should not be included as text in the file. Were the computer terminal equipped with two keyboards, it would be a simple matter to enter the commands at one and the text at the other! In the real world, the single keyboard is made to do double duty by receiving and interpreting characters in two different ways, as commands to be acted upon or as text to be inserted in the file, by making **vi** understand characters differently at different times. Accordingly, **vi** is said to be in *command mode*, meaning that **vi** will attempt to interpret any character typed at the keyboard as a command; or in *insertion mode*, meaning that characters typed at the keyboard will be understood to be text and will be placed in the editing buffer along with any text that is already there.

Since **vi** accepts characters in two different modes and responds to them in two different ways, it is obviously important to be able to switch between the two modes. It might be imagined that the most straightforward scheme for doing so would be to have a special key on the keyboard for toggling from one mode to the other. A more complicated but elegant alternative might conceivably be to have **vi** itself determine from context which mode the user probably needs at any given time and to do the necessary switching all by itself. In fact, both solutions are only half good, so both have been half accepted by the designers of **vi**. Changing from insertion mode to command mode is mostly done by manual switching, while changing from command to insertion mode happens automatically.

The ESCAPE character is used by **vi** as a mode switch. Whenever this key is struck, **vi** attempts to change over to command mode. If already in command mode, **vi** does nothing in response to ESCAPE; it will, however, object loudly by bleeping the terminal bell, buzzer, or noisemaker. Some experienced **vi** users have the habit of punctuating their commands with liberal helpings of ESCAPE characters, just to be sure. The result can be noisy and annoying. Nevertheless, **vi** will always end up in command mode in response to an ESCAPE keystroke. Hence, if in doubt, press ESCAPE!

Insertion mode is entered automatically whenever the command being entered at the keyboard requires it. For example, the `i` command says, in effect, "insert into the text buffer the characters that follow". Once in insertion mode, any printable character as well as most others are entered into the text buffer. Any significance the same characters might have as commands is totally ignored. Only a few characters—notably ESCAPE—are intercepted and acted upon, rather than being placed into the text. But almost any character, including ESCAPE, can be included in the text by prefixing it with control-V.

Editor Commands

Cursor control, despite its importance, forms only a small part of the **vi** command repertoire. Other commands include text insertion and deletion; text alteration and searching; file manipulation; display management; and of course an inevitable miscellaneous category. All commands are typed while **vi** is in command mode (some versions of the **vi** manual use the term *quiescent state*). Most commands are not echoed on the screen as they are typed; some appear on the bottom screen line because verification is needed, or for some other good reason.

Most **vi** commands involve a single basic keystroke each (i.e., the command verbs are generally single characters), but these keystrokes are frequently augmented by numeric arguments or other qualifiers. Thus, the typical command may be made up of several characters. Any command can be abandoned before it is fully typed, by striking the ESCAPE key. In general, this key serves to terminate a command and causes it to be executed; however, if the command is incomplete, it cannot be executed and will therefore be abandoned. A corollary of this argument follows: if unsure whether **vi** is prepared to accept commands, the user may strike the ESCAPE key a few times. If **vi** wasn't in a receptive mood before, it will be after!

The DELETE key may be used to abandon whatever activity is currently in progress. It may be used to cancel wrong instructions, once their execution has begun. Disaster relief is also provided by the u ("undo") command, which can be employed to reverse the unfortunate effect of almost any incorrect command after it has been executed. Of course, the u command can only be used to go back one step, for a second u will simply undo the first!

While editing with **vi**, the terminal screen is used as a "window" on the text buffer. In most installations, the entire screen is used as the text window; in some, only part of the screen is used. The default window size is half the screen height for slow terminals and the full screen height for fast ones.

The display window can be moved to expose different parts of the buffer to view. It may be moved forward or back along the buffer in four different ways: a full window height at a time, or a partial window height at a time; forward or backward. There are four commands for doing so, all communicated by control characters:

control-F	forward a window
control-B	backward a window
control-D	forward part of a window ("down")
control-U	backward part of a window ("up")

When **vi** is first started, the partial-window commands scroll up or down half the window size. The amount of scrolling can be reset, by prefixing either command with a number. The number is taken to show how many lines to scroll; it is not only used in the command executed immediately but is remembered for all future control-D and control-U commands.

Just precisely how the window movement is carried out depends on the terminal type. There are so-called intelligent terminals, with plenty of built-in memory used to buffer text. Such terminals can carry out nearly all the above operations by scrolling text already stored in the terminal. At the other end of the intelligence spectrum, there are terminals which can only scroll in the "down" direction, to simulate printing. Backward movements then require erasing the screen and rewriting whatever should be there. With many users loading down the system or when using a slow communication line, the result can be less than joyous.

Local Commands

Local commands in **vi** are commands that perform actions at the place where the editing cursor happens to be currently. They all deal with insertion, deletion, or rearrangement of text and yield results clearly visible on the screen; local commands have no "hidden" effect. They are easy to use both because they are exceedingly brief—only one, or at the most two, characters long—and because not many of them are essential. There actually exist more than a dozen distinct commands in this family, but four or five are all that the average **vi** user really needs.

Text Insertion

Insertion of new text in the editing buffer requires the user to switch from command mode into insertion mode and eventually to switch back again. These mode switches are performed by the *insert* and *append* commands `i` and `a`. Switching back is invariably effected by an ESCAPE keystroke, so that insertion and appending of text take the form

`i`*text to be inserted before the cursor character*ESC

and

`a`*text to be placed after the cursor character*ESC

Like practically all other **vi** commands, `i` and `a` do not show on the screen; neither are the ESCAPEs echoed in visible form. The inserted text, on the other hand, is displayed because it has been placed into the text buffer, and the screen is supposed to represent a true image of the buffer contents. Anyhow, seeing the text makes typing a lot easier!

In addition to the `i` and `a` commands, which insert text before and after the cursor character respectively, there are two similar commands `I` and `A`. These insert and append before and after the *current line*, the line on which the cursor happens to be. Handy, no doubt; but also quite inessential, for it does not take much work to move the cursor around.

A pair of commands closely related to `i` and `a` are `o` and `O`. Either will create a blank line, move the cursor to it, and switch to insertion mode:

`o`*text to be inserted on a new line after the current one*ESC
`O`*text to be inserted on a new line before the current one*ESC

A moment's reflection will show that `o` and `O` do nothing that cannot be done by combinations of other, perhaps more elementary, **vi** commands.

For example, the effect of `o` is readily obtained by moving the cursor to the beginning of the next line and inserting text with `i`; or appending with `A` and making the first inserted keystroke RETURN; or indeed in several other ways which the imaginative user can readily construct. There is not much economy in work either; the keystrokes involved are

`o`	1 keystroke
`j I`	2 keystrokes
RET `i`	2 keystrokes
`A` RET	2 keystrokes
`$ a` RET	3 keystrokes

Saving a keystroke or two is clearly meaningless for a user about to type in a manuscript of 2000 words.

The apparent duplication of commands here, and elsewhere in **vi**, probably arises from two causes rooted in history. First, **vi** was initially developed in the era of single computers serving large numbers of concurrent users—woefully slow computers working into highly unintelligent terminals by today's standards. Irritating delays can occur between command keystrokes, making it attractive to concentrate a lot of activities into single commands. A second likely cause is the development of **vi** in a university, an environment of brilliant but idiosyncratic and voluble people with widely differing preferences, where compromise is sometimes best struck by heaping together all contending views. The resulting multiplicity of commands is not necessarily bad; after all, some can always be ignored!

Command Repetition

Any command which changes the text buffer content can be repeated without reentering the command keystrokes. The dot command `.` may be used instead: it repeats the previous action. For example, deletion of several lines is easiest to accomplish by deleting the first with a dd command, then getting rid of each succeeding one by a single `.` keystroke. To choose a slightly more imaginative example: there is no need to type the ruler line

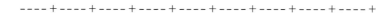

by pecking away laboriously at repeated minus signs; it suffices to insert the initial string of four minuses and a plus, then to replicate it with the `.` command as many times as desired.

A cautionary point must be made about the `.` command: it only applies to commands which change the text buffer content. In other words, it repeats the last *text alteration*. Cursor movements, which may change the display but make no change to the text, do not count; `.` always seeks out and repeats whatever the most recent text alteration may have been. If a lot of cursor movement and screen rearrangement have occurred since the last change, the result may well be a surprise. Fortunately, u will undo one (but only one!) . command.

Erasure and Replacement

Correction of text errors or alteration of characters for any other reason is readily effected in **vi**, as in most other screen editors, by erasing the offending characters and inserting new ones. Erasure in its simplest form is achieved by the x command, which erases the character under the editing cursor, or by X, which erases the character immediately to the left of the cursor. To replace it with another, a text insertion may then be performed with the i command.

Because replacement of a single wrong character with one or more others is a common operation, **vi** provides a composite command s. It combines erasure and insertion; in other words, it erases the character under the cursor and immediately places **vi** in insertion mode. All text following s is inserted into the text buffer, until insert mode is terminated by the usual ESCAPE. Whether s is really necessary is unclear; it cannot do anything that cannot be done in other ways and it rarely saves much work.

Replacement of a single erroneous character using x and i requires four keystrokes; replacement by s takes three. There is a command verb r which allows erasure and replacement of one (and only one) character with two keystrokes, obviously the minimum possible. Entering r erases the character under the cursor and then replaces it with the character typed next after the command itself. No ESCAPE is necessary because exactly one replacement character is allowed. Although there are other ways of doing the job, this command is much more convenient than x followed by i for making many small corrections.

The r command also exists in a "large" version R, which replaces characters by overwriting the existing text. It bears a resemblance to i in that it inserts characters into the text, but differs in that every character inserted replaces, i.e., overwrites, an existing character. The replacement process is terminated, as might be expected, by means of ESCAPE.

Text Markers

When working with large files, it is often necessary to page back and forth between various points in the text. To simplify this process, **vi** permits the user to set markers at any desired point in the text buffer. Markers are temporary mileposts established expressly as spots to which the user may wish to return from time to time.

A text marker is an invisible character, one placed in the file but not visible on the screen. Although its location is initially specified by the cursor, the marker resides at a fixed place within the text subsequently. Markers are single characters planted at the cursor location by means of the **vi** command `m`, as in

```
ma
```

While the marker cannot be seen, it certainly can be found again. The cursor will be moved to marker a immediately, from anywhere in the file, in response to the command

```
`a
```

Note that the two single quote marks ' and ` are not interchangeable; one slants to the right, the other to the left. Both are perfectly acceptable commands but have differing meanings: the down-slanting one (also called the back quote or grave accent) makes `a represent the exact location of the marker while 'a refers to the beginning of the marked line.

Markers are handy to have when two parts of a file must be compared and brought into agreement. When consulting reference books, most people find themselves using all the fingers of one hand as bookmarks while trying to sort out which index references to pursue or how to resolve apparent contradictions between statements on different pages. Markers set by **vi** are the electronic equivalent of fingers, for they permit flicking back and forth between two text segments rapidly without needing to trouble about the intervening material.

Range Commands

Many, perhaps even most, **vi** commands instruct **vi** to do something with a *range* of text. For purposes of this discussion, a range is the portion of text spanned by the present cursor position and another specific point or *target* in the text file. The deletion of a block of text, for example, involves a range command, for it specifies that the text located between the cursor position and a target point is to be removed. Similarly, a cursor movement spans a range, taking the cursor from its erstwhile position to a specific target point. Although a large fraction of **vi** commands make use of range information, only a few command verbs are actually employed in range commands, far fewer than might appear at first glance. However, **vi** understands a large number of different range-delimiting targets. This section therefore sets out a selection of target types, then lists and illustrates the range commands themselves.

Command Structure

Range commands, more than any other feature of **vi**, are probably responsible for the complex and heavyweight appearance that **vi** often presents to novice users. They are actually easy to master; the grammar of range commands is quite simple. On the other hand, an extensive vocabulary is available for constructing such command sentences. A simple grammar and a large vocabulary make light work for the beginner—one need not learn all the words at once—but there is a lot of room for growth later on.

A range command in **vi** always has the same general structure. It always specifies a target, a uniquely identified place in the text, and may include a verb clause to tell **vi** what to do with the range. The verb clause comprises a command verb and possibly the name of a temporary buffer in which fragments of text are stored pending further action. The command form is always

[[<*buffer*>] <*command verb*>] <*target*>

where the square brackets denote optional items. Curiously enough, the command verb itself is optional, while the target to be aimed at is not.

Making range commands work requires some consideration of what can be a target, what verbs are available, and how to manage buffers. These matters will be dealt with in the following, beginning with that most essential ingredient, the target that delimits the range of a command.

Target Types

Ranges of text begin at the cursor position and end at a target. Every possible target must be a single, uniquely defined, character; the requirement of uniqueness aside, however, it could be almost anything anywhere. It is easy to gain the mistaken impression that all conceivable targets have been included in **vi**, so great is the number of ways targets may be defined. The principal target symbols are shown in Table 7.1. Incredible as it may seem, this list is still not complete! Fortunately it is unnecessary to remember all of these, for many differ only a little in their effect.

In the early days of computing when terminal response was often very slow, software designers tried hard to minimize the number of keystrokes required for any particular operation. While this consideration may still be important on a busy afternoon in large multiuser systems—it is annoying to be forced to type extra slowly while the machine decides whether to listen—most people now believe that a small, effective set of command verbs good for just about everything is preferable to a vast arsenal of special-purpose tools. Keystrokes are a minor consideration with most people who spend hours at a keyboard; it is much more important to avoid

TABLE 7.1.

Target identifier	Description
h	character to left
j	character below
k	character above
l	character to the right (or use SPACE)
n|	*n*th character position in current line
-	left edge of previous line
0	left edge of the current line
+	left edge of next line (or use RETURN)
$	next right edge of the text line
*n*G	left edge of the *n*th line in the file
G	left edge of the last line in the file
b, B	next word beginning to the left
e, E	next word end to the right
w, W	next word beginning to the right
(	left to beginning of a sentence
)	right to beginning of a sentence
{	left to beginning of a paragraph
}	right to beginning of a paragraph
t*c*, f*c*	right to the character *c* in this line
T*c*, F*c*	left to the character *c* in this line
/*str*RET	right to the character string *str*
?*str*RET	left to the character string *str*
\`*x*	place where the marker *x* is set
'*x*	beginning of the line containing marker *x*

mental fatigue by using simple command sequences that make logical sense. Deleting five lines, for example, is possible in **vi** with just three keystrokes, but it is necessary to stop to count the lines first. Most users prefer to delete one at a time, saying what amounts to "delete one; repeat;. . .; repeat"; how far the work has progressed is immediately visible on the screen. Although the latter approach takes a few more keystrokes, many people prefer it because the activity is both visually guided and interactive—just precisely the characteristics **vi** was supposed to contribute in the first place!

Most of the targets in Table 7.1 are probably self-explanatory, or nearly so. Others, however, may need a few words of description. The upper and lower case versions of B, E, and W arise because **vi** is prepared to accept two definitions—"small" and "big"—of just what constitutes a word. Under the smaller definition, a word is a string composed entirely of alphabetic characters or entirely of nonalphabetic characters; under the larger one, a word is a string of characters which contains no blanks, tabs, or newlines. Hence, a string containing punctuation marks, such as /usr/spool/lp/interface, would be counted as eight words under the "small word" definition (usr, spool, lp, and interface count as one word each, and so does each slant /) but it is a single word under the "big word" definition. The f,F and t,T pairings refer to targets right and left of the present cursor position and in the current line; lowercase commands search forward, uppercase backward. `F` and `T` are almost the same thing, but `f`*c* is targeted at the next character *c* while `t`*c* aims at the character *before* the next *c*. Few users bother to worry about the difference; they habitually use one or the other and make the necessary one-character adjustment with the `h` and `l` keys as need dictates.

Range Specification

To make using **vi** really flexible—and a bit more complicated—most of the targets shown in Table 7.1 may be embellished with a multiplier. The multiplier *n* always precedes the target symbol (with no intervening spaces!) and effectively makes the target the *n*th occurrence of the object indicated. The general form of a target specification is therefore

<multiplier><identifier>

For example,

```
3(
```

identifies the third sentence break to the right as the target, and

4/drabRET

aims at the fourth occurrence of the character string `drab`, counting from the present position of the cursor. Where the target is defined by giving several characters, as in the search 4/drabRET, the actual target location is one character in the string (keeping in mind that a target is always exactly one character), though which one depends on the direction of search. Except in rare circumstances, it is really not worth the bother to know whether, for example, the first character of a search string is included in the range or not; it is easier to assume that it is and to make any necessary one-character adjustments afterward.

All the target identifiers shown in the Table 7.1 may have multipliers attached, except for those which can occur only once in the file so that a search for their *n*th occurrence is guaranteed to be fruitless. These exceptions are as follows:

n|	*n*th character position in current line
0	left edge of the current line
*n*G	left edge of the *n*th line in the file
G	left edge of the last line in the file
'*x*	place where the marker *x* is set
'*x*	beginning of the line containing marker *x*

The most obvious are *n* | and *n*G, which already have multipliers of sorts. G, which refers to the last line, denotes a unique fixed location; similarly, 0 is a natural exception, for at any moment there exists only one current line.

It may be worth noting that some of the target locations are defined only in relation to the cursor while others are absolute. For example, "five characters left from the cursor" is clearly a cursor-relative location, while "left edge of ninth line in the file" is an absolute place, always the same no matter where the cursor may be located currently.

Moving the Editing Cursor

A curious point about the **vi** editor is that there is no "move" command for moving the cursor. Instead, there are various range delimiting targets, symbols that stand for places in the text file. What look to the novice like commands for moving the cursor are in reality merely symbols for place names, targets for cursor movements (or indeed other **vi** operations) to aim at. Naming a target while **vi** is in command mode is tantamount to saying "move the cursor to that place".

At first glance the lack of a verb to move the cursor may seem strange; on second thought, it is reasonable enough (or do users simply become accustomed to the strangely surrealistic logic of Unix?). All range command verbs do two things: perform some action and, if appropriate, move the cursor to the target end of the range. A cursor movement thus amounts to no action whatever, followed by a move. No action whatever is appropriately enough requested by no command verb. Consequently, moving the cursor requires no action verb, followed by the target specification:

<target>

In other words, a cursor movement is regarded as a null command followed by a range specification. This arrangement may well be open to some criticism as being not entirely obvious to the novice user, even if it does effect the greatest conceivable economy in the number of keystrokes.

Deletion of Text

Targets are used by **vi** not only to move the cursor but also to define the ranges of several other commands. These include deleting, moving, or changing of text segments. Deletion in **vi** always removes a range of text which begins at the location of the cursor and ends at the specified target. The general form of the delete command is

d *<target>*

where <*target*> is any valid target. All the characters between the current cursor location and the target are deleted; it does not matter whether the cursor is located before or after the target in the file. Examples, beginning with the simple and moving on to more complicated ones, are:

dw	delete rightward to the beginning of the next word
d0	delete leftward to the beginning of this line
d5h	delete five characters to leftward
d2j	delete to corresponding position two lines down
d3)	delete the rest of this sentence and the next two
d2}	delete rest of this paragraph and all of the next
dG	delete from cursor to the end of the file
d'u	delete from cursor to the marker u

Strangely, this tidy logical structure cannot include a command that simply deletes the current line. The current line is not a range because it is not in general spanned by the cursor location and some definable target; it therefore refuses to fit into the otherwise very neat scheme shown here. On the other hand, deletion of the current line is obviously a useful activity. To get around this problem, a special command is provided:

dd	deletes the current line
d*n*d	deletes the current line and the next *n*-1 as well

Deletions in **vi** do not annihilate text without trace but remove it to an invisible storage buffer. They should properly be thought of as throwing sections of text into a garbage bin, rather than as destroying them. So long as the bin has not yet been littered with other garbage, an inadvertently discarded item can still be retrieved from the trash can and resurrected. To retrieve it and put it back where it came from the u ("undo") command is normally employed. The existence of such a trash depository, a temporary storage buffer for discarded text, is essential to make the undo command work at all; if there were no copy of the discarded text, how would **vi** know what is to be undone?

Moving and Copying Text

When a text segment is deleted by the d command, it is removed from the editing buffer and placed into a temporary discard buffer. The u command can be used to replace it in its original location; but a more interesting possibility is to reinsert the discarded text elsewhere. The p command serves just this purpose: it retrieves whatever is in the discard buffer and inserts it at the current cursor location. In other words, a section of text may be moved from one place to another in a document by discarding it with the d command, then moving the cursor to the new, desired location and placing the text there with the p command. The word "there" can have two different meanings, depending on the nature of the text deletion. If whole lines were deleted, as with a dd command, then the lines are inserted as lines, immediately following the line on which the cursor sits. On the other hand, if characters were deleted, as for example with the x command, the placement is made following the cursor position within the line.

The ability of a p command to replace lost characters leads to an interesting and fast way of curing a letter inversion, one of the most common typing problems. Suppose, for example, that the word *example* had been mistyped as *exmaple*. Placing the cursor over the *m*, the x command removes the letter *m*, leaving *exaple*—with the cursor covering the *a*. The p command copies into the text whatever is in the deletion buffer (here just the letter *m*) at the right edge of the cursor position, after the letter *a*. The inversion is thus cured by placing the cursor over the first of the two letters and giving the commands xp.

Multiple copies of a text segment may be made by repeated p commands. One simple method is to delete the wanted text segment with the d command, then to undo the damage immediately with a p command. The result of this apparently useless activity is to leave a copy of the desired text segment in the discard buffer. Further p commands will then place duplicates wherever desired.

To simplify work and to avoid any risk of inadvertent harm to the original text, **vi** provides a special command y ("yank") which has the effect of d followed by P; that is, it copies a text segment into the discard buffer without altering the text itself. A range command of the same form as d, y accepts all the normal target specifications and behaves just as might be expected.

Changing Text

One of the most frequent editorial activities undertaken by anyone with a bit of writing to get through is text alteration. In drafts of reports or articles, changes of wording often occur: an awkward sentence, for example, might be improved by substitution of a noun clause for a simple pronoun. Typically, the change required might involve a few or a half-dozen words. It can be achieved easily enough, eliminating the erroneous material with a d command, then inserting the new text with i or a. However, **vi** provides a combined command c ("change") able to do the entire job. It is another range command:

c *<target>*

When a c command is executed, the text in its range is first eliminated, then the new material is inserted. On most terminals, the deletion is not immediately shown by rearranging the screen contents, but only by placing a dollar sign at the target to serve as a visible marker of the range. As with the other range commands, the target may be to the right or left of the cursor; it does not matter. Text insertions of course always proceed from left to right. If the target is to the left of the cursor when the command is issued, the display positions of the target and cursor are swapped to make the inserted text run in the natural direction. Of course, the c command always copies the text to be changed into the delete buffer so that a subsequent u is able to undo the change. If desired, the p command can then be used to fetch the old (unchanged) text segment and place it at some other location.

The c command is really equivalent to d followed by a, so it should not be surprising that the structural deficiency suffered by d is repeated here: the current line cannot be the object of a c command because it is not necessarily spanned by the demarcating pair of cursor and target. This problem is solved in the same way here as it was for deletions, by inventing a special command. In analogy with dd,

cc	changes the current line
c*n*c	changes the current line and the next *n*-1 as well

In screen displays it is easy to eliminate and scroll whole lines; changing the content of an individual line of characters is a slower process. The cc and c*n*c commands therefore perform visible deletion on the screen and at the same time open up a new line for editing.

Delete and Save Buffers

Deletion buffering is a mechanism clearly fundamental to most range commands of **vi**. The management and use of delete buffers are not quite so simple as might seem at first glance, however, for **vi** does more than just maintain a delete buffer for the text yanked or deleted—it keeps nine of them! Text obtained by a d or y command is placed in the first buffer. But as editing proceeds, **vi** moves deleted or yanked text from the first buffer to the second, from the second to the third, and so on down the line; recovery from grievous error is therefore possible not merely to the extent of a single u command but to nine levels of recovery. To extract text from a particular buffer, the p command is prefixed by the buffer identification, as in

```
"3p
```

in which the text from buffer 3 is placed at the cursor location. The nine buffers are sequentially numbered from "1 to "9 and text is moved through them in numerical order.

Not only the p command but the c, d, and y commands also can be prefixed with buffer names. Thus, the full form of a range command in **vi** is

<buffer> <command predicate> <target>

In addition to the nine buffers automatically managed in response to d and y commands, **vi** has an additional 26 text buffers identified by alphabetic characters. These are not used by **vi** in any automatic procedure; they are entirely at the user's disposal as temporary storage areas. Text may be written into them or extracted from them by any range command. For example, one simple way of reversing the order of three paragraphs of text is to delete them in order, requesting the deleted text to be placed into three separate buffers, then to put them back with p commands in inverted order.

The text buffers are addressed similarly to their numbered counterparts: a double quote mark followed by a letter. Both capital and small letters are used to refer to the same buffers. The difference is that when a buffer is addressed by the small letter, as in `"k`, its existing content (if any) is overwritten, while use of the capital letter `"K` implies that the new text is appended to whatever was already there. Examples can range from very simple to absurdly complex:

`"3p`	place a copy of the text from buffer 3 at the cursor location
`"bc(`	change the rest of this sentence but keep a copy of the original in buffer b
`"Dy2/nil`RET	append a copy of the text from here to the second occurrence of the character string `nil` without changing the text now in the editing buffer

Although the makeup of such commands is logical and consistent, it probably contributes toward making users feel that **vi** is a complicated program. It is not easy to convince a novice that `"Xd3?A`RET is an obvious and self-evident statement!

Global Commands in **vi**

A few **vi** commands are neither local in effect nor do they affect a range of text. They are global in the sense that they act on the text buffer without reference to the editing cursor. Some global commands are obvious while others represent truly obscure recesses of **vi**. Happily, there are only a few global commands, even though they include some of fundamental importance—like ZZ, the command for exiting gracefully from **vi**!

Undoing

Especially for beginning users of **vi**, the u (undo) command is a boon. It undoes the effect of the last command that made any change in the text buffer content, thus restoring the buffer to its previous state. The cursor position is not included in what is undone; hence, u cannot be used to return the cursor to its previous position. Quite the contrary: if the cursor has been moved a long distance since the last deletion or insertion, so that the effect of u would not be visible on the screen, **vi** moves the cursor and the screen display in such a way as to make the effect clearly visible. In other words, every effort is made to guard against unwelcome or unseen surprises.

An old chestnut of editor design, indeed of many areas of the software art, is the philosophical question posed by *undo*: what exactly is meant by two successive requests to undo? In some software systems, successive undoings effectively roll back history. **vi**, on the other hand, takes a mathematician's attitude: a negation of a negation results in an identity. In other words, a second u undoes the first; any odd number of u commands is equivalent to one and any even number achieves nothing.

Old hands at using **vi** make extensive use of u as well. A mildly nasty aspect of **vi** is that almost all command verbs are only one character long, with the corollary that almost every keystroke corresponds to a command. This circumstance can lead to surprises if, for example, the user accustomed to office word processors forgets to switch to insertion mode with an `i` or a command and simply proceeds to type in some text instead. Starting to type *For example*. . . will result in

`Fo`	move to next *o* leftward in the current line
`r`	substitute a blank for the *o*
`e`	move to next word-end
`x`	delete last character of word
`a`	start appending text
. . .	and so on

Any reasonable English text is likely to contain an a or an `i`, so an insertion will probably take place sooner or later—though at an unexpected place and possibly after some damage hard to locate. The u command cannot yield a full recovery in all circumstances, but it is certainly helpful.

Exiting

There are several ways of exiting from **vi**. Only one is recommended: the `ZZ` command. It checks whether any changes have been made to the text buffer and writes out the new file contents if so. In other words, `ZZ` makes sure the newly edited file contents have been properly saved, then exits tidily.

An alternative way of exiting is through the **ex** command : q, about which more later. That is a dangerous route, however, for it is possible to escape from **vi** without having saved the edited text at all: fine for experts, but fraught with hazard for the novice!

Using **ex** Commands from **vi**

The **vi** editor is actually not a complete editor program, but only the interactive portion of a composite editor system that includes both **vi** and the keyboard-oriented editor **ex**. This fact explains some otherwise startling shortcomings in **vi**: there are no provisions for switching files, no search-and-replace function, no graceful way of exiting without writing to the input file. All these, and numerous other facilities, are provided by **ex** and not duplicated by **vi**; instead, **vi** is made to pass on commands to **ex**. The command-passing mechanism can handle exactly one command at a time, so any action that **ex** can take in response to a single command line is available to the **vi** user also.

Passing Commands to **ex**

The **ex** editor is a classical keyboard editor. It handles two input streams: a command input and a text input. It also has two outputs: a message stream and an output text file. When operated by itself, without reference to **vi**, the command input and message output are connected to the user terminal, while the text files are files in the normal sense of the word. When **ex** is operated in conjunction with **vi**, both have access to the same files; command input to **ex** consists of keyboard lines passed on by **vi**. Messages sent to the user by **ex** are shown on the screen, mildly filtered by **vi** to avoid undue interference.

When operating by itself, **ex** prompts the user for commands by showing a colon : at the left edge of the screen. The signal for **vi** to transmit a command to **ex** is also a colon, but one typed by the user. For example, the command verb to quit an editing session under **ex** is the single character q, so to quit editing with **vi**, it suffices to say

```
:q
```

Other **ex** commands are handled similarly. It should be noted, incidentally, that the q command is *not* a synonym for the **vi** command ZZ; unlike ZZ, **q** quits without saving the contents of the editing buffer. This command is of value to **vi** users when things have gone wrong, the edit buffer content is irretrievably botched, and the only reasonable course of action is to scrap the whole mess.

Incorrect or ill-advised use of the q command can have serious consequences. To ward off disaster, **ex** tries to spot dangerous actions and refuses any commands it considers suspect. Its objections can be overridden by attaching an exclamation mark to the command, as in

```
:q!
```

to say, in effect, "do not argue, I know what I am doing." Responsibility for any consequent disaster of course lies entirely with the user.

Reading, Writing, and Filing

Like its older brother **ed**, **ex** understands commands for writing and reading files. The `r` command reads in a named file at the location of the editing cursor, thus effectively performing an insertion of one file into the middle of another. The command takes the obvious form

```
:r filename
```

Once inserted in the editing buffer, the files are effectively merged and no longer have any separate identity. Of course, the reading is done in the usual Unix fashion, without affecting the original file.

The w command is used for writing out buffer contents to files. It is used much like the `r` command, but with the difference that, if desired, only part of the buffer need be written. Thus, the commands

```
:w wholefile
:1,10 w partfile
```

will copy the entire buffer content into `wholefile`, and lines 1 through 10 of the buffer into another file `partfile`. The line numbers may be given as numbers or in any of the various symbolic formats permitted by **ex** and **ed**. The buffer content is not changed by writing.

The **ex** and **vi** editors keep track of the file name so as to know where to deposit the edited copy. At times it is desirable to switch file names. The memory area in which the file name is remembered can have a different file name written into it by the `f` command:

```
:f newname
```

This command is useful if several different versions, with different names, need to be fabricated from a single root file.

There is no provision in any of the Unix editors for automatically saving backup copies of the original (unedited) file. Since the w command does not alter the content of the editing buffer, it is a good idea to write out the buffer every ten or fifteen minutes during long editing sessions, especially on small computers. Files on disk are relatively secure, whereas even a minor power interruption, not to mention a system crash, can destroy editing buffer contents totally. Very long editing sessions are perhaps even better safeguarded by taking copies of the file every hour or two on a removable backup medium such as a floppy disk.

In program development it is often wise to secure a backup copy of the source file before beginning a serious session of editing, compilation, and testing and to delete it only after ensuring that the alterations had the intended effect. These backup copies represent insurance against human error, not machine malfunction. Such extra copies entail a very small cost in file space if editing scripts are created with the Unix **diff** command. These list only the differences between files, in a form that can later be used to convert the old copies into new, or vice versa.

Sophisticated search-and-replace functions are provided under **ex**. These are similar to the facilities provided under **ed** and will be found discussed at some length further below.

Reaching for Another Shell

Both **ex** and **ed** provide an escape to the shell without forcing the user to leave the editor. When the command

```
:!abcdefg
```

is given to **vi**, **vi** strips off the colon (which it recognizes as the sign of an **ex** command) and passes the string `!abcdefg` to ex. In turn, **ex** strips off the exclamation mark (which it recognizes as the sign of a shell command), asks the kernel to start a new shell, and passes `abcdefg` to the new shell as a command. After the command has been executed, the shell returns control to **ex**, which hands it back to **vi** again.

At first glance, passing commands from program to program may seem to be of doubtful use. Consider, however, the following situation. A large program file is open for editing under **vi**, the cursor is located in the right spot, and the time has come to insert at that point a subprogram known to be in another file. Unfortunately, the file name which seemed obvious at the time has now managed to escape, so there is nothing to do but consult some file directories to find it. Issuing the command

```
:!ls -l ../which
```

permits the user to have a look at this directory without leaving the editor, to find out the missing file name and to continue work. In fact, nothing stops the user from making some quick corrections on the lost file by launching another copy of **vi**,

```
:!vi ../which/lost
```

before reading it into the main program file and resuming work.

Customizing **vi**

An important reason why **vi** should be a widely respected editor program, despite its shortcomings as compared to state-of-the-art word processors, is that few design decisions made in creating **vi** are forever fixed. Many characteristics of **vi** can be altered by the user to suit **vi** to particular jobs or to please in matters of taste. The principles underlying such customization are given in this section, along with a few examples of what might be considered appropriate parameter settings.

Abbreviations

Abbreviations and macros are tools for shortening work both in text entry and in subsequent text editing and processing. An abbreviation is exactly what its name implies: a short form to represent some longer expression or character string.

Abbreviations are useful for writing decent English despite the tendency, particularly of technical authors, to indulge in short forms as accepted by particular disciplines or trades. Every technical jargon includes a host of short forms, as indeed does everyday speech. The computer professions in particular seem to delight in prose such as

Being part of the CPU, the ALU accesses RAM via the MAR.

To turn computer argot into something resembling English, the user can define a set of abbreviations to have meanings, as, for example,

```
:ab CPU central processing unit
:ab ALU arithmetic and logic unit
:ab RAM random access memory
:ab MAR memory address register
```

These definitions are entered at the keyboard (and terminated with RETURN) while **vi** is in command mode. When the above sentence is subsequently typed at the terminal, the text buffer and screen both show

```
Being part of the central processing unit, the
arithmetic and logic unit accesses random access
memory via the memory address register.
```

Abbreviations are recognized and acted upon by **vi** while in insertion mode, never in command mode. During text entry, words are checked against the list of abbreviations and synonymous full forms are substituted. Substitution is undertaken only if the full word entered at the keyboard exactly matches the abbreviation, so that the string ALU in ALUM and ALUMINUM would not be replaced in the above example. When no longer required, the command

```
:una ALU
```

can be used to remove ALU from the list of recognized abbreviations.

Command Macros

Macros are like abbreviations, but they are recognized only in command mode. A macro is therefore no more and no less than an extension to the **vi** language, the definition of a new command verb. An only slightly contrived example is furnished by the macro declaration

```
:map v bdwwP
```

which means that whenever the character v is entered at the keyboard in command mode, the character string bdwwP is to be understood instead. This string will be interpreted as

b	move cursor left to the next word beginning
dw	delete that word
w	move right to the next word beginning
P	place the deleted word to the left

all of which says in simple English: exchange the two words. Applying these commands, the character string

```
this character is not long forgotten
```

turns into

```
this character is long not forgotten
```

if the cursor was initially under the *o* in *not*. Many useful extensions to **vi** can be made in this way, either on a temporary basis or more or less permanently. Since macros must be defined in terms of already existing commands, they cannot endow **vi** with any actions it could not perform before; but they certainly can make work faster and more agreeable.

A note of caution may be in order. Macros are strings of commands, so they are really programs written in the **vi** language and need debugging just like any other programs. The **vi** language is subtle and terse so debugging is not always easy. The five-character macro shown above, for example, contains a bug not immediately obvious to most people (it fails if the cursor is at the beginning of a line). A second, perhaps even trickier, problem is that macro names must not contain characters that might be misunderstood; a macro name beginning with d, for example, would be exceedingly dangerous! Macro names are therefore somewhat constrained, safe characters being any that **vi** does not already use for something else:

```
^A ^K ^O ^T ^V ^W ^X K V g q v * _
```

Other characters can certainly be used but may entail some risk. At the very least, debugging should be done using some "scrap" text!

Macros are susceptible to a particularly wicked variety of bug. When a macro name is replaced by the defining command string, the commands in the string are executed as if they had been typed at the keyboard. If the command string should contain a reference to the macro name itself, the macro substitution is made and interpreted up to the point where the macro name occurs; then the macro is substituted for the name and interpretation is begun again. This process then continues recursively! For example, mistyping the character string bdwwP in the example above as

```
:map v bdwvP
```

causes the entire text buffer content to be reduced to a few punctuation marks by a single request for the macro v.

The set of currently defined macros can be viewed by using the macro definition command :map without any arguments, and existing macros may be cancelled by :unmap. In spite of the warnings given, macros are a very useful tool for anyone interested in retuning **vi** even slightly.

Options

Many habits of **vi** can be altered by resetting internal numeric or logical parameters. These settings, called *options* in the manuals, are dealt with by the :set command. One particular option, which will serve to illustrate the point, deals with searches implied by the / and ? target identifiers. Such searches normally continue to the end of the file and then "wrap around" to its beginning, so that the entire file will be searched no matter where the search was begun. At times, users may wish to search only to the end of the file. The command

```
:set nowrapscan
```

will defeat wrap-around in searching, and the command

```
:set wrapscan
```

will turn it on again when required. Options available total between three and four dozen, depending on the version of **vi**; they include window size management, scrolling speed, default line width, checking for control character inclusion in the file, tab stops, and a great deal more. The command `:set`, with no arguments, displays what options have been set since **vi** started running; the command

```
:set all
```

displays the entire list of options available and their present settings.

The `.exrc` File

Every time **vi** starts up, the file called `.exrc` is read, if it exists, and interpreted as a set of **vi** commands. Customizing **vi** is therefore best done by creating an `.exrc` file, to contain option settings, macros, or indeed anything that **vi** is able to recognize as a command.

A simple example of customization may be helpful here. The IBM PC keyboard has a keypad often used to steer the cursor, as shown on the left in Figure 7.3. When struck, these keys actually send out three characters each: an ESCAPE (which echoes as `^[`), followed by `[`, followed by a capital letter. The character sequences are shown in the middle portion of Figure 7.3, while the right-hand part shows the **vi** commands which correspond to the cursor movements marked on the keytops.

To make the keypad function under **vi** as marked, a set of macros must be defined, one for each key, so that the character sequences actually sent by the keys are recognized as macro names; **vi** will then substitute

7 Home	8 ↑	9 PgUp
4 ←	5	6 →
1 End	2 ↓	3 PgDn

^[[H	^[[A	^[[G
^[[D	^[[E	^[[C
^[[F	^[[B	^[[I

H	k	^F
h	M	l
L	j	^B

FIGURE 7.3. Control keypad of a small computer, its character sequences and corresponding **vi** commands. `^[` denotes the ESCAPE character.

the appropriate characters shown on the right. Such a set of macros is incorporated in the .exrc file

```
:set nowrapscan
:set window=18
:map ^[[A k
:map ^[[B j
:map ^[[C l
:map ^[[D h
:map ^[[E M
:map ^[[F L
:map ^[[G ^F
:map ^[[H H
:map ^[[I ^B
```

To insert the control characters and the ESCAPEs into a file with **vi**, they must be preceded with control-V; for example, one types

control-V ESCAPE `[ I` *control-V control-B*

to get the last of the macro definitions right. If placed in file `.exrc` and left there permanently, these macros are loaded automatically every time **vi** is invoked. Clearly, the same technique can be used to customize **vi** to any other terminal or computer.

Text Entry with vi

Writing plain prose text with **vi** is not only possible, it can even be agreeable; many books and innumerable technical reports have been written with this editor. In its default form, **vi** is usable for writing, as it is for programming; but better use can result from slight adaptation to the task.

People accustomed to office word processors can be forgiven for disliking the line orientation of **vi**, for it is pleasing to type text without worrying about line ends. Although there is no way **vi** can be made to format lines automatically, there is provision for automatic insertion of line ends. Requesting

```
:set wrapmargin=8
```

requires **vi** to insert line ends automatically, with as much text as possible on each line but with no line exceeding 72 characters (screen width of 80 characters less 8 for the wrap margin) in length. The line ends inserted will be genuine RETURN keystrokes, so the text is organized in lines just as it would have been manually. However, there is no need to pay heed to the line ends any more. Of course, the margin width can be reset at any time. Resetting it to zero, however, defeats the automatic insertion of line ends.

The text processing facilities normally provided under Unix include one or more large packages of macros for text formatting. These provide numerous combinations of paragraph and section styles, saving the writer a good deal of trouble. Two options provided by **ex**, paragraphs and sections, store character strings which can subsequently be recognized by **nroff** or **troff** as macro indentifications. They allow customizing **vi** to the user's preferences in typographic style.

Computer Programming with **vi**

For writing computer programs in most conventional programming languages, and even some unconventional ones, **vi** provides options that can make life a little easier. Three of these bear particular mention: autoindentation, line numbering, and parenthesis matching.

Every line entered at the keyboard will be preceeded by exactly as many blank character spaces as its predecessor, provided autoindentation is turned on with the command

```
:set autoindent
```

The result is that formatting styles common for Pascal or Fortran programs follow naturally and automatically:

```
begin
   read(tops);
   twopower := 2;
   threepower := 3;
   while threepower < tops do
   begin
      twopower := twopower * 2;
      threepower := threepower * 3;
   end;
   writeln(tops, twopower, threepower);
end;
```

Much to the liking of some programmers, and much to the dislike of some others, the *number* option attaches a line number to every line automatically:

```
262  begin
263     read(tops);
264     twopower := 2;
265     threepower := 3;
```

```
    while threepower < tops do
    begin
       twopower := twopower * 2;
       threepower := threepower * 3;
    end;
    writeln(tops, twopower, threepower);
end;
```

Languages such as Lisp and C, indeed even Fortran, sometimes involve many nested parentheses or brackets, in the manner of

```
KQ = IP(IK(IJ(1,II(L)), IK(IJ(2,II(L-1)), K), L))
```

Such statements can be a prolific source of program errors. The *showmatch* option of **vi** may be turned on to help here. Whenever a closing parenthesis is typed, this option causes the cursor to travel to the matching opening parenthesis for a second or so, then to return. The hand is quicker than the eye, so it is possible to miss the cursor action; nevertheless, a great many puzzling compiler messages can be avoided by this means.

Computer program writing can be simplified considerably by creating a `.exrc` file containing any desired keyboard reconfiguring macros, plus

```
:set autoindent
:set showmatch
:set number
:map v a   ^[
```

where `^[` is the echo of a control-V followed by ESCAPE. The macro at the end of this file inserts three blank spaces for program indentations. It is better than tab characters because tab settings on the terminal do not necessarily correspond to the tab settings on the printer.

A minor inconvenience of **vi** is that there can only be one `.exrc` file in any one directory. The rather different requirements of text processing and program writing suggest that different `.exrc` files should be invoked. There are several clever ways of getting around this problem; the easiest is undoubtedly to keep separate directories for programs and text, with an appropriate `.exrc` file in each.

The **ed** Line Editor

Long the main editor furnished with the Unix system, **ed** has suffered a relative decline in popularity as **vi** has become the normal working tool of programmers and writers alike. Like **vi**, **ed** is a line editor and expects text to be organized into lines separated by newline characters. Aside from minor exceptions, its commands are compatible with those of **ex**, so users of **vi** and **ex** generally find themselves quite at home with **ed**.

Line Numbers

Like **vi**, **ed** regards the text buffer content as a set of lines, a line being simply a string of any printable characters including blanks and terminated by a newline character. Unlike **vi**, **ed** does not have an editing cursor; but it does maintain a line pointer which identifies one particular line in the file as being the current line. For example, a small text file might contain the character sequence

```
This is a small\ntext file to\ndemonstrate editing.
```

Here \n represents the newline character (ASCII 012 octal). When this file is copied into the text buffer for editing, **ed** will regard it as containing three lines, with a pointer pointing at one of them:

```
        1   This is a small
  →     2   text file to
        3   demonstrate editing.
```

ed permits reference to lines by number. It assigns the number 1 to the first line in the file and numbers the rest sequentially. Whenever any new lines are inserted in the buffer, or any lines are deleted, **ed** automatically renumbers all lines then and there.Neither line numbers nor the pointer ever appear on the terminal screen, however, so the user does not see the renumbering taking place.

Because the first line in the buffer is always numbered 1, it is always easy to locate.However, the number of the last line is not usually known so the symbol $ is used to denote it. Similarly, the user does not usually wish to keep track of the current line number; the symbol . (pronounced "dot") may be used instead. Both symbols may be employed in any **ed** command which refers to line numbers. In other words, text normally appears to the user as

```
        1   This is a larger
        2   text file which
            ....
  →     .   This is the current line
            ....
        $   and this line is the last.
```

It is rarely worth worrying about the actual numerical values of . and $; the symbols are used in practically all cases.

Editor Commands

Most of the text manipulation commands used by **ed** contain a single command verb. The verb may refer to a particular segment of text, in which case it is augmented by a line number or a range identified by a pair of line numbers. Of course, the symbols . and $ may be substituted for line numbers where appropriate. The usual form of an **ed** command is

[[*linenumber,*] *linenumber*] *verb*

All command verbs are made up of just a single character. For example, p ("print") may be used to display lines on the screen. The command

```
1,$ p
```

will cause the entire buffer content to be listed (the range is from line 1 to line $, the last line in the buffer). Other commands available in **ed** are

a	*append*	appends more lines at a specified place
c	*change*	changes specified lines to new material
d	*delete*	deletes specified lines
e	*edit*	sets edit buffer to contain a given file
f	*filename*	prints a remembered filename
g	*global*	applies following commands to whole buffer
i	*insert*	inserts lines at the specified place
m	*move*	moves lines to a new place (cut and paste)
p	*pointer*	positions pointer and displays lines
q	*quit*	exits from the editor, to the Unix shell
r	*read*	reads a file into the editing buffer
s	*substitute*	substitutes new character string for old
v		applies following commands selectively
w	*write*	writes buffer contents into a file
=		shows current numeric value of . or $
!		passes the following command to the shell

Where a line number is required for a command to make sense (e.g., for the p command), but the user does not supply one, **ed** assumes that the current line number is meant. In other words, commands with line numbers omitted are executed as if the dot symbol . had been included in the command.

Line numbers and line number ranges must make sense, otherwise **ed** will ignore them. Line numbers below 1, or above $, are not acceptable, and ranges must always ask for line numbers in ascending order. For example, line 0 cannot be printed, nor can all lines from number 12 to number 8.

Because **ed** is normally operated in an interactive fashion, any errors in commands can be identified immediately as they occur. They are signalled by the single error message provided by **ed**, a question mark ? displayed at the left-hand screen edge.

Pointer Manipulation and Text Examination

Lines in the editing buffer may be displayed with the p (''pointer'' or ''print'') command. Displaying causes the line pointer to move to the last line displayed. Thus, the p command may be used not only to cause display but also to move the pointer about.

In general, one or two line numbers precede the command letter p. If only one number is supplied, it is understood to denote the desired line; two line numbers are taken to identify a range. The p command is specially privileged among **ed** commands: if a command is issued with the command verb omitted, p is understood by default. Thus, it is not necessary to type

```
5 p
```

to position the pointer at the fifth line of text; it suffices to enter

```
5
```

In addition to numeric values and the symbols . and $, the line number identification may contain addition and subtraction operations. For example,

```
.-1,$-10 p
```

will cause display to start at the buffer line preceding the current pointer position and to continue until the 10th last line in the buffer. Because it is permissible to omit p, the same effect will result from the abbreviated command

```
.-1,$-10
```

Because **ed** always assumes that the dot . is meant if line number information is omitted,

```
-1,$-10
```

is also acceptable. There is a difference between signed and unsigned positive numbers; 5 is understood to denote the fifth line in the buffer, whereas +5 is interpreted to mean .+5 and therefore denotes the fifth line counted from the current pointer position. No ambiguity can arise with negative signs, since the lowest line number in the buffer is always 1.

Under the syntax rules of **ed**, very few unacceptable command lines can be devised, for **ed** employs an extensive set of rules to fill in missing information. The limiting case arises when trying to abbreviate

```
. p
```

which requests display of the current line. The rules allow both the letter p and the dot to be omitted, for both will be supplied by default. Typing a blank line (just pressing RETURN) should therefore display the current line. In fact, this ultimate abbreviation forms an exception to the rules: a blank line is interpreted as equivalent to

```
.+1 p
```

While nobody likes exceptions to rules, this one is quite beneficial because it permits displaying a succession of lines, one at a time, simply by pressing the RETURN key.

Inserting, Appending, and Deleting Text

Text insertion in **ed** follows the same principles as in **vi**, but with one major exception: inserting or appending is done before or behind the current line, not the current cursor position. Since **ed** is a strictly line-oriented editor, it follows also that the text to be inserted must be made up of one or more complete lines; partial lines or individual characters cannot be inserted. Insertion is terminated by typing a dot . as the first (and only) character of a new line. For example,

```
i
This is an inserted line
and this is another.
.
```

results in insertion of the two lines shown (but not of the i and the dot .) in the editing buffer. When an insertion is completed, the current line pointer remains at the last line inserted. There is an a ("append") command as well as an i, just as there is in **vi**. When either is used, lines are automatically renumbered to take account of the new insertions.

Lines are deleted using the d command, which is a range command just like p and employs the same syntax conventions. Thus,

d	deletes the current line
1,2 d	deletes the first and second lines in the buffer
-1,+1 d	deletes current line, plus one before and after
1,$ d	deletes the entire buffer contents

After a deletion, the pointer is set to the line following the last line deleted—unless that was the last line in the buffer, in which case the pointer is set to $.

A group of lines can be deleted and immediately replaced with the c ("change") command, which deletes the specified lines and leaves **ed** in insertion mode. For example, the current line and the two immediately adjacent lines are removed and replaced by a single line, by

```
.-1,.+1 c
This line replaces three old ones.
```

As might be expected, the syntax rules of c are exactly those of d and i combined.

String Searching and Replacing

Instead of line numbers, **ed** will accept line identification in the form of a character string delimited fore and aft by the slant /, as in `/line/`. For example,

```
/line/,/example/ p
```

causes display of a range of lines determined as follows. The first line to be displayed is the first line after the current line which contains the character string `line`; the last line is the first line thereafter to contain the string `example`. In other words, `/example/` means "the next line to contain `example`". Of course, the rule still applies that p is assumed if no other command letter appears. Hence,

```
/line/,/example/
```

causes an action similar to that described above, while the single string

```
/line/
```

causes the next line to contain `line` to be found and displayed. Note that the character string `line` need not coincide with the word *line*; the search may turn up such other strings as *line*man, col*line*ar, fe*line*, mil*line*ry. Searching always proceeds in the natural text sequence. But if the search is not successful when the end of the buffer is reached, searching is continued on a "wrap-around" basis, as if line 1 followed line $. If the search is totally unsuccessful, **ed** will simply display a question mark.

When a particular character string has been found, another can be substituted for it using the s command. Thus,

```
1,5 s/use/employment/
```

will find all first occurrences of the string `use` in the first five lines of the editing buffer and substitute `employment` for `use`.

Null strings are acceptable in substitutions. If by a slip of the finger the string `use7` was typed instead of `use`, correction could be achieved by either

```
s/use7/use/
```

or

```
s/7//
```

The latter merely substitutes "no characters" for `7`. Note that since no line number range was given, **ed** will assume that the current line was meant, as if `.,.s/7//` had been typed.

Substitution is occasionally required for all occurrences of a word or character string. The `s` command can achieve global replacement, if the g ("global") command is attached to it. For example,

```
1,$ s/use/employment/gp
```

will replace all occurrences (as specified by g) of `use` in the entire edit buffer (lines 1,$) by `employment` and will display on the screen every line in which the replacement is made. The latter echoing is useful for detecting unwanted changes, since global replacement of `use` will result in am*use*ment being replaced by the unintended am*employment*ment!

Cut and Paste Operations

In "cut and paste" operations text is rearranged by moving entire paragraphs or sentences. To do so, **ed** permits moving groups of lines by means of the `m` ("move") command. This command removes a group of lines and inserts them elsewhere. For example,

```
-5,. m +7
```

moves six lines (`.-5` to `.` inclusive) so that they follow line `.+7` after the command has been executed. It should be noted that the `m` command requires a total of three line numbers: two (or one) preceding, to identify the range of lines to be moved, and one following the `m`, to specify where to move them to. Of course, the line specifications may be either numeric or contextual; the command

```
/necessary/,/example/ m .-5
```

could be used to move an entire paragraph beginning with a line containing `necessary` and ending with the first line thereafter to contain `example`.

File Handling by the Editor

File handling by **ed** is similar to the file handling done by **ex** (and therefore **vi**). However, there are a few small differences. The first concerns the `r` command, as, for example,

```
r filename
```

which under **vi** reads in a file at the current cursor location. In **ed**, it is considered more natural for such reading to append at the end of the text buffer, so that

```
r firstfile
r secondfile
```

causes two files to be read into the buffer and concatenated.

To exit from **ed**, the q (''quit'') command is issued. This command has probably caused more grief to beginners than any other, because the q command quits the editor without writing out the buffer content. In other words, issuing a q without a preceding w command will simply abandon whatever work may have been expended in editing. Writing out the edit buffer content is the responsibility of the user!

Chapter 8

Text Preparation and Processing

Everybody who computes needs to do some text processing from time to time. Even scientific programmers must be able to prepare program documentation to accompany their cleverly constructed source code. Others may be directly concerned with text in its more usual sense—manuscripts, letters, and documents. Unix has traditionally catered for both needs better than most other operating systems.

Tools and Facilities

The Unix system includes an unusually good set of software tools for text preparation, editing, and formatting. Many, indeed probably the great majority, of its users at Bell Laboratories during the 1970s employed Unix not to compute numbers, nor to develop operating systems, but to set up and format text. The Unix programming team responded to this need by creating many utility programs, well thought out and carefully implemented. These were quickly incorporated in the succession of standard system releases. Other text processing utilities developed outside the Bell environment, yet many remained well within the Unix tradition. Techniques developed for use with Unix have profoundly influenced practically all text processing software ever since. Users acquainted with office word processors will be interested to discover within Unix the roots of many methods now considered conventional.

Text Files and Processes

Text preparation involves two distinct facets, which might be termed material and intellectual. The material aspect of text is the physical presentation and arrangement of characters and lines on the page, the layout of paragraphs and the choice of typographic style. Its intellectual or literary side concerns content rather than form and thus includes matters of style, phrasing, grammar, and orthography. Both are important to the writer, whether of poems or programs. Both are provided for in standard Unix software.

The design philosophy underlying Unix is to provide flexible general-purpose tools for individually simple jobs and to allow users to combine them for specific tasks. This viewpoint is perhaps more clearly expressed and more extensively carried into practice in text processing software than in any other part of Unix. Subdividing the task of writing into parts is best begun by separating form from content, as indeed happens in Unix software. Creating an attractive physical arrangement of text, a task generally called *formatting*, is taken care of by programs that do not care about content. *En revanche*, as it were, content is analyzed by programs that do not care about physical layout.

Text files must clearly contain information about both content and form. The content part may appear more or less self-explanatory. Characters were invented, after all, expressly for the purpose of writing down words and sentences, so Unix ordinary files which simply consist of strings of characters seem ideally suited to contain formatless text. Physical layout of text—text placement on the page, choice of typeface, size, and balance of white space—is another matter. It is incorporated in text files as a set of formatting directives or, as they are usually called in the manuals, *requests*. These specify margin widths, indicate what typefaces are to be used, determine page lengths, and generally tie down exactly what the writer had in mind. In other words, a text file under Unix ordinarily contains two interlaced sets of character strings: those which specify content and those which specify form. Either can be altered without affecting the other. This sort of file structure is essential if the task of formatting text is to be separable from the task of writing and editing its content, if programs are to be created to affect either aspect of a text file independently of the other.

Text Formatting Programs

To prepare properly formatted and attractive documents, software facilities are required far beyond the minimal level provided by editor programs such as **vi** or **ed**. The main formatting program available under the Unix system is **nroff** (pronounced *en-roff*). The structure and style of **nroff** derive from an earlier precursor program **roff**, now obsolete but said to be still in use at some Unix installations. The command structure of **roff** and **nroff** has been widely accepted by the text processing community; indeed, numerous commercial word processors otherwise unrelated to **nroff** have borrowed it. **nroff** will justify margins, place footnotes at the bottom of the page, number pages, center titles, indent paragraphs, and take care of a thousand things normally expected of a professional typesetter.

In addition to **nroff**, which produces output suitably formatted for printing terminals and line printers, all releases of Unix provide some version of **troff** (*tee-roff*), a program similar to **nroff** in principle but capable of producing book-quality output from a phototypesetting machine or laser printer. The distinction is straightforward enough: **troff** knows about different fonts and different type sizes, while **nroff** does not. The two are mutually compatible, in the sense that **nroff** requests are a subset of all **troff** requests; **troff** will happily execute requests intended for **nroff** and **nroff** will do likewise so far as the printer used can rise to the task. The full command language of **nroff** and **troff** is extensive and not easy to master. A small subset, some fifteen or twenty requests, fortunately suffices to do practically everything required in routine report writing. This chapter describes it in sufficient detail to enable users to cope with simple documents.

The Unix system includes a wide range of further formatting aids to the report writer. For mathematical typesetting (equations and the like) there exists a program called **eqn**; for setting up tables, there is **tbl**, a table editor. The **troff** and **eqn** programs are able to drive an ordinary printing terminal, but obviously they cannot do anything the terminal cannot do. To realize their full potential, they require a phototypesetting machine or laser printer. Because such are rare (compared to terminals), these programs will interest a smaller community than **nroff**, so they are described here in less detail than the more fundamental text formatting software.

A note of caution should perhaps be introduced about **troff** and its various clever derivatives. Typesetting—in particular mathematical typesetting—is a skilled craft not easily learned overnight. On first encountering **troff** and **eqn**, most writers are enchanted with the power to determine both content and form of their work, for they are instinctively aware that art includes not only an intellectual element but also an aesthetic one. Only later does the realization dawn that the art of making beautiful books involves two crafts, writing and typography; the typographer's craft is demanding and the author who wishes to take full charge of typography must be prepared to spend time at it. Where the layout requirements exceed those of typewriting, the writer certainly ought to experiment with **troff** for a day or two, but it may be wise to entrust the final job to an expert.

Programs for Writers

For checking documents to find spelling errors, Unix software includes a program called (not surprisingly) **spell**. Similarly, stylistic errors can sometimes be caught by the programs **diction** and **style**—though writing style is a matter of taste. In addition, the Unix system includes various utility programs able to compare, sort, and modify files. These are often convenient for text processing. However, they are more broadly useful than that; they are therefore described in *Chapter 6: Facilities and Utilities*.

The **nroff** Text Formatter

Editing programs such as **vi** or **ed** used by themselves are satisfactory for developing and correcting computer programs, in which the layout and formatting of the text are more or less fixed. On the other hand, reports, manuscripts, and other purely textual matter look better if certain essentially cosmetic operations are performed. For example, it is often thought desirable to move words across line ends and to insert blank spaces so right-hand margins come out straight. Such operations are performed under Unix by **troff** and **nroff**, text formatting programs included in practically all releases and versions of the Unix system. **nroff** reads a file containing the "raw" text and writes an output file containing the same text, reformatted in accordance with appropriate requests. The requests are embedded in the text file itself.

The **nroff** Command Language

In essence, **nroff** may be regarded as a processor for a batch programming language, in which program commands operate on data (the raw text itself) in a prescribed fashion. Every command in this language begins at the left-hand margin, preceded by a . (dot) to identify it as a command. For example, the request

```
.pl 55
```

sets the page length to 55 lines. An automatic line counter in **nroff** keeps track of how many lines have been printed and causes a new page to be started whenever 55 lines of output have been generated. To produce the above paragraph and heading, the following text might have been set up using **vi**:

```
.pl 55
.ll 50
The nroff Command Language
.sp 1
.ti 6
In essence, nroff may be regarded
```

```
as a processor for a batch programming
language, in which program commands operate on data
(the raw text itself) in
a prescribed fashion. Every command
in this language begins at the left-hand margin,
preceded by a . (dot) to identify it as a command.
.sp 2
```

The requests at the head of this text segment instruct **nroff** to make the page length 55 lines and the line length 50 characters, to insert a blank line after the heading, and to indent 6 characters at the start of the paragraph. The text itself is furnished to **nroff** in lines of random length. **nroff** removes the line breaks from the text and inserts new ones so it will fit into the specified page layout. After processing, the sample text shown looks much tidier:

```
The nroff Command Language

      In   essence,   nroff   may   be   regarded   as   a
processor   for   a   batch   programming   language,   in
which  program  commands  operate  on  data  (the  raw
text   itself)   in   a   prescribed   fashion.   Every
command  in  this  language  begins  at  the  left-hand
margin,  preceded  by  a  .  (dot)  to  identify  it  as  a
command.
```

The document content is not altered by **nroff** in any way; only the formatting requests are translated into the page layout. Form and content make up two interlaced data streams, with **nroff** acting on one stream but not the other. Because there is only one file, running **nroff** is a simple matter:

```
$ nroff datafile | lpr
```

nroff feeds the standard output, so redirecting or piping is necessary if the output is not to go to the terminal screen.

Basic **nroff** Requests

Every **nroff** request begins with the dot (or sometimes the apostrophe) at the left margin and contains precisely two other characters. The characters may be followed by a space, then by a signed or unsigned number. Unsigned numbers mean just what they say; for example, `.pl 55` means "make the page length 55 lines". If the number is preceded by a + sign it is understood to say "add to the previous value", so `.pl +55` means "make the page length 55 lines longer than it was up to now". Correspondingly, the - sign (as in `.pl -55`) means "shorten the the page length by 55 lines". In practically all cases, a missing numeric argument is taken as 1 (page length = 66 is one of the rare exceptions). The numeric values are subject to a host of restrictions, but most of these are not worth mentioning because they are obvious: line and page lengths must not become negative, paragraph indentations must not exceed the line length, and so on.

All the numeric values that **nroff** is obliged to know—such as line spacing and line length—have initial values set when **nroff** is first started up. The average user happy to fill pages 66 lines long with single-spaced 65-character lines (on most printers, the right numbers for 8.5 inch by 11 inch paper) therefore need not bother setting page and line lengths. The same goes for non-numeric option settings; **nroff** will insert enough blank spaces between words to make left and right margins straight, unless instructed otherwise.

The full **nroff** language includes nearly a hundred requests, a truly formidable list. Fortunately, a very modest subset is enough to permit working with ordinary text. The informal overview given here actually deals with fewer than two dozen requests, but these probably suffice to cover a great many requirements.

Filling and Adjusting

Text is really a one-dimensional entity, a string of characters. The purpose of any text formatter is to map this one-dimensional continuum onto a two-dimensional page in accordance with some set of rules. The first rule is to cut up the text into "lines" by inserting line breaks. This is done by removing any existing line breaks, then forming each new line by taking as many words as possible without overflowing the permissible line length. In **nroff** terminology, this process is called *filling*. A second rule of text formatting, often though not always applied, is to *adjust* all lines to have equal length so the output document has straight left and right margins. Adjusting is done by inserting blanks next to existing blanks. The result can be excellent if lines are long and words short, otherwise "white rivers" can occur in the text. Sometimes adjusting is not desired; **nroff** permits turning it off with the `.na` ("no adjustment") request and on again with the `.ad` ("adjust") request. No adjusting does not mean no filling; lines are still made as long as they can be. For example,

```
     In essence, nroff may be regarded as a
processor for a batch programming language, in
which program commands operate on data (the raw
text itself) in a prescribed fashion. Every
command in this language begins at the left-hand
margin, preceded by a . (dot) to identify it as a
command.
```

is filled exactly the same way as in the first example, but no extra blanks are inserted for adjustment.

Filling of lines may on occasion not be desirable (for example, if printing out a table!). It can be turned off by the .nf ("no fill") request and back on again with the .fi ("fill") request. With filling turned off, input text lines are copied to the output with line breaks intact, even if the lines then exceed the specified line length:

```
      In essence, nroff may be regarded
as a processor for a batch programming
language, in which program commands operate on data
(the raw text itself) in
a prescribed fashion. Every command
in this language begins at the left-hand margin,
preceded by a . (dot) to identify it as a command.
```

It is worth noting that the paragraph indentation in the first line is inserted even though filling is turned off. In other words, the input lines are not simply copied exactly as they come; other **nroff** requests still apply.

Adjustment without filling makes little sense, so the .nf request turns off both filling and adjusting. There is no way to turn adjusting on if filling is off; the .ad request is simply ignored after .nf. Similarly, the .fi request turns both filling and adjustment on again, unless the adjustment has been deliberately turned off.

Centered lines, often used in titles, are never filled by **nroff**. The .ce ("center") request causes the next line to be copied into the output exactly as it is, but with enough blanks inserted at the left edge to make the text appear at the center. The .ce request may specify that more than a single line is to be centered. For example, .ce 3 causes each of the next three lines to be centered.

When filling, **nroff** removes all line breaks and inserts new ones. Where a line break is definitely wanted, as at the end of a paragraph, the .br ("break") request is used. This request causes a line break to be placed in exactly the place where it occurs, no matter what the effect on filling. In addition to .br, a host of other nroff requests introduce forced line breaks. For example, .fi and .nf both do. These implied breaks may be suppressed by using the apostrophe instead of the dot at the left margin; the .fi request thus introduces a break, the 'fi request does not.

Page Layout

A new page is started in the output file by the request .bp ("begin page"). It causes a line break as well as a page break; that is, it will not delay starting a new page until the current output line is complete. If a page break is wanted at the next natural line end but not earlier, 'bp can be used.

Left and right margins are set in **nroff** by the `.ll` *N* ("line length *N*") and `.po` ("page offset *N*") requests. The former defines line length, the latter moves the entire line *N* spaces to the right. There are no requests for moving margins, so the user can never set the left margin beyond the right! Page length is controlled by `.pl` *N*, as discussed above. These requests may be issued at any time and take effect at the next line end or page end. None of them causes a line break.

When started up, **nroff** is set for single-spaced output. If double line spacing is desired, the `.ls 2` ("line spacing") request is used. Triple, quadruple, or wider line spacing may also be asked for by including the appropriate number with `.ls`. If a single block of *N* blank lines is desired, the request `.sp` *N* is employed. It causes the printer to produce *N* blank lines. A break is caused by `.sp` but not by the `.ls` request. Both accept only absolute numeric arguments: it is not possible to increase or decrease spacing by `.ls +1` and `.ls -1`. However, no number at all is understood to mean `1`, so `.sp` and `.sp 1` are equivalent.

Paragraph indentations are achieved by the `.ti` *N* ("temporary indent") request, which causes a break. "Temporary" means that only a single line is indented. The `.in` *N* ("indent") request is similar, but indents all subsequent lines. These two may be used in combination to cause indented text to be preceded by item numbers or other identifiers. Indentations may be added to or subtracted, but the total indentation is not allowed to be negative. Hence, the "hanging" paragraph style, in which the first word sticks out beyond the left edge of the text, can be produced easily but cannot run out into the left margin proper. The input file

```
.in +5
.ti -5
In essence, nroff may be regarded
as a processor for a batch programming
language, in which program commands operate on data
(the raw text itself) in
a prescribed fashion. Every command
in this language begins at the left-hand margin,
preceded by a . (dot) to identify it as a command.
.in -5
```

thus produces

```
In  essence,  nroff  may  be  regarded  as  a  processor
     for  a  batch  programming  language,  in  which
     program  commands  operate  on  data  (the  raw
     text  itself)  in  a  prescribed  fashion.  Every
     command  in  this  language  begins  at  the  left-
     hand   margin,   preceded   by   a   .(dot)   to
     identify it as a command.
```

Word emphasis in **nroff** is available by boldfacing, which really means double printing, and by underlining. Underlining is usually the more effective by far. The `.ul` *N* request causes all alphanumeric characters (but not the blanks) in the next *N* lines to be underlined. This request does not cause a break, so that a single word may be underlined:

```
.ti 5
In essence,
.ul
nroff
may be regarded
as a processor for a batch programming
language, in which program commands operate on data
(the raw text itself) in
a prescribed fashion. Every command
```

The word **nroff** will now appear underlined in an otherwise normal, justified, paragraph whose first line is indented five spaces:

```
     In  essence,  nroff  may  be  regarded  as  a
processor  for  a  batch  programming  language,  in
which  program  commands  operate  on  data  (the  raw
text  itself)  in  a  prescribed  fashion.  Every
```

It is possible to underline several lines with the `.ul` request, much as the `.ce` request permits centering several lines. However, the value of such prolific underlining is questionable.

Hyphenation

The English language lends itself particularly well to the fill-and-adjust process because it is an almost uninflected language whose sentences include large numbers of "little" words—articles, prepositions, conjunctions, auxiliary verbs. Despite that, large streams of white space still mar the appearance of printed text when line lengths must be kept short, as in two-column magazine articles or scientific papers. Good formatting of text therefore requires hyphenation.

Hyphenation is carried out by **nroff** only in response to the `.hy` request; no hyphenation is done unless the user asks for it. It is turned off again with the `.nh` request. To find good places to hyphenate, **nroff** overfills the line, then backtracks to locate a consonant or string of consonants that will permit word division. For example,

```
     In  essence,  nroff  may  be  regarded  as  a  pro-
cessor  for  a  batch  programming  language,  in  which
```

```
formatting requests operate on data (the unformat-
ted text itself) in a prescribed fashion. Every
formatting request in this language begins at the
left-hand margin, preceded by a . (dot) to iden-
tify it as a command.
```

Hyphenation is an onerous task which can only be accomplished passably, never perfectly, because the rules of hyphenation in English are keyed to syllables and phonemes, not to characters. For example, the word *present* must be divided differently as emphasis shifts: "I would like to *pre-sent* to you my *pres-ent* spouse." No computer program is likely to achieve that in the near future.

To decide the fate of their own words, **nroff** provides users a selection of mechanisms for manual control. The crudest of these is naturally the .nh request which defeats hyphenation altogether. The next level of refinement is still automatic, but a little neater; it consists of allowing the .hy request to be restricted by a numeric argument, as in

```
.hy 4
```

The numeric arguments are purely symbolic, not really numbers. Their meanings are

2 do not hyphenate on the last line before a page break
4 do not divide off the last two characters of a word
8 do not divide off the first two characters of a word

Values may be added arithmetically. For example, 12 denotes 4 and 8: not less than three characters are to be divided off.

Some words should never be divided and some should only be divided at places which nroff does not guess correctly. Such cases can be handled by using the hyphenation indicator character `\%`. It may be included somewhere in a word, as in `pres\%ent`, to show where hyphenation is permitted. Prefixing a word with this character, as in `\%fashion`, means that the word must not be divided at all.

Margin Characters

When text is revised and corrected, as often happens with software manuals or with successive revised drafts of manuscripts, simply handing readers a copy of the new version is not good enough. More often than not, the key question "what is new?" must be answered at the outset. **nroff** provides a mechanism for identifying alterations by printing a margin character at the right edges of output lines. Printing of the margin character begins when the .mc request appears, showing which character is to be used. It ends when the .mc request reappears without a character specified, effectively saying "from here on use nothing as the margin character." The writer is of course obliged to insert these requests; they will not appear automatically. For example, the asterisk * is used as the marker character in

```
In essence, nroff may be regarded
as a processor for a batch programming
.mc *
language, in which formatting requests operate on data
(the unformatted text itself) in
a prescribed fashion. Every formatting request
.mc
in this language begins at the left-hand margin,
preceded by a . (dot) to identify it as a command.
```

Here three lines have been rewritten; the revision is identified by first requesting an asterisk as the margin character, then switching it off again. The output then contains asterisks next to every line that contains any part of any marked line after filling is done:

```
     In   essence,   nroff   may   be   regarded   as   a
processor  for  a  batch  programming  language,  in    *
which  formatting  requests  operate  on  data  (the    *
unformatted  text  itself)  in  a  prescribed  fashion.  *
Every  formatting  request  in  this  language  begins
at  the  left-hand  margin,  preceded  by  a  .  (dot)  to
identify it as a command.
```

In principle, the writer is entirely responsible for turning marginal markings on and off. However, the standard Unix program **diff** compares two files and creates an editor script able to create one out of the other. It is not hard to write a shell script to insert .mc requests into such an editor script, thereby automating the process of comparing two files and marking changes. Where continuous and extensive revision of documents is frequent, creating appropriate shell scripts is well worth the trouble. In fact, a shell script to place .mc requests is available in some Unix systems as part of the standard release package.

Using **nroff** to Advantage

Although many simple documents can be prepared effectively using no more than a dozen or two built-in **nroff** requests, the preparation of more ambitious texts can benefit greatly from the use of various programming facilities provided by **nroff**. The most important of these are macros, traps, and registers, devices that permit users to write text processing programs in which the **nroff** requests themselves play the part of a programming language. In effect, every user and every project can acquire a specialized text processor suited to its own purposes.

Defining and Using Macros

The true power of **nroff** lies in the fact that the user is allowed to define new requests (macrorequests, or *macros*) in terms of requests already known to the system. Experienced **nroff** users in fact employ only a few of the system requests directly and do almost everything with macros. The Unix system itself provides several libraries of predefined macros, so users often blend system-provided macros with their own. To define a new macrorequest, it is only necessary to write out its definition as a string of known requests (which may of course include known macros), then to identify it as a macro definition by the `.de` ("define") request in front and `..` ("end of definition") behind. When **nroff** is called on to execute the new request, it simply copies the definition and executes it step by step.

To give a simple example, paragraph breaks can be inserted by defining the `.PA` request to mean exactly what the user desires: a blank line and an indentation of five spaces. The macro definition is entered as

```
.de PA
.sp
.ti 5
..
```

To cause paragraph breaks, `.PA` as newly defined is used instead of any other requests. **nroff** will actually substitute and execute the pair of requests which form its definition, so one request entered by the user is able to do the job of two. The real point, however, is not merely to save a little typing; it arises when the user decides that more white space between paragraphs and a deeper indentation would produce a better looking document. There is no need to alter the text at all; instead, the above macro definition is replaced by

```
.de PA
.sp
.ti 8
..
```

and a job is done which would probably never have been attempted otherwise!

Macros may include instructions, as in the example above, text lines, and arguments. Arguments may be almost any character strings, numeric or alphabetic. They are included in the macro definition as symbols of the form `\\$1`, `\\$2`, . . . up to `\\$9`; when the macro definition is copied, these place holders are replaced by actual values. For example, the paragraph break request above could be set up as

```
.de PA
.sp \\$1
.ti \\$2
..
```

and then invoked by the request

```
.PA 2 8
```

A double blank line and an eight-space indentation will result, just as if the actual values had been written into the macro definition.

Arguments passed to macros can be alphabetic strings. For example, the macro

```
.de DW
.bp
.sp 4
.ce
Appointments for \\$1
.sp 2
.ti 5
..
```

might be suitable for creating a personal appointment calendar. It may be used to begin a new week, for example, by

```
.DW "Monday"
```

The result will be to start a new page with the centered title

```
Appointments for Monday
```

with some blank space above and below. Other days of the week are then given the same treatment. Whatever text may follow is indented in good paragraph form.

Traps, Headers, and Page Numbers

Traps may be planted in any **nroff** input file by the .wh (''when'') request. This request has the general form .wh *N mc*. It causes the macro *mc* to be invoked whenever the line counter (on the current page) reaches *N*, that is, after the *N*th line of every page of output. If *N* is zero or positive, lines are counted from the top of the page, if *N* is negative, lines are counted from the bottom.

Traps are commonly used to create page headers and page footers. To begin printing six line widths (usually one inch) below the top edge of the paper and to stop printing six line widths above the bottom edge, traps are set at those places:

```
.wh 0 HD
.wh -7 FT"
```

These invoke the macro `.HD` at the very start of the page and the macro `.FT` when exactly six lines remain (the trap is placed *after* the seventh last line). The macros themselves can be very simple, amounting to no more than insertion of blank lines and beginning a new page:

```
.de HD
'sp 6
..
.de FT
'bp
..
```

The `'sp` and `'bp` requests are prefixed with an apostrophe rather than a dot, to suppress the line break that would otherwise result.

Complicated header and footer macros are often used in manuscripts to insert running titles or to reverse page numbering formats for even and odd numbered pages. For such purposes, the `.tl` ("title") request is very convenient. Inclusion of

```
.tl 'Leftstuff'middlestuff'Rightstuff'
```

in the input file will cause the string `Leftstuff` to be set flush to the left margin, `Rightstuff` to be placed flush to the right margin, and `mid-dlestuff` to be centered between them:

```
Leftstuff                    middlestuff                    Rightstuff
```

This command must fit on one line, thereby all but guaranteeing that the line length is sufficient to house the whole lot!

Page numbering can be effected with the `.tl` request, which has a peculiar property: whenever the % sign appears in any of the alphabetic strings in the `.tl` request, it is replaced by the current page number. Hence, the header macro

```
.de HD
'sp 3
```

```
'tl 'Draft Manuscript''Page %'
'sp 2
..
```

will left-adjust the words Draft Manuscript and right-adjust the page number. Right-adjustment will shift the word Page leftward so that Page 3 and Page 103 will not have the character P in the same location, but the character 3 will occupy corresponding places on the two pages.

Traps are usually set at the beginning of a file and left on. However, it may be desirable to alter them if the printout format is changed in midfile. Trap removal and resetting are achieved with the .wh request. To be precise, .wh *N mc* does not *invoke* the macro *mc* at line *N*; it *alters the name of the macro to be invoked* at line *N* to *mc*. Hence, issuing the instruction .wh *N* (with no macro name given) resets the name from *mc* to blank, causing no action to be taken at place *N*.

Strings and Number Registers

Page headers and footers often include not only page numbers but running heads or titles. Typically, a page header in a book will have a two-part title, with the title of the book itself on the left and the chapter name on the right; alternatively, the chapter name and current section title may appear. A header of the latter type might be produced by the macro

```
.de HD
'sp 3
'tl 'Languages and Compilers''The C Language'
'sp 2
..
```

which is invoked at the head of every page. The difficulty with this approach is that the HD macro will need to be redefined at the beginning of every section because the section title changes. It works, but it is a bit too fussy.

The **nroff** command language includes a form of variable called the *string*, a sequence of characters with a name. The name is usually two characters long (a one-character version with slightly different rules also exists) and should not duplicate the name of any request or macro. A string name is assigned a value by the .ds (“define string”) request,

```
.ds SC "The C Language"
```

No separate declaration is required to create the string name SC; assigning it a value also defines it to exist. A string value may be inserted anywhere in an **nroff** request or macro by mentioning its name, prefixed with the strange character sequence *(. The page header shown above may be made somewhat more flexible by leaving the section title variable:

```
.de HD
'sp 3
'tl 'Languages and Compilers''\\*(SC'
'sp 2
..
```

It may seem that the victory gained is at best pyrrhic, for now the string SC must be redefined at the start of every section instead of the three-part title. Furthermore, nothing in this arrangement guarantees that the string SC will be identical to the section title, as it should be. Both problems are cured at one stroke if section titles are inserted by a title macro:

```
.de ST
.sp 2
.ds SC \\$1
.tl '\\*(SC'''
.sp
..
```

The single macro request

```
.ST
```

now prints the section title and redefines the running head at the same time.

Numeric variables can be handled within **nroff** in a way similar to strings. They are called *number registers* and are also referred to by name. Number register names are subject to much the same rules as string names and macro names. A number register is set up and assigned a value just as a string would be; for example,

```
.nr SN 0
```

assigns the value 0 to number register SN. Because number registers are frequently used in **nroff** as counters, autoincrementation and autodecrementation are provided, and the standard increment is part of the value assignment. Thus,

```
.nr SN 0 1
```

assigns the current value 0 and the increment size 1. When the character string \\n(SC is encountered by **nroff**, the current value contained in SC is inserted in the text; but when \\n+(SC or \\n-(SC occur, the value of SC is incremented or decremented first and the new value is inserted in text.

Using number registers as counters is convenient for numbering sections, equations, figures, tables, indeed anything and everything that needs to be numbered. For example, to number the sections of a manuscript, a number register SN is set up at the start, with an initial value 0 and an increment of 1, as shown above. Printing of the section title is then preceded by incrementing and printing the section number:

```
.de ST
.sp 2
.ds SC \\$1
.tl '\\n+(SN.   \\*(SC'''
.sp
..
```

A major advantage of using number register values is that sections are automatically renumbered if a section is deleted or another added—all without human intervention!

Diversions

Diversions are temporary but invisible data files into which text may be written for retrieval and later reuse. A common use of diversions is for making footnotes. The footnote text is typed into the input file adjacent to the point where the footnote is referenced; but instead of being printed, the footnote text is sent to a diversion. When the main text approaches the bottom of the page, the diverted text is fetched and incorporated at its rightful place.

Diversions look to the **nroff** user much like macros. They have two-character names like macros and are incorporated into the text like macros. To divert text into diversion CT the .di request is used twice, once to begin the diversion and then again to end it:

```
.di CT
     ... text ...
.di
```

Recovering the text afterward is similar to incorporating a macro in the **nroff** file:

```
.CT
```

The diversion may of course include any alphanumeric text at all—even **nroff** requests or macros.

An alternative request is .da, which is similar to .di but *appends* to the text already in ST instead of replacing the content of ST as .di would do. In this way, text can be gathered from many places into a single diversion. One example of such gathering is making up tables of contents. In principle, the table of contents of a book is a collection of the chapter, section, and subsection titles as they appear in the main text, with page numbers appended. The easiest way to compile it is therefore to make copies of the titles as the text is formatted, noting the page numbers. This task can be entrusted to the .ST macro with a little extra added:

```
.de ST
.sp 2
.ds SC \\$1
.tl '\\n+(SN.   \\*(SC'''
.sp
.da CT
.tl '\\n(SN.   \\*(SC''%'
.da
..
```

The final three lines, just before the macro terminator, append to diversion CT. One line is sent to the diversion, comprising the section number (numeric register SN), the section name (string SC), and the page number (%). When **nroff** finishes reading the input text, CT contains the complete table of contents; it remains only to fetch it and perhaps to tidy it up a bit.

Standard Macro Libraries

For users with more or less routine document preparation requirements, there exist libraries of prewritten **nroff** macros, so even novice users can gain access to much of the power of **nroff** without needing to write any macros of their own. Two are currently distributed: *-ms* and *-mm*.

The *-ms* macro library is the older of the two libraries. It was particularly designed for scientific manuscripts, technical reports, and similar literature. It provides a set of macros for commonly encountered constructions, such as

.FS to .FE	footnote start and end
.KS to .KE	keep blocks of text together
.LP	unindented (left flush) paragraphs
.NH	numbered headings
.PP	indented paragraphs
.SH	simple (unnumbered) headings
.TL	titling

and many others. Multicolumn formatting, as often used for technical papers, is available, with the column arrangement automatically set up.

The newer *-mm* (“memorandum macros”) package is larger, more heavily parametrized, and more flexible. For the same reason, it can also be a little more difficult to use than *-ms*. The choice is often limited by the habit of system suppliers to include one or the other, but not both, with the Unix system.

Other Text Formatting Programs

In addition to **ed** and **nroff**, which are fundamental tools for almost every user, Unix provides three other programs: **troff**, **eqn**, and **tbl**. All three are text formatting tools in the same generic family as **nroff**. They are intended for driving a phototypesetting machine and can produce output of excellent quality. In fact, the popularity of Unix in its early years was based largely on the ease with which large numbers of sophisticated technical reports, scientific papers, and even books could be produced by engineers, scientists, and secretaries, working to tight schedules without any of the usual tools of the printing trade.

The **troff** Text Formatter

The **troff** formatter is in principle similar to **nroff**, but there are striking changes in hardware performance. The phototypesetter (unlike a standard terminal) is capable of producing several different fonts, so that boldface, italic, and varying sizes of type can be intermixed with the font selected as standard. User selectable parameters include not only the font to be used, but also the character size and line spacing, plus of course the overall page format: line length, default indentation, tabs, page size, page numbering, etc. The phototypesetter is in principle capable of drawing almost anything; it is able to move both horizontally and vertically, creating inked area as it goes. Hence, the selection of fonts is limited less by the hardware than the cleverness of the embedded software. Character and line sizes are variable, so there is no longer much sense in instructions like “page length 51 lines”; it is more sensible and useful to say “page length 8.5 inches”.

Font changes can occur anywhere in a text, and although they could be handled by standard **nroff**-like request lines beginning with a dot at the left margin, setting single words in italic or boldface by this method becomes messy. Various **troff** functions are therefore introduced by an *escape character*, which is usually the reverse slant \ but which may be altered by the user. For example, the character sequence `\fB` changes to a boldface font when encountered anywhere in the text.

Command lines used in **troff** are similar in structure to those employed by **nroff**, but a much wider range of possibilities exists. In fact, the **troff** and **nroff** requests are deliberately created so that the **nroff** command interpreter can understand **troff** requests and can make substitutions within the limited capabilities of its printing device. It is thus correct to say that **troff** files can be processed by **nroff**; but hardware functions not locally available obviously cannot be used. Since the **nroff** and **troff** command sets are both programming languages, any **troff** script must be debugged and corrected before it can be finally printed. Debugging cannot be undertaken with much hope of success if the hardware functions are not available. Users without phototypesetting equipment, and with little hope of obtaining access to any, are probably well advised to stick with **nroff**!

Equation Processing with **eqn** and **neqn**

Much scientific text involves mathematical equations or chemical formulae, whose typesetting requires special symbols and mixed fonts as well as critical placement in both the horizontal and vertical directions. In principle, all the necessary phototypesetter motions and font selection can be handled by **troff**. In practice, the detailed work required to make **troff** do so is finicky, error-prone, and unattractively time-consuming. To lighten this load, Unix contains **eqn**, a utility capable of writing **troff** request sequences for equations. To allow dealing with simple equations and to enable users to proofread **troff** text quickly, there is also **neqn**; it produces output suitable for **nroff**.

Mathematical usage includes a great deal of convention and standardization. Scalar variables are set in light face italic, vectors in bold roman; names of trigonometric functions appear in lightface roman, their arguments in italic. Superscripts and subscripts are reduced in size by a conventional amount and offset by a standard height difference. The **eqn** package knows a good deal about these conventions but almost nothing about mathematics. It accepts input instructions in an essentially verbal language which describes equations and transcribes these verbal instructions into **troff** requests for font changes, vertical or horizontal motions, and special symbols (e.g., integral signs). Its input will typically contain text like

```
2 pi sum from k=0 to 20 A sub k cos (k omega t + psi sub k)
```

to denote a 20-term Fourier series. **eqn** will recognize "pi", "omega", and "psi" as Greek letters and "sum" as a summation sign. It will automatically reduce the size of the subscripts identified by "sub" and will choose italic or roman fonts for the remaining characters as appropriate. On the other hand, it knows next to nothing about mathematics, just as **troff** knows next to nothing about English. It will happily typeset rank garbage that hardly even resembles mathematics.

The **eqn** package works as a preprocessor to **troff**. To use **eqn**, the mathematical portions of text are marked off with special delimiters (.EQ and .EN for starting and ending equations), thereby indicating that translation is required. All unmarked text, which normally includes standard **troff** requests and text, passes through to the output unaltered. Thus, the output of **eqn** is actually the **troff** text that could have been produced, albeit laboriously and with errors, by a human programmer. However, this intermediate text is hardly ever seen by a human eye, for under Unix it is easiest to pipe the **eqn** output directly to **troff**:

```
$ eqn textfile | troff
```

The output then appears as if **eqn** and **troff** constituted a single program.

Since **troff** requests are fully acceptable to **nroff**, it is in principle possible to use **eqn** or **neqn** to set up equations for **nroff** as well. However, the results are rarely attractive; mathematical typesetting does benefit greatly from the availability of Greek characters and multiple fonts.

Table Manipulation with **tbl**

Tabular matter is often difficult to set up quickly with normal editing programs. For one thing, columns in tables are justified in many different ways, as may be seen in the following simple example:

```
        Average Annual Increase Rates

       Industry        Class   Increase

       Electronics       B        1.25
       Construction     AA       12.7
       Aircraft          K      103.
```

Here one column is left-justified, one right-justified, and one justified to keep the decimal points in line. Many other variations are encountered: inclusion of special symbols, ruling of boxes around tables, and so on.

The **tbl** program is another **troff** preprocessor which allows tables to be set up using specialized commands. These commands, along with the tabular data, are encased in delimiters that identify material to be processed by **tbl**: .TS to start the table and .TE to end it.When **tbl** is run, all material marked as tables is processed into a string of **troff** requests; the rest is passed through unmodified. As in the case of **eqn**, the result is the same as if a human operator had produced the same request string.

The principles involved in using **tbl** are delightfully simple; complexities only arise when large, complicated tables need to be dealt with. In spirit, processing of tables is viewed as being much like processing of straight text: form is separated from content so that formatting instructions can be issued without reference to the tabular data. Every table to be processed by **tbl** takes the general form

> .TS
> *global options;*
> *format image* .
> data
> .TE

The global options take up one input line; they specify such matters as whether the table is to be centered on the page and whether a box is to be ruled around it. This line is always terminated by a semicolon. The format image is an abstract representation of the table, one line of the image corresponding to one (or more) lines of the table. It shows the type of entries to be placed in each column and how they are to be formatted. The example above is generated by the following input file:

```
.TS
center;
c s s
c s s
l c r
c s s
l c n .
Average Annual Increase Rates

Industry        Class   Increase

Electronics     B       1.25
Construction    AA      12.7
Aircraft        K       103.
.TE
```

The format image contains fewer lines than the table; this situation is common, for the rule is that the last line of the image is used again and again until all data are exhausted. This last line, in other words, describes the body of the table. It contains three letters to show that the table has three columns; `l`, `c`, and `n` denote left-adjusted alphabetic entries, centered alphabetic entries, and numeric (aligned decimal point) entries. The heading lines which precede the tabulated data are similar; the three column headings are identified by `l`, `c`, and `r` to request left alignment, centering, and right alignment. The main column header is centered; the character `s` in the second and third columns says that the first column is allowed to swallow the space that might otherwise have been allocated to the others. The last line of the format image is terminated by `.` (dot).

The data to be entered into a table are simply typed row by row, with tab characters as column spacers. When the raw **tbl** input file is viewed on a terminal or printer, data thus usually appear in left-aligned columns whose precise placement depends on how the tab stops on the terminal are set.

The **eqn** and **tbl** preprocessors may of course be combined by a pipeline,

```
$ eqn inputfile | tbl | troff > outputfile
```

Invoking the preprocessors costs little, since any text not flagged for preprocessing is simply passed through unmodified. **tbl** can be used with **nroff** as easily as with **troff**, provided the limitations of **nroff** are respected: there must be no changes of type size, style, or other attributes that a plain printing terminal cannot manage.

Spelling and Typographic Errors

Despite the best intentions, spelling errors and typographic errors will creep in when text is prepared. Unix provides a certain measure of error-proofing by allowing text to be checked against a built-in spelling dictionary. The spelling check may of course also turn up typographic errors.

The Dictionary Check

The basic facility in Unix for checking spelling is a program called **spell**. **spell** is invariably used with a spelling dictionary. It reads the text file to be checked and identifies as words all character strings encased by suitable combinations of terminator characters—blanks, line ends, and punctuation marks. Each word is then checked against entries in a spelling dictionary. In most Unix implementations, the dictionary resides in file `/usr/dict/words`, but in some installations it may be located elsewhere. **spell** produces as output a list of words not found in the dictionary, which therefore qualify as potential spelling errors.

Spelling checking is a fascinating problem in both lexicography and computer science. To spot misspellings, it is helpful to know what to expect, so that a detailed analysis of each word is indicated. People automatically recognize the word *recreation* as being composed of the prefix *re-*, the stem *creat-*, and the suffix *-tion*, the composition being subject to rules which drop one of the two *t*'s that would arise from agglutinating *re-creat-tion*. People, as a rule, will therefore spot recreattion as being misspelled even if the word is not a familiar one. For a computer program to do as well is not at all easy. The rules are complicated, the stems many and confusing.

The **spell** program can be run in two ways: it may be asked to accept only words found in the dictionary in their exact forms, or it may consider correct all words formed from dictionary words by applying a limited set of word transformation rules. When asked to check for literal accuracy, without applying any transformation rules, many words may be flagged as possibly erroneous, because *project*, *projective*, and *projectively* will be considered unrelated; each will be accepted only if it appears in the dictionary in precisely that form. Under the word transformation rules, possessive endings, various prefixes such as *re-*, *in-*, and a variety of suffixes (*-tion*, *-ing*) are all sorted out nicely. In a few cases they may be spotted incorrectly, for the English language is simply not so consistent as to permit encoding all valid transformation rules in a program of reasonable size. Nevertheless, it is surprising and pleasing how few real mistakes **spell** actually does make when operated this way.

Running **spell**

As one might well expect, the **spell** program is operated just like any other Unix command: it uses the standard input unless file names are provided, and it delivers the results to the standard output unless redirected. Typically,

```
$ spell -b +unixdict manuscript > errors
```

will cause the file `manuscript` to be scanned for unrecognized words, choosing British spellings in preference to American ones (about which more below) and accepting the words listed in the user-supplied file `unixdict` in addition to those found in the standard dictionary. The output is directed to file `errors`.

Several options are available under **spell**. Of these, **-v** and **-b** deserve special mention. The **-v** option flags all words not found in the dictionary in exactly the same form as they occur in the text file; no derivations (possessives, adverbial endings, plurals, etc.) are accepted. However, all plausible derivations that can be constructed from the words in the dictionary are shown. The **-x** option views the world in a complementary light and shows every stem from which a word could plausibly have been derived. To give an example, the output produced by the **-v** option of **spell** takes the following form:

```
+s          additions
+s          adds
+ing        applying
+s          besides
```

```
+ed        collected
+ion+s     constructions
-y+ies     copies
+d         created
-e+ion     derivation
-e+ion+s   derivations
+s         does
+s         errors
```

Brief study will show that every derived word in this list was arrived at by a different route. Most have added suffixes, but several have dropped letters as well, for example, *derivations* which is obtained from the root *derive* listed in the dictionary.

Because the **-v** and **-x** options go into considerable detail in analyzing the makeup of individual words, they will at times signal invalid derivations or derivations that might be valid but could be arrived at in several ways. In the report shown above, the word *does* is shown—but the derivation shown does not identify it as the third person form of a common auxiliary verb. In spite of what one might have expected, **spell** views this word as a noun, meaning a herd of female deer. Hard indeed is the lot of the English lexicographer!

Comfortingly, **spell** provides a "British" switch (the **-b** option) to make room for people who do not fancy American spellings. British and American spellings differ a good deal. There are distinct forms for many words as well as for several common suffixes. **spell** provides the option of examining for either form of spelling, but it does so by providing alternate valid dictionary entries. As a result, **spell** can proofread text that conforms to either one standard or the other, but not to mixtures. Some inconvenience may well be felt by Canadians or Australians, who frequently choose American spellings for some words, British for others. Under the rules as understood by **spell**, anyone who favors *colour* and *odour* is not permitted the *z* in *recognize*—not even if used with absolute consistency—and is required to spell *tyre* with a *y*.

Mixed tastes in spelling can be accommodated, more or less, by two techniques, neither wholly satisfactory. One way, useful to people who generally stick by one convention but wander off to use the other for some words, is to collect a file of personal deviations and to include them as a + option (as illustrated above). The other, handy where the mixing is extensive, is to run with the command

```
$ spell textfile | spell -b | errorfile
```

In this way any acceptable spelling is guaranteed to pass muster. Unfortunately, there is no consistency check so that mixing British and American spellings for the same word in a single document will not be spotted.

Typographic Errors

The easiest way of finding typographic errors in text is to employ **spell**; words such as *ditcionary* and *dicctionary* will be flagged as suspect and can then be picked out. If there are only a few distinct typographic errors, they can be corrected easily enough with the **vi** editor. If there are a great many, one of the fancier batch-mode editors can be used instead.

One variety of typographic error spotting program simply scans words and reports as suspect any character string which does not satisfy certain rules (e.g., three consonants in a row are suspect). Such checkers are fast, but often unreliable. None is provided with most standard Unix releases.

It should be kept in mind that any existing program designed to find misspellings or mistypings can only look for errors in individual words; it will not perform textual analysis. Hence, typographic errors can never be spotted if they produce semantic nonsense out of lexically acceptable words; for example, *test* in place of *text* will pass all spelling checks. Similarly, errors in homonyms (similar-sounding but differently spelled words), such as *waist* and *waste*, cannot be located by spelling checkers.

style and **diction**

Two programs are provided under most Unix releases for assisting the writer with style improvement. Both attempt to provide the sort of critique expected of a tutor in Freshman English: they say "too many compound sentences made up with semicolon splices" or "say *now*, not *at this point in time*". The human tutor can be unfair but understanding, having apprehended the objective in view. Being mere computer programs, **style** and **diction** are totally unforgiving but impartial; they report what they regard as facts and leave the user to judge whether the facts are useful.

The **style** program analyzes the grammatical structure of a document and produces several statistical indicators to show how the text might be improved, or indeed whether improvement is needed. The analysis is purely formal; **style** makes no pretense to understand the content. **diction** attempts to criticize content, or at least its wording, by looking for phrases it considers inelegant or downright bad.

Readability Grades

A fundamental form of output always produced by **style**, almost independently of the options the user may specify, is a listing of readability grades. These stem from the world of public education and therefore report their findings in terms of grades—meaning that text with a grade level of 8 is within the ability of Grade 8 pupils to comprehend. Because the analysis **style** makes is purely structural, such indices are likewise; **style** will happily assign readability grades to well-formed sentences made up of pure nonsense words or to sentences in foreign languages.

Four different indices are computed, corresponding to four different authoritative studies on readability. In all four, the readability grade is a function of both sentence length and word length. The formulae used differ a little: two count characters to determine word length, while the other two attempt to count syllables. None takes account of the things most readers of technical text really find difficult: complicated technical terms, symbols and abbreviations that readers were expected to remember from three chapters ago, a presupposition of familiarity with the residue calculus (or with recent writings on comparative paraliterature, as the case may be). The gradings are therefore guides of a sort but should not be taken too seriously.

Invoking and using **style** is much like using any other Unix utility. **style** is given a set of options and an input file name or names to work on, the output being placed in the standard output. **style** can be downright garrulous under some options, so the output is usually best channeled to a file. For the introductory chapter of this book, stored in file `intro`,

```
$ style intro | tee intro.styl | more
```

produces the output shown in Figure 8.1.

Readability grades around 14 imply that college students should on the whole have no difficulty with this text. However, in the real world there is a lot more to readability than just word length, so **style** obviously reports a great many other things as well. These will be discussed next.

Sentence Analysis

Surprising as it may seem, useful grammatical analysis of plain English really can be carried out by computer programs of tolerable complexity. **style** proceeds by first identifying sentences, then parsing each one in turn. The parse is carried out partly by referring to a vocabulary of common words, partly on a structural basis. The findings are reported in a statistical summary as shown above.

Basic statistics include the total numbers of words and sentences in the document analyzed and the lengths of sentences. The report includes average, maximum, and minimum sentence lengths, also the number of very short and unusually long sentences. Sentences more than ten words above average are judged to be unusual, as are any that fall short of the average by five or more.

```
readability grades:
   (Kincaid) 14.3        (auto) 14.6
   (Coleman-Liau) 13.0  (Flesch) 15.2 (35.4)
sentence info:
   no. sent 179 no. wds 4274
   av sent leng 23.9 av word leng 5.11
   no. questions 3 no. imperatives 0
   no. nonfunc wds 2627  61.5%   av leng  6.47
   short sent (<19) 30% (54) long sent (>34) 12% (22)
   longest sent 57 wds at sent 24
   shortest sent 5 wds at sent 79
sentence types:
   simple  37% (67) complex  36% (65)
   compound  15% (26) compound-complex  12% (21)
word usage:
   verb types as % of total verbs
   tobe  38% (159) aux  14% (56) inf  20% (84)
   passives as % of non-inf verbs  24% (80)
   types as % of total
   prep 11.6% (494) conj 3.8% (161) adv 6.9% (294)
   noun 25.7% (1100) adj 20.6% (880) pron 4.4% (187)
   nominalizations   2 % (75)
sentence beginnings:
   subject opener: noun (29) pron (23) pos (3)
                   adj (34) art (31) tot  67%
   prep  13% (23) adv   7% (13)
   verb   2% (4)  sub_conj   4% (8) conj   2% (3)
   expletives   4% (8)
```

FIGURE 8.1. Output of **style** for analysis of the introductory chapter of this book.

Word lengths are not subjected to the same searching scrutiny as sentences; presumably the author can spot a long word as easily as a program! A more significant issue is that English, a practically uninflected language, includes in any real sentence a large number of "little" words: articles, particles, conjunctions, prepositions. Such important small items are referred to as *function words* in the report generated by **style**. Their number is often larger than one might imagine; in the report of Fig. 8.1, they account for almost 40% of the words in the chapter. Accuracy in assessing text is improved by reporting word length statistics two ways: first for all except the function words, then for all words in the text. The difference is significant; in the chapter shown here, the "little" words average 2.86 characters in length while the others have a mean length of 6.47. Of significance is the variation in the latter with writing style, for the function words are the same in practically all writing: *the*, *for*, *in*, *to*, and so on.

Sentence structure is also analyzed by **style**, with all sentences classified into *simple*, *compound* (containing two principal clauses), *complex* (one principal and one dependent clause), and *compound-complex*. No easy recipe can be given for sentence structure, except that most people seem to think it should be varied. Charles Dickens and Tom Wolfe are interesting to read at least partly because they vary their sentences from short and simple to multiply compound-complex. Thomas Hardy, on the other hand, is generally considered difficult to read because his sentences are both long and intricate.

What can be said for variety in sentence structure can be said equally well for ways of starting sentences: variety is the spice of life. **style** therefore reports in some detail what parts of speech were used to begin sentences, from nouns to subordinating conjunctions.

Word Usage

What words are used (and how) has an obvious effect on writing style, so **style** classifies the parts of speech and reports on word use. Verbs in particular are given searching analysis. They are classified by their use as auxiliaries or otherwise, and they are scrutinized to distinguish active from passive voice. There is a part of the English-teaching community which believes the passive voice should be avoided at almost any cost because it is terribly difficult to understand; but the scientific community generally prefers the passive because it reflects a long tradition of dealing with impersonal fact rather than personal experience or opinion.

While statistical information on word usage may be of some value, a much more interesting use of style results from the `-P` option of **style**. Under this option, the detailed analysis of each sentence is shown in an output file generally much longer than the input file. For example, the sentence

```
The Unix time-sharing system is rapidly becoming one of the
most popular computer operating systems ever designed.
```

is mapped into the output file as

```
art     The
adj     Unix
adj     time-sharing
noun    system
be      is
adv     rapidly
verb    becoming
pron    one
prep    of
art     the
adj     most
adj     popular
adj     computer
adj     operating
noun    systems
adv     ever
adj     designed
```

The analysis uses both lexical and structural data: *most*, *computer*, and *operating* are all spotted as adjectives, even though *computer* may look like a noun, *operating* like a verb.

Admittedly, there is no point in reading reams of output merely to discover that *rapidly* is an adverb. A useful purpose is served, on the other hand, by asking **style** to report in great detail wherever a sentence is convoluted, full of difficult words and ideas, hard to read and hard to grasp. If **style** is confused by a welter of present participles masquerading as adjectives, is it not likely that some readers will be too?

Phrasing and Style

The **diction** program actually does what **style** promises: it gives hints for improving the aesthetics and stylistics of prose. Unfortunately, **diction** is a critic, not a teacher—it only looks for things it does not like. In use, **diction** acts and feels different from **style** in every possible way. One program, after all, deals with statistical facts, something computers are really quite good at, but the other can do no more than carp at things it believes are bad. It is a useful program, *faute de mieux*; one just wishes it were better.

When invoked, **diction** strips the text of its capitals and most of its punctuation, then seeks out words and phrases it thinks bad. The output of **diction** consists of all the sentences that contain one or more of the offending phrases, with the offenders shown in brackets:

```
 introduction the unix time sharing system is rapidly
becoming[ one of the ] most popular computer operating
systems ever designed.
```

To obtain clarification about the phrases marked, including suggestions for improvement or more appropriate synonyms, the **explain** program may be run. **explain** asks the user to type in the phrase to be explained and suggests alternatives if it knows any. Thus,

```
$ explain
phrase?
one of the
use "one, a" for "one of the"
phrase?
```

This example illustrates both the strengths and weaknesses of **diction**. No doubt *one of the* is an overused phrase and probably deserves flagging. Two alternatives are suggested by **explain**; clearly neither is appropriate, though it would admittedly be unreasonable to expect a computer program to know that. In this way, **diction** incorrectly picks out large numbers of non-errors. Not only do these unwarranted criticisms irritate the user, they lead him to ignore the real ones, as in the story of the little boy who cried "Wolf!"

The **diction–explain** pair was developed at the University of California at Berkeley and shows it in its choice of blacklisted phrases. The list includes many illiteracies and sophomorisms:

absolutely complete
added increments
adequate enough
and etc
another additional
as regards
at about
at this point in time
in back of
basic fundamentals
basically
brief in duration
collaborate together

Unfortunately, the overuse of perfectly good words by undergraduates apparently led to the inclusion of words which not only deserve to be used but make for vigorous or precise writing:

actual
accomplished
aggregate
assistance
awful
commence
compensation
conjecture
construct
contemplate
demean
demonstrate
discontinue

Blacklisting of these words may help some less literate members of the community, but it is a misery for others.

Practical Use of **style** and **diction**

Allowed to run unchecked, both **style** and **diction** like to generate piles of unwanted trash. The key to effective use of either is selectivity; ways must be found to make the programs filter out useless output before it even arrives in a file or on a terminal screen. While no single method is wholly agreeable to everybody, a few general hints may be broadly useful.

The **style** program can be made selective by requesting output of only those sentences which meet some specified criterion. Readability index and sentence length are available as criteria, so it is possible to have a look at very long or very complicated sentences only, ignoring the rest. Less usefully, sentences containing the passive voice or beginning with an expletive can be selected. Curiously, it is only possible to ask for the difficult sentences of a file; no provision is made in **style** for the easy ones. Thus, **style** lends itself to revision tending to reduce the readability grade of a document, but there is no easy way to make a boringly straightforward text more interesting to a sophisticated audience.

To make **diction** genuinely useful is harder but rewarding. **diction** looks for phrases listed in its blacklist file, usually `/usr/lib/dict.d`, and **explain** searches through `/usr/lib/explain.d` for suggestions to make. If these files are absent, then `dict.d` and `explain.d` are presumably elsewhere and can be tracked down with

```
$ find / -name dict.d -print
```

Modification of these files is not strictly necessary to make **diction** behave better; the user can substitute a pair of files for those provided in the system release. However, it is no use throwing out all the 500 or more phrases in `/usr/lib/dict.d` just because there are some silly ones. It is better to copy the system-provided file, then to use an edited version. The same goes for `/usr/lib/explain.d`.

Editing the **diction** files is easy enough since they are text files and contain one phrase per line. The only sticky point is that the phrases as listed must be exact matches for character strings in the text file after capitals and most punctuation marks have been stripped. Thus, words should be separated by exactly one space and the phrase should have one space preceding and following to ensure that partial words will not be spotted. For example, the file entries

```
 haggle
hood
 huge profits
~ brotherhood
```

will cause the phrases `[ haggle ]` and `[ huge profits ]` to be marked, along with all words ending in *-hood*: `mother[hood ]`, `man[ hood ]`. The latter is spotted when a suffix because it is not prefixed by a leading blank. The word *brotherhood* is not flagged, however, because the tilde ~ character beginning a line is understood to mean acceptance.

The file `/usr/lib/explain.d` is organized similarly, one line per explanation, with the bad phrase first, the preferred form following.

The Unix manuals hint that a 50% useful hit rate for **diction** should be regarded as good. With some clever customization, most users should be able to do better. However, it pays to walk slowly and carefully, not making changes in the phrase blacklist too quickly!

Chapter 9

Languages and Compilers

While some Unix users are only interested in running ready-made programs, others wish to make at least occasional use of the program development facilities available under this system. They find themselves well served; because the Unix operating system is widely used, compiler writers have found it worthwhile to produce language compilers to run under it. This chapter provides an overview of the programming languages generally available, giving details on the most important and popular.

Programming Languages Available

Though only a few languages are furnished with standard Unix system releases, support software is of high quality. The C language is almost always furnished with the system. A Fortran compiler is often included; Pascal appears a little less frequently. However, numerous other language compilers are available for almost all Unix-derived operating systems. Proprietary versions of Unix, particularly those destined for the newer computer hardware configurations, may offer such further languages as Lisp or Ada. The result is a rich haul indeed, comprising most of the programming languages commonly employed in scientific work as well as several others whose primary orientation is to commercial data processing.

Structured Languages

The key language of the Unix system, in which most of the system itself is written, is a language called C. The basic Unix software tool kit invariably includes a C compiler. A structured high-level language, C bears some resemblance to both Fortran and Pascal but retains closer ties to the computing machine than either. C occupies a special role in the Unix structure because some other high-level languages are processed at least part way by the C compiler. An important benefit of this arrangement is that subprograms or procedures originating in different high-level languages can often be intermixed.

Pascal is also supported under virtually all Unix systems; indeed several Unix-compatible Pascal compilers are now in existence. Unfortunately, Versions 6 and 7 of Unix as released by Western Electric did not include a Pascal compiler, so several "unofficial" Pascals appeared. However, the University of California, Berkeley 4.2 BSD version of Unix includes a Pascal compiler which has gained wide acceptance. It is available in many Unix installations and is therefore briefly described in this chapter.

The Ada language is not yet widely supported—as yet there are few full Ada compilers in existence anywhere—but it is sure to become widespread before long. Ada is a structured language and has been specified by the United States Department of Defense as its preferred high-level language.

Turning to non-numeric computing, the Lisp and Prolog languages have been linked to Unix for several years; so has Cobol, the most widespread standard commercial data processing language. Basic was initially supported under Unix, presumably as a result of outside pressure since its characteristics and spirit run counter to the general design philosophy of Unix. Interest in Basic has waned as the computer user community has come to recognize that Basic really is very basic.

Fortran

The best known and most widely used high-level language for scientific computing is undoubtedly Fortran. Despite its many acknowledged shortcomings, engineers and physicists habitually use almost nothing else. Fortran was intended for scientific computing from the outset; indeed, its name was coined as an acronym for *FOR*mula *TRAN*slator. It has been in use for almost a third of a century, so there now exists a large amount of acquired programming expertise in the scientific community and also an immense pool of Fortran software. For serious scientific computing, Fortran will probably remain the language of choice for many years to come. No operating system can be considered a serious candidate for large-scale computing if it does not support at least one version of Fortran, so despite their apparent distaste for this language, the Bell Laboratories

Unix software team did make Fortran available. A Fortran compiler may be missing, however, from repackaged versions of the Unix system primarily intended for business data processing.

Versions of Unix that include Fortran compilers normally also support a Fortran dialect called Ratfor (*rat*ional *For*tran), which permits structured forms similar to those of Pascal or C. There is no Ratfor compiler; instead, Ratfor is translated into ordinary Fortran by a preprocessor called **ratfor**. A reverse translator, for turning Fortran into Ratfor, also exists.

A Veritable Babel

Turning from the "official" languages distributed in the standard Unix package, and from Pascal which is so widespread that it is at least "semiofficial", the Unix system user is faced with a veritable Babel. The languages available under Unix in some form include almost everything imaginable.

Snobol, APL, and Algol 68 are three established high-level languages for which compilers are available under Unix. While none of them is furnished with the standard system releases, various Unix systems do support them and they are fairly widely used. Modula-2 compilers are less widespread but they do exist. Cobol appears to be running satisfactorily at various installations, while Lisp and Prolog are employed by many workers in artificial intelligence. Basic has been available since the early Version 6 and Version 7 releases, though one might well enquire why it should be when such a wide range of better languages exists.

There is one language always available under any operating system, which is absolutely not transportable—the native assembler language of the host machine. Very little use need—or should—be made of it in Unix systems because most user needs are covered by C. However, there do arise some occasions when use of machine instructions is essential and for those occasions an assembler is imperative. Of course, it is not practical to give details here of the assemblers for all, or even a significant number, of the many machines on which Unix now runs. Assembler language programming therefore rates no more than a brief mention in this chapter.

Fortran 77

The Fortran language is supported under most Unix systems in its most recent version, Fortran 77. Fortran was first introduced in the late 1950s and was brought into standard form ten years later, the nominal date of the standard being 1966. The need for another revision became obvious some time thereafter and led to the creation of Fortran 77, a new standard.

Almost all the old standard Fortran (Fortran 66) is included as a subset of the Unix dialect of Fortran 77, so Fortran 66 programs usually run without difficulty.

Because Fortran is well known, no attempt is made here to describe the language itself. People not acquainted with Fortran but interested in learning about it are well advised to begin by reading one of the many excellent introductory textbooks on this language.

The **f77** Fortran 77 Compiler

The normal Fortran language compiler available in most Unix systems is **f77**, which implements the Fortran 77 standard.

Unlike many compilers, **f77** does not translate Fortran directly to assembler code or machine language. Instead, it produces C intermediate code. This approach to compilation implies that many features of C, which are not considered part of Fortran under the standard rules, become acceptable automatically. For example, recursive subroutine calls are not permitted in standard Fortran, but they are accepted in **f77** Fortran. All Unix system calls and library subroutines which are available through C become available through Fortran also. Compiling Fortran into C intermediate code further implies that procedures written in the two languages may be intermixed: Fortran programs can use C functions as if they had been written in Fortran and C functions can call Fortran subroutines equally well. Indeed, the intermixing extends to any other language, past or future, whose compilation passes through C intermediate code.

In **f77** Fortran there are also some variations from the Fortran 77 standard not easy to explain in terms of C dependence. Few compiler writers have ever created Fortran compilers true to the published standard; the temptation to extend and improve is too strong to resist. **f77** is no exception: it does accept (almost) any correct Fortran 77 program but it also provides additional features not part of the Fortran 77 standard. Fortran 77 rules are violated by **f77** only in a few minor ways. The enhancements and added features are rather more numerous. Both the improvements and the exceptions will be treated in detail below.

Non-Unix Fortran Compilers

Many Unix-derived operating systems now available use the Unix kernel and shell as originated by Bell Laboratories but employ language processors produced by other software makers. Microcomputer implementations of Unix or Unix-like systems in particular tend to use nonstandard compilers.

Many of the Fortran compilers now running on personal computers under Unix began life on small machines intended for the now almost forgotten CP/M operating system, which was keyed to the 8080 and Z80 eight-bit processor chips. As CP/M approached obsolescence, several compiler makers modified their code to cater for newer processor chips; at the same time, others entered the marketplace with entirely new compilers. These were usually not oriented to Unix and therefore produced machine language code directly without passing through C intermediate code. There is nothing inherently wrong with such compilers; indeed, some are said to produce faster running code than **f77**. However, they are wholly independent and do not use the common facilities provided by the Unix system for all language compilers. The machine code they produce cannot be combined with machine code produced by the Unix C compiler, so mixing of subprograms originating from several different languages is only possible in roundabout ways, if at all.

Running Fortran Programs

The compilation, loading, and execution of a Fortran program under any operating system is a complicated affair involving a sequence of processes. Fortunately, there is no need for most Unix users to see the complexities, because the commands needed to run simple jobs are pipelined and appear to the user as a single command. To run a Fortran 77 program stored in file `fortprog`, it suffices to enter the command

```
$ f77 fortprog
```

When the shell prompt $ next appears, an executable object program called **a.out** will be found in the user's current directory. It contains the machine language code corresponding to `fortprog`. It can be moved to a more sensible name, if desired; in any case, it can be executed. A more sensible name, say `newfile`, can also be specified in the command itself, following the option flag **-o**; for example,

```
$ f77 -o newfile fortprog
```

The **f77** user may request various other options. Those most directly concerned with program debugging are probably **-onetrip**, **-u**, **-w**, and **-C**. The **-onetrip** option makes all *do* loops execute at least once, by arranging for the index to be checked at the end of the loop. The **-u** option causes all variables to be undefined at the start, thus forcing the programmer to declare every variable explicitly (as happens automatically in Algol or Pascal). Many subtle programming errors can be caught in this way. Warning messages are suppressed by the **-w** option. Very usefully in mathematical work, **-C** causes all array subscripts to be checked during program execution, to ensure that they do not exceed array bounds.

Like any good compiler, **f77** permits an enormous variety of options.

These are shared with the C compiler, the assembler, and the loader, through a unified structure of option names and letters. Details of this structure will be found below, in the section on compilation and linking.

Textual Extensions to Fortran 77

Numerous extensions to Fortran 77 are accepted by **f77**, but many of them affect only a small minority of users. Those likely to prove of general interest involve formatting of program text, extensions to data types, and some rule relaxations on input and output.

Program form in standard Fortran 77 continues the tradition of the 80-column punch card: Fortran text must be placed in columns 7 to 72. Statement numbers, if there are any, belong in column positions 1 to 5, and any character in column 6 means that the statement in the previous card is being continued on a second or subsequent card image. **f77** is much more tolerant than the Fortran 77 standard in such matters. Lines may be of any convenient length and may be typed anywhere in the available space. Continuation lines must contain an ampersand (the & character) in the leftmost character position, with Fortran text following anywhere thereafter. Statement numbers are separated from statement text by a tab character.

While the Fortran 77 standard recognizes only the 26 uppercase alphabetic characters, one should not be surprised to find that **f77** shares the general Unix addiction to lowercase. In an attempt to achieve compatibility with the standard, **f77** works in lowercase only and translates all characters from upper case to lower (except in character constants). It is possible, however, to suppress this translation; uppercase characters are then regarded as distinct from their lowercase brothers, so that `sum` and `Sum` become distinct variables. Fortran keywords are only recognized in lowercase form, so that when character translation is suppressed,

`subroutine x(a, b)` is considered normal,
`subroutine x(A, b)` is all right, but different;
`SUBROUTINE x(a, b)` is unacceptable,

because `subroutine` is recognized as a Fortran keyword but `SUBROUTINE` is not. Within character string constants, either case is acceptable.

In program text, the Hollerith character construction of Fortran 66 may be employed for character string constants and for initializing noncharacter variables in data statements, even though the Fortran 77 standard does not care for it. For example, one may communicate a string of 23 characters by

```
23hthis ' is an apostrophe
```

or analogously for uppercase characters. Such usage is particularly convenient where the string contains the apostrophe character, which Fortran 77 uses to delimit strings. **f77** allows an alternative way of handling the apostrophe problem, through the provision of two standard quote characters, `'` and `"`. A character string may be started with either and is considered terminated at its second occurrence. Hence,

```
"this ' is an apostrophe"
```

will also work nicely. The Hollerith construction was standard in Fortran 66, so its inclusion in **f77** makes for program compatibility.

To strengthen compatibility with C, **f77** also recognizes certain character combinations beginning with a reverse slant to be single special characters, not the two-character combinations that they seem to be. These are

`\n`	new line	`\f`	form feed (new page)
`\t`	tab character	`\0`	null character
`\b`	backspace character	`\\`	reverse slant \
`\'`	apostrophe '	`\"`	quotation mark "

The existence of these combinations provides yet a third solution to the apostrophe problem:

```
'this \' is an apostrophe'
```

which may be a little less elegant than those above, but works.

Extensions to Language Scope

The Fortran accepted by **f77** includes two data types not wholly standard, as well as one entirely unknown to programmers in conventional Fortran. The declarations

```
integer*2 j
double complex z1
```

are accepted by **f77**. Experienced programmers will no doubt guess that the first allocates two bytes (a 16-bit word) of memory for variable `j`. The second declaration makes variable `z1` both double precision and complex, thus occupying four times the storage allocated to an ordinary real number. The standard Fortran functions applicable to complex numbers, such as `cabs(z1)`, `cexp(z1)`, etc. cannot be used with the double complex data type. To cope, it was necessary for the designers of **f77** to introduce functions applicable to complex data in two parallel families, exactly as the original designers of Fortran provided real functions in both single and double precision versions. Function names beginning with c, like csqrt(z1), are used with single precision complex numbers, while functions whose names begin with z, like zsqrt(z1), are used with double complex arguments. Happily, a similar family of function pairs is not required for long and short integers; one can write, for example, iabs(ij), without worrying about whether ij is long or short. In other words, integer type mixing works just fine in integer functions.

A new data type, which is perhaps a bit less obvious, might be best introduced by the declarations

```
implicit undefined (a-z)
integer ij; real a1, bnx
```

The first declaration invalidates the Fortran convention that any symbol beginning with the letters i to n is an integer and any other symbol must be a real number; it says that no variable will be considered acceptable unless its type has been explicitly declared. The next two declarations (typed on one line!) then create the specific variables ij, a1, bnx. It is conventional in Algol, Pascal, C, and some other languages to require every variable to be declared explicitly. The same discipline can be imposed on the Fortran programmer by declaring everything to be undefined at the start. As one might expect, no operations of any kind are permissible with undefined data.

Data statements serve to initialize variable values. In **f77**, bit strings may be specified in a data statement for any variable declared logical, real, or integer. The bit strings may be given in one of three notations: binary, octal, or hexadecimal, as in

```
data a, b, c /b'10010', o'477', z'2f'/
```

Care must be taken, if both long and short integers are used, to specify only as many bits as the variable actually contains.

Finally, a truly convenient nonstandard feature of **f77** is the include statement. In normal usage, it takes the form

```
include textfile
```

where textfile is the name of a file containing Fortran statements. **f77** does not translate this statement; instead, it causes textfile to be copied into the Fortran program in place of the include statement. Blocks of Fortran text needed in many subroutines, such as array dimensions, common statements, and equivalences, can be placed in a single file and included in numerous places in a Fortran program (e.g., at the head of each subroutine). An immense amount of debugging and editing labor can be saved during program development, since changes in array dimensions or variable declarations will be carried through all program segments automatically if they are changed in just the single file containing the declarations.

Fortran 77 Input and Output

In principle, all Fortran input and output operations are directed to logical input-output units identified by numbers. **f77** recognizes logical units 0 through 9 as being valid. Three unit assignments are made at the start of any program run and remain in force unless changed by the program:

> *unit 5* is the standard input, usually the keyboard;
> *unit 6* is the standard output, usually the screen;
> *unit 0* is the standard error output, usually the screen.

The remaining seven Fortran logical units are automatically connected to seven formatted sequential files when program execution starts. Unit 1 is connected to file `fort.1`, unit 2 to file `fort.2`, and so on. These files are located in the user's current directory (default directory) at the time the program is run. The files `fort.1`, . . ., `fort.9` are actually created only if the program attempts to access them so users need not bother to open them, nor to remove them if they were not used.

Fortran logical unit assignments to files can be altered at any time, using the Fortran 77 open and `close` statements. In their simplest form, these are

```
open (2, file='filename')
close (2)
```

The open statement attaches a file to a Fortran logical unit. In the normal course of events, the file could be a Unix special file, if input or output from a specific physical device (e.g., the keyboard) is expected; or it could be an ordinary file. The file name must be encased in apostrophes to satisfy the rules of Fortran 77; in all other respects it is a normal file name. If the unit was previously attached to another file, that file is detached automatically before the new attachment is made. The `close` statement detaches whatever file was attached to a logical unit, leaving the logical unit free.

Fortran files may be formatted or unformatted (binary) and they may permit either sequential or direct access. The Unix system supports all four types of file, handling them all as ordinary files. Newline characters are written at ends of records and newline characters are expected as record terminators on input. Internally, direct access files are handled by moving the file pointer. For Unix to know how far to move the pointer, the record length must be declared (in bytes) when a direct access file is opened. For example, the Fortran statement

```
      open (unit = 2, file = phonebook, form = formatted,
    & access = direct, recl = 60, status = old, err = 999)
```

opens phonebook as an already existing formatted direct access file with a record length of 60 bytes and connects it to logical unit 2.

When first opened, sequential files have their pointers positioned at their ends. In this way, writing can be done naturally, by appending to the already existing file content. Attempts to read, on the other hand, will produce an end-of-file indication. To read a file, it is therefore necessary to rewind it first.

When reading numeric input, **f77** takes a somewhat more relaxed attitude to formatting than the Fortran 77 standard prescribes. The standard Fortran format statement is oriented to card images (column counts in format statements), while **f77** attempts to preserve its orientation to the screen display terminal. Commas are therefore accepted as data separators between numeric fields, overriding the field widths shown in the format statements. For example, the format specification `2f12.0` will be satisfied by the character string

```
    1.2758, 3.7
```

despite its failure to respect the format specification. This broadmindedness is unfortunately only applicable to numeric data. There is no convenient way to extend the same leniency to character string variables, for the comma itself could be a legitimate part of a character string.

Fortran 77 Rule Violations

Little that is specified by the Fortran 77 standard is not implemented in **f77**. The exceptions include

(1) the treatment of double precision variables in `common` or `equivalence` statements,

(2) the treatment of character-valued variables when passed as subroutine arguments, and

(3) the treatment of tab (absolute tab and leftward tab) format control codes in sequential files or devices.

Happily, the rules are violated only in cases most ordinary programmers never run into, so they are not aware that differences exist. The rarity of any malfunctions makes the shock doubly great when violations do occur, hence the warnings given here.

The first exception above only arises on computers where the hardware requires all double precision variables to start at even word locations. If there is any problem, a diagnostic message is issued, so unwelcome surprises are rare. Unfortunately, some machines care about even address boundaries, others do not. Hence **f77** cannot be made totally machine independent.

The second exception results from the way character variables are handled by **f77**, which in turn stems at least partly from a desire to remain compatible with C. Again, a warning message is issued if there appears to be any difficulty. Problems of this kind can always be cured by a few `external` declarations.

The third exception arises from a logical inconsistency in Fortran 77, or rather from inclusion in the standard of assumptions about how the language is implemented. Backing up (as implied by a left tab) is clearly not possible on any truly sequential device or file. The Fortran 77 standard seems to assume that the input or output of any sequential device is sufficiently buffered to allow backing up at least within the current record, but the **f77** dialect of Fortran does not make a similar assumption about genuinely sequential devices (e.g., a terminal display screen). Attempts to back up where Unix will not allow it lead to execution-time error messages.

Ratfor: A Rational Fortran

Ratfor is an extended form of Fortran which includes many of the control structures familiar in Pascal and C. Initially introduced as part of the Unix system, Ratfor has recently found wider acceptance. Several other operating systems now have Ratfor preprocessors available.

The **ratfor** Preprocessor

The Fortran language has long been the language favored by scientific programmers for various reasons including its almost universal acceptance. Computer scientists generally consider Fortran an unattractive antique because it contains neither the syntactic niceties that make for clean program structure nor the flexible data structures provided by Pascal, Ada, and other newer languages.

Short of redefining the Fortran language, there is not much to be done about its paucity of data types. But deficiencies in syntax lend themselves to treatment by language preprocessors. The Ratfor language represents a welcome step in this direction. In contrast to other extended Fortran dialects, Ratfor text is never actually compiled, only translated into standard Fortran. Ratfor is therefore locked to the Unix system only to the extent of the Ratfor-to-Fortran conversion; from there on, the programs will run anywhere that a Fortran compiler can be found. Using the normal Unix language translators, the sequence from Ratfor to executable code thus passes through four intermediate forms, of which two are human-readable languages:

Ratfor	translates to	*Fortran*
Fortran	translates to	*C intermediate code*
C intermediate code	translates to	*assembler language*
assembler	translates to	*relocatable object code*
relocatable object code	translates to	*executable object code*

The multiplicity of intermediate forms implies that program segments originating in other languages, or created at other times, can be grafted on to the structure easily and naturally. On the other hand, all the necessary processes are usually pipelined together to form a single compile-and-load pass; thus, the average user need never even know what intermediate stages existed.

Program Text Formatting in Ratfor

Ratfor strikes the newcomer at first glance as being a free-format version of Fortran. Statements may be placed anywhere on a line and may be continued on as many lines as desired. Continuation characters are not needed. The **ratfor** preprocessor will reformat statements to begin in column 7 and will supply continuation characters in column 6 where necessary. Multiple statements on one line are permitted, with the semicolon (the ; character) used to separate them. Semicolons are also permitted (but not required) if a statement ends at a line end. **ratfor** does try to spot incomplete statements and assumes that continuation across a line end is meant if a line ends with a character that implies arithmetic or logical operations to follow:

```
+ * = , | & ( _
```

The underscore (the _ character) can be used to force **ratfor** to understand that a continuation is meant. Underscore characters are not reproduced in the Fortran output. Semicolons and underscores can always be used to dispel confusion about statement ends and continuations.

Statement numbers may be entered anywhere in a Ratfor line, but of course they must always precede the statement itself. In fact, **ratfor** assumes that any number at the beginning of a line is a statement number and places it in columns 1-5 of the Fortran output. However, the structure of Ratfor is such that statement numbers are likely to occur rarely in the Ratfor text.

The comparison operators generally used to form Fortran logical expressions may be replaced in Ratfor by symbols a little closer to their mathematical origins. They are subsequently translated by **ratfor** into their usual Fortran equivalents:

```
==  becomes  .eq.     <   becomes  .lt.     !=  becomes  .ne.
>            .gt.     <=           .le.     &            .and.
>=           .ge.     !            .not.    |            .or.
```

While experienced Fortran programmers may find expressions like `x.gt.0` natural, many people would prefer `x>0`.

Ratfor is deliberately designed so that the **ratfor** preprocessor need not understand any Fortran. Sometimes it seems desirable to prevent **ratfor** from even attempting to read Fortran lines, and for this purpose the percent mark (the % character) at the beginning of a line is used. Any line that begins with the % character is copied into the Fortran output unaltered except for removal of the % sign itself. In Ratfor jargon, the % character when so used is called the *transparency operator* because every line marked with it passes through **ratfor** unseen and unprocessed.

Statement Groups and `if` Statements

Ratfor control flow strongly resembles that of Algol or Pascal; indeed, it is surprising how little translation is required to produce standard Fortran out of Ratfor programs that hardly look like Fortran at all. A key Ratfor idea is to use *statement groups* (like Pascal compound statements) where Fortran ordinarily allows only single statements. A statement group is exactly what its name says: a group of statements which logically belong together and which may be inserted in Ratfor text wherever the Fortran rules would allow a single statement. Statement groups are identified by enclosing them in braces `{...}`. To give a simple example, the Fortran `if` statement permits conditional execution of just one statement, while Ratfor allows several actions to be requested in one statement group:

```
if (x<0) {call errmsg; answer = 0.0; return}
```

In ordinary Fortran, the equivalent would read

```
      if (x .ge. 0) go to 100
      call errmsg
```

```
      answer = 0.0
      return
  100 continue
```

Few statement numbers and very few go to statements are needed in Ratfor. Many of the inverted-if constructs of Fortran are also eliminated: Ratfor makes it easy to say "if x is negative, do this. . ." rather than "if x is not negative, don't do this. . ." as illustrated by the Fortran example above.

Ratfor allows an *if–then–else* construct to be used with statement groups, in the natural form

```
if (x<0) then {a = res; j = 1} else {a = -res; j = 0}
```

This form is cleaner and tidier than its Fortran 66 equivalent, which requires at least one *if*-inversion (below, left). It is less verbose than its Fortran 77 equivalent (below, right) and distinctly easier to read than either:

```
     if (x .ge. 0) go to 10        if (x .lt. 0) then
     a = res                       a = res
     j = 1                         j = 1
     go to 20                      else
  10 a = -res                      a = -res
     j = 0                         j = 0
  20 continue                      endif
```

Ratfor *if–then* and *if–then–else* constructs can be nested. Intermixing the two in nested constructs could lead to ambiguity, for it may not always be clear to which *if* an *else* belongs because every *if* does not necessarily require an *else*. The ambiguity is resolved by a simple rule: an *else* belongs to the most recent preceding *if* not matched by another *else*.

Program Loops in Ratfor

Ratfor provides four convenient looping constructs which all permit one statement group to be repeated. Pascal programmers will recognize them instantly; for others, they are perhaps best introduced by examples:

```
do i = 1,10 {. . . statements . . . }
for (i = n; i > 0; i = i+1) { . . . statements . . .}
while (x>0) {. . . statements . . .}
repeat {. . . statements . . .} until (x > 0)
```

Unlike its Fortran counterpart, the Ratfor *do* statement does not require a range ("from here down to statement number so-and-so") to be defined; its range is always exactly one statement group. Otherwise, it is similar to an ordinary Fortran *do* loop. In fact, **ratfor** translates the Ratfor *do* statement into an ordinary Fortran *do* loop, so the rules of loop indexing are ultimately those of the Fortran compiler which will follow **ratfor**.

The *for* loop provides a very flexible looping structure. Like the *do* loop, it is guided by an integer loop index. The index is initialized at some value when the loop is first entered. During each trip around the loop, it is examined to see whether it meets the prescribed terminating condition and is then altered according to a prescribed rule. The initial value, terminating condition, and alteration rule are listed in the parentheses following the keyword *for*. Initialization and alteration may be performed by any one Fortran statement, and the condition may be any valid logical expression. Since "any one Fortran statement" may well be a subroutine call, progression through a *for* loop can take place in infinitely many ways. The **ratfor** preprocessor creates Fortran code which tests for loop completion first and performs the index alteration only after loop completion. Thus, the loop indexed `for(i=10; i<0; i=i+1)` will not be executed at all. Looping backwards or looping through chains of pointers is easy with *for* loops.

The *while* loop and the *repeat-until* loop are index-free. Both merely examine a logical condition and continue if it is met (*while* loop) or not met (*repeat-until*). The condition must be a single valid Fortran logical expression, but this rule is not excessively harsh because the expression may involve a call to a separately defined logical function. The *while* loop tests for the condition before executing the statement group, so it is possible that the statement group will not be executed at all. The *repeat-until* condition is tested after loop completion; its statement group will therefore be executed at least once.

Ratfor allows two additional statements, `next` and `break`, to be embedded in the statement groups controlled by loops. Any statement group in any type of loop can be cut short by the Ratfor statement `next`. Unconditional exit from any type of loop is caused by the statement `break`. The `next` statement only skips the remainder of the statement group. What happens next depends on the type of loop. In a *for* loop the index is incremented; the other three loop types proceed to test the loop terminating condition.

Text Insertions and Substitutions

Two kinds of Ratfor statement permit text substitution: `define` and `include`. The `define` statement allows a character string value to be assigned to a name:

```
define long 500
```

Wherever the name `long` appears in any subsequent Ratfor text, the character string `500` is substituted. Calling `long` a name implies that the character string `long` is recognized as such only if immediately preceded and followed by characters other than alphanumeric. Thus, the program segment

```
define long 500
dimension xarray(long); oblong = x + 27.5
```

will become on translation

```
dimension xarray(500)
oblong = x + 27.5
```

because the string `long` in the `dimension` statement has nonalphanumeric characters fore and aft so it constitutes a name in the foregoing sense; but in the arithmetic assignment next following, `long` is preceded by the alphabetic character b so it is not a name. The `define` statement is useful for achieving much the same effects as the `parameter` statement of Fortran 77. However, it is much more powerful because the name may be defined to stand for any character string whatever; it is not required to denote a single numeric value. For example, many Fortran programmers ask for intermediate printouts during program debugging either through subroutine calls, say

```
call dump
```

or by simply inserting `write` statements into program code. Under Ratfor, temporary printout requests are easy to create by including in the program a line containing a particular character string, say `print1`, wherever printout is required. Subsequently,

```
define print1 call dump
```

or

```
define print1 write(6,100)x,y,z
```

will cause printout statements to be inserted as required. When the program has been satisfactorily debugged, altering just one statement,

```
define print1 continue
```

turns all the printout requests into harmless `continue` statements.

The `include` statement of Ratfor is similar to the corresponding statement of Fortran 77:

```
include filename
```

causes the file `filename` to be found and copied into the program text, replacing the `include` statement. It is convenient for inserting multiple copies of the same text, such as `common` blocks or globally applicable parameter definitions, while maintaining only one actual copy of the text. Any editing changes in the master text then automatically appear everywhere.

Ambiguity and Duplication

A fundamental principle of Ratfor design is that **ratfor** should not understand, nor for the most part recognize, the Fortran language. Some potential difficulties may arise from this fact.

In Fortran, keywords are not reserved and may be used as variable names, subroutine names, common block labels, and so on. Thus,

```
call call
```

may look a bit curious, but it is perfectly valid Fortran. The compiler will sort out that the first `call` is a Fortran keyword, the second a subroutine name! However, **ratfor** cannot do the same because it does not know Fortran. Ratfor keywords are therefore reserved. It is not permissible in Ratfor to use `call` as the name of a subroutine, nor `if` as the name of an integer variable.

Any dubious lines can be dealt with by placing % signs in the first column, thereby preventing **ratfor** from reading them. The arithmetic `if` statement, for example, must be handled in this way, otherwise **ratfor** will spot the keyword `if` and attempt to process the rest as an ordinary logical `if` statement. Similarly, the `include` statement may be intended for action by **f77** at a later time. It can be shielded from **ratfor** by the % sign which **ratfor** will remove, thereby exposing the statement to **f77**.

Using **ratfor**

ratfor can be invoked in two ways: by itself or as part of an **f77** run. If Ratfor text is placed in a file whose name terminates with `.r` (e.g., `text.r`), **f77** will automatically include **ratfor** as the first step in the Fortran pipeline. Thus, the command

```
$ f77 text.r
```

will cause the file `text.r` to be translated to Fortran, compiled, linked, and loaded into an executable object file called **a.out**.

If only a translation to Fortran is desired, without compilation, the command **ratfor** will invoke the preprocessor on its own. Some quite straightforward options are provided with **ratfor**. If none are specified, output compatible with the **f77** compiler is produced. However, Fortran text agreeable to other compilers can be provided as an alternative.

Reverse Processing with **struct**

Fortran programs can be made easier to maintain by using the convenience features of Ratfor. To do so with already existing Fortran programs, it is necessary first to invert the translation process so as to generate a Ratfor program from the Fortran source code. The **struct** program does precisely this, producing reasonable Ratfor from either Fortran 66 or Fortran 77 text.

Like the result of any reverse translation process, the inversion produced by **struct** is not unique. Options are therefore provided, to allow a measure of control over the Ratfor text produced by **struct**. Most **struct** options can be safely ignored because their effects are not critical. For example, `break` statements might be tidier than `goto` statements, but neither will really hurt. Nevertheless, there are a few possible pitfalls; some statements may appear to translate without difficulty while producing troublesome output. For example, the use of Ratfor keywords as Fortran variable names in the original source code may yield nonsense without seeming to do so. Conversion of a large program is therefore best done in several passes, inverting the program using **struct** and following up with **ratfor** to check whether the inversion ran into any snags. The resulting files can be compared by **diff** to see whether any significant differences exist. At least two round trips through the **struct–ratfor** cycle may be necessary, otherwise the formatting of the Fortran text will not be similar in the two files and **diff** will report numerous differences of no consequence to the Fortran compiler.

Translation of old Fortran 66 programs to Fortran 77 can be achieved by a similar means. The Fortran 66 program is turned into Ratfor by **struct**, then into Fortran 77 by **ratfor**. The automatic translation frequently needs to be augmented by manual editing of a few really nasty patches, especially if the Fortran 66 program is old and was produced by highly experienced programmers; large programs of the late 1960s or early 1970s sometimes contain clever tricks for saving memory, too clever for **struct** to handle. They are usually obvious enough once they have been located.

Non-Unix Ratfor

Programs written in Ratfor are much easier to read, easier to maintain, and easier to move to different computer operating systems than programs written in Fortran. At the same time, they are usable wherever a Fortran program is usable because Ratfor is always converted to Fortran before compilation; as far as the compiler can tell, Ratfor programs *are* Fortran programs. The Ratfor programmer thus works in a more agreeable language than Fortran, yet has ready access to existing Fortran facilities and subroutine libraries.

Ratfor translators are usually furnished with any Unix system that supports Fortran. Where the Fortran compiler is separately acquired from a third-party source, **ratfor** may well be missing. In such cases, a Ratfor translator is still easily acquired and installed. There exist several translators which were written in Ratfor itself and which can therefore be installed (after translation into Fortran) wherever a Fortran compiler is available. Such "foreign" Ratfor translators may not provide `define` and `include` statements in their full generality but may have other agreeable facilities by way of compensation.

The C Language

The language C is the prime language of the Unix system. Unix and C are related because they were developed concurrently and grew together, the needs of the system shaping the language while ideas about the language led to system revision. In many respects C represents a halfway house between true high-level languages (like Pascal or Algol, which strive to be machine independent) and assembler languages entirely keyed to the structure of a particular computer. Since C recognizes the various lower-level entities of interest to the system programmer, it is considered by many an ideal language for writing operating systems. C compilers are now available under several operating systems of widely varying character, not merely under Unix.

In this chapter, C occupies a position slightly different from Fortran and Pascal. Nearly all C programmers are already acquainted with the Unix system or another similar operating system; people usually learn the language because they work with the system, not often the other way around. On the other hand, many experienced Fortran or Pascal programmers are newcomers to both C and Unix. Consequently, this section is intended primarily for programmers already acquainted with other high-level languages. It describes the main characteristics of C, how C is related to other languages, and hints at why its authors should have deemed a new language necessary at all. The discussion given here is not sufficient to learn programming in C; for that, the definitive book by Kernighan and Ritchie should be consulted.

Most C compilers distributed with Unix or Unix-like systems derive from the original Bell Laboratories version and are therefore (almost by definition!) authoritative. They do not violate the C standard in any significant way. Nevertheless, they were produced years before there was a published and agreed standard for the C language, so some deviations are likely to be found in due course.

General Characteristics of C

The structure of C places it midway between Fortran and Pascal, with the significant difference that C understands some machine dependent facts of life deliberately ignored by the other two languages. Although the C language is more or less machine-independent, C programs frequently are not. Unlike Pascal or Algol, C implicitly assumes a twos complement binary machine of fixed and finite word length. It presupposes that characters are represented by single bytes or by byte-like subsections of words. Within these constraints, easily met by many computers, C provides a large set of data types and operators, almost as large as one might expect in a machine language. Bit-level operations such as shifts and maskings, logical unions and intersections, are as easy in C as in machine language. C includes various constructs customarily found in assembler languages but not in high-level languages: address values, indices, incrementation and decrementation operators. At the same time, C contains most of the mathematical capabilities of Fortran or Pascal.

As compared to Fortran, C may be considered a superior language in at least one major respect: its greater richness in data types and data structures. After all, the only data structure conveniently available in Fortran is the array. Even fairly elementary constructs such as linked lists and trees cause great difficulty in Fortran while they are easily dealt with in either C or Pascal. C may be preferred to Pascal for a different reason, one perhaps a little more controversial: it is not a block-structured language in the Algol or Pascal sense. It therefore permits separate compilation of program modules and makes it easy to ascertain the scope of variables. Program modularity and separate compilation have made Fortran the darling of the scientific computing community. The design of C takes this requirement very seriously, so much so that the standard Unix compilers for Fortran and C share a considerable amount of code.

Structure of C Programs

A C program consists of one or more *functions*, each possessing zero or more arguments. A function is comparable in form and purpose to a function in Fortran or Pascal. Functions in C have names; the function `example` is invoked by mentioning its name, with its arguments listed in parentheses:

```
example (a,b,c);
```

There is nothing to correspond to the Fortran subroutine or the Pascal procedure; in C, the function does everything. Functions without arguments may exist, but parentheses are required even if there are no arguments, as in `example2()`. A function is declared to exist by naming it, with a dummy argument list, and giving the set of C statements that define it. The set of defining statements is enclosed in braces, as in

```
example2 (. . . arguments . . .)
        { . . . C statements . . . }
```

A function generally involves computation with its arguments and also with variables purely internal to itself. Arguments given in the argument list of a function are defined ahead of the left brace that begins the body of the function itself:

```
addup (a, b)
        int a, b;
        {       int z;
                z = a + b;
                return z; }
```

This function computes the sum of two integers *a* and *b*. As in Pascal, semicolons serve to terminate statements. In contrast to Pascal, however, they are terminators, not separators; a semicolon is required after the last statement.

A function returns a value, that is, it may appear in C statements in all contexts where an arithmetic value is expected. By default, all functions are considered to return integer values. If desired, the function value may be of any other data type acceptable in C, but a type declaration must then precede the function name. Thus,

```
double dexample (x, y)
        int x, y;
        { . . .
        . . . }
```

defines a function `dexample` which returns a double precision value. Functions may also perform other activities, such as reading a character or writing a block to tape. Where a function value is in principle not explicitly necessary, it is often used as a success flag. For example, a function which copies one file to another may return the integer value 1 if the operation was carried out successfully and the value 0 if not (e.g., if the file to be copied was not found).

There is no such thing in C as a "main program" in the Fortran sense; instead, there is one privileged function name `main`. Execution of a C program always begins with `main`, which in turn must invoke any other functions required. Although `main` is privileged in this way, it is a function and its declaration must contain parentheses. When a C program is run under Unix, the arguments declared for `main` are passed on to or from the kernel, so that the program becomes almost an extension of the operating system itself. The form of a typical C program is illustrated by the following simple example:

```
main ()
        {     int a, b, c;
              do     {
                 scanf("%d", &a); scanf("%d", &b);
                 c = addup(a, b);
                 printf("%d + %d = %d0, a, b, c); }
              while (c != 0);
        }
addup (a, b)
        int a, b;
        {     int z;
              z = a + b;
              return z; }
```

It is noteworthy that the function addup`(x, y)` is not defined inside the `main()` function, as a Pascal procedure might be; it resides outside, like a Fortran subroutine. C functions are defined separately, not in nested blocks. As may be evident from the example, braces `{...}` are used to turn a whole string of statements into a single compound statement, much like the braces used in Ratfor or the Pascal **begin** and **end** brackets. Even though details differ, the punctuation rules of C resemble those of Pascal in principle.

No special statement exists in C for defining a function, a strange break with habit for both Fortran and Pascal programmers. If the C compiler encounters a previously unknown name followed by a left parenthesis, it assumes that the name identifies a function and remembers it as a function name. The rules for exiting from a function are also more liberal than those of Pascal or Fortran. Control is returned to the calling program when execution logically reaches the closing brace, even without a return statement. A return statement does exist, but its use is optional in most circumstances.

Recursion is permitted in a C function, that is, a function may invoke itself. On the other hand, functions may not be defined within functions. In this respect, C differs fundamentally from Pascal or Modula-2 and the structure of a C program resembles that of a Fortran program much more closely than the procedures-within-procedures nesting of Pascal. This arrangement makes for both structural simplicity and simplicity in compilation. Unlike Pascal but like Fortran, C easily allows separate compilation of individual functions. Furthermore, their structural similarity allows the

C and Fortran compilers to translate both languages into a common intermediate code and to process them in an identical fashion thereafter. Fortran, C, and assembler language programs may therefore be intermixed, so different sections of a large program can be written in different languages chosen to suit each processing task.

All C variables are passed to functions by *value*, not by *name*. In effect, duplicate local variables are created when a function is called and values are assigned to the duplicates. The function operates on the duplicates only and therefore cannot affect the variables or constants in the function that called it into action. If modification of variables in the calling function is really desired, the equivalent of a call by name is possible in C through the mechanism of *pointers*.

The sequence in which C functions are called into play is controlled by program flow mechanisms resembling those of Pascal and Ratfor: `if` statements have a similar form, a *for . . . while* construct exists, and the `case` of Pascal reappears under the Algol name of `switch`.

Constants, Variables, and Pointers

The C language contains an unusually rich set of fundamental data types, each requiring a different amount of memory. The memory allocated depends on the machine word length and memory organization. Machine word lengths of 16, 32, and 36 bits are common and implementations of Unix for each of these have been in common use for some years now. The data types available in C and the number of memory bits allocated to each are given in Table 9.1. Most types in this table, excepting perhaps `unsigned`, will be familiar to experienced programmers. Type `unsigned` is useful for indexing operations, counting, or addressing where sign is not a consideration. All numerical operations on unsigned integers are done in straight (uncomplemented) binary arithmetic. The other integer types are stored in twos complement notation and arithmetic is performed accordingly. There is no type `logical` or `boolean` in the C language. However, logical operations are defined on integers. C considers any nonzero value to signify *true* and zero to denote *false*.

TABLE 9.1. Memory bits per C variable

Data type as defined in C		Machine word		
Name	Characteristics	16	32	36
`int`	signed integer	16	32	36
`char`	single character	8	8	9
`short`	integer (short)	16	16	36
`long`	integer (long)	32	32	36
`unsigned`	nonnegative integer	16	16	36
`float`	floating point	32	32	36
`double`	double precision	64	64	72

All variables must be declared in a C program; a new variable may never be introduced by simply using it. Fortran programmers feel this insistence on strong typing of variables contrasts strangely with the lack of a function declaration statement but Pascal and Algol programmers find themselves quite at home. In C, the usual place for declarations is at the head of each function. A declaration consists of a type name, followed by a list of variables:

```
float a, b, c;
int i, j, k;
```

The scope of a variable is confined to the function in which it is defined; it is undefined outside. Variables can be made `external` by declaring them outside any function, for example,

```
int x,y;
main () {nt f,g; ...funct(a,b) ...{
funct (p,q) int p,q; {extern int x,y; ...}
```

`extern` variables are somewhat like Pascal variables declared in the outermost block. They permit global use of values, perhaps resembling variables in a Fortran `common` declaration, but neater and easier because variable identification is always by name, not by storage position in a `common` block. Mercifully, there is no precise analogue of the Fortran `equivalence`, which many programmers find a rich source of particularly difficult bugs.

Pointers are widely used in C, much like pointers in Pascal. The value of a pointer is the memory address of the variable to which it points. There is no declaration `pointer`; instead, they are declared implicitly by saying, for example, "p is a pointer containing the address of a floating-point variable":

```
float *p;
```

The asterisk operator implies "the variable to which p points". Its inverse is the ampersand: &x is the pointer to (i.e. the address of) the variable x. Pointers and variables are associated implicitly by assignment statements. For example,

```
p = &x;
y = *p;
```

In pointer manipulation, the different word lengths associated with different variable types are taken care of automatically. Thus, there are in reality several different kinds of pointer, one corresponding to each possible data type.

Arrays in C are in principle one-dimensional. They are established by a type declaration statement like

```
float a [5];
```

Indexing of arrays always starts at zero, so this declaration says that array components `a[0]` to `a[4]` inclusive exist. Two-dimensional arrays are declared as arrays of one-dimensional arrays. Arrays are declared by attaching the number of repetitions, in square brackets, to an existing variable or array declaration. Thus,

```
float x [5] [3];
```

is equivalent to the Fortran declaration `real x (3,5)`. Array storage is by *rows* (Fortran programmers take note!): the rightmost index varies fastest.

C knows about various constants: *integer*, *floating*, *character*, and *string*. All floating constants are automatically taken to be double length; the exponential or E notation therefore covers both single and double precision. Character constants are placed between apostrophes, e.g. `'A'`. They can be used in arithmetic; however, their numeric values may vary from one installation to another. There also exists a set of character constants, principally used to represent nonprinting characters, denoted by two-character sequences. The main ones are `\n` (the newline character), `\r` (carriage return), `\b` (backspace), and `\t` (tab). Any desired bit pattern may be placed in a character constant as *nnn*, where *nnn* is an unsigned octal number of one to three digits. A string constant is a string of characters encased in quotes, as in "`string constant`". They can be placed into character arrays of the appropriate size.

Arithmetic and Logical Operations

As programming languages go, C recognizes and uses an immense set of operators. Operators come in four principal classes: unary, binary, relational, and assignment.

Unary operators are used as prefixes to values (variables, constants, or functions), as is customary in almost any programming language. For example, one writes

```
x = !x
```

to indicate logical complementation (negation) of the variable *x*. Other unary operators are used in a similar fashion. An exception is formed by the operators `++` and `--`, which increment or decrement the operand, respectively. These operators may be applied either before or after evaluation of the operand (including a single variable) to which they relate. They are positioned before the expression if predecrementation is required, after it if postdecrementation or postincrementation is intended. For example, ++x indicates incrementation prior to evaluation, while x++ asks for incrementation afterward. While predecrementation and postincrementation are notions familiar to most machine language programmers, they are not frequently encountered in high-level languages. They are included in the full set of available unary operators in Table 9.2.

Manipulative binary operations in C make up an unusually rich set. They all employ infix notation, so that the operator op connecting variables x and y always appears in C expressions in the form x op y. The re-

TABLE 9.2. Operators used in C

<table>
<tr><td></td><td>Unary operators</td></tr>
<tr><td>*</td><td>indirection (compute the value associated with a pointer)</td></tr>
<tr><td>&</td><td>pointer creation (compute pointer associated with a value)</td></tr>
<tr><td>-</td><td>arithmetic negation (negative of the value)</td></tr>
<tr><td>!</td><td>logical negation (zero produces 1, nonzero produces 0)</td></tr>
<tr><td>~</td><td>bitwise (ones) complement of an integer variable</td></tr>
<tr><td>++</td><td>following operand incremented before evaluation (e.g. ++x)</td></tr>
<tr><td>--</td><td>following operand decremented before evaluation (e.g. --x)</td></tr>
<tr><td>++</td><td>preceding operand incremented after evaluation (e.g. x++)</td></tr>
<tr><td>--</td><td>preceding operand decremented after evaluation (e.g. x--)</td></tr>
<tr><td>(type)</td><td>typename in parentheses preceding operand converts type</td></tr>
<tr><td>sizeof</td><td>size (in characters) of following operand or type name</td></tr>
<tr><td></td><td>Binary operators</td></tr>
<tr><td>*</td><td>multiply the two operands</td></tr>
<tr><td>/</td><td>divide, truncating if operands are integers</td></tr>
<tr><td>%</td><td>find remainder from integer division</td></tr>
<tr><td>+</td><td>add the operands</td></tr>
<tr><td>-</td><td>subtract</td></tr>
<tr><td><<</td><td>shift first operand left the given number of bits</td></tr>
<tr><td>>></td><td>shift first operand right the given number of bits</td></tr>
<tr><td>&</td><td>bitwise AND (boolean product) of the two operands</td></tr>
<tr><td>^</td><td>bitwise exclusive OR of the two integral operands</td></tr>
<tr><td>|</td><td>bitwise inclusive OR of the two integral operands</td></tr>
<tr><td>&&</td><td>logical AND (yields 1 if both nonzero, 0 otherwise)</td></tr>
<tr><td>||</td><td>logical OR (yields 1 if either operand nonzero, 0 otherwise)</td></tr>
<tr><td></td><td>Relational operators</td></tr>
<tr><td><</td><td>less than</td></tr>
<tr><td>></td><td>greater than</td></tr>
<tr><td><=</td><td>less than or equal to</td></tr>
<tr><td>>=</td><td>greater than or equal to</td></tr>
<tr><td>==</td><td>equal to</td></tr>
<tr><td>!=</td><td>not equal to</td></tr>
</table>

lational operators are similar to those in other high-level programming languages. The full set of both manipulative and relational binary operators is shown in Table 9.2. Despite the large variety provided, not everything imaginable is included; for instance, there is no exponentiation operator.

C also contains an unusual variety of assignment symbols. The equal sign = is used in its Fortran sense, but it may be augmented by a binary operator sign to indicate an operation on the variable itself. For example,

```
x += 2;    means   x = x + 2;
x -= 2;    means   x = x - 2;
```

and similar meanings apply for the *=, /=, %=, <<=, >>=, &=, ^=, and != operators. As far as the underlying bit manipulations are concerned, the precise meaning of an operator is further affected by the data types on which it operates. For example, the symbol + placed between two unsigned integers does not lead to the same manipulative operations as + placed between two real (type *float*) variables.

Structures

C permits use of entities called structures, denoted by `struct`, to simplify data handling. A structure is a set of data objects (not necessarily of the same type) identified by a common name. It closely resembles a `record` in Pascal. For example, a structure may be defined by

```
struct day
    {int date;
     char month [9];
     int year;
    } x, y;
```

Henceforth, *x* and *y* are understood to have the structure described in the declaration. Once the structure has been defined, other variables of the same type may be created by a simple declaration

```
struct day birthday;
```

without repeating the details of what the structure must contain.

Two operations are permitted on structures: (1) setting a pointer to the address of a structure with the & operator, as in `&birthday`, and (2) accessing one of its members. Fetching (accessing) uses syntax similar to that in Pascal: the generic structural component name is suffixed to a specific variable name. The two are separated by a dot. For example,

```
x = birthday.year;
birthday.year = y;
```

But

```
birthday = another;
```

is not permitted in C, because structures cannot be passed or copied directly, nor can they be made into function arguments. This restriction is not nearly so severe as it might seem, for much the same effect can be achieved by equating or manipulating pointers to structures.

Input and Output with C

In principle, C has no input and output statements. However, there does exist a library of standard functions including both primitive (character level) and formatted input and output. It may be requested from the loader by the **-l** option, as, for example, in

```
$ cc filename -lS
```

Here **S** denotes the standard library. The standard library relies on various macros and external variables; they are included in a C program by

```
#include <stdio.h>
```

The angle brackets instead of quotation marks mean that the file in question is system supplied, not a user file.

For formatted output, the `printf(...)` function is invoked. Its arguments may include character strings containing text to be output, variables, and possibly conversion (formatting) control. Output can be produced as signed or unsigned decimal, octal, or hexadecimal integers; real numbers in plain decimal or exponential notation; or as characters. The field width to be occupied, whether left or right justification is desired within the field, and the number of digits to be printed for each variable are matters controllable by appropriate arguments. Formatted input uses the `scanf(...)` function and follows much the same rules, with one significant exception: the arguments of `scanf()` must always be pointers to variables, not the variables themselves.

The C Preprocessor

Before they are translated into lower-level code, C programs are passed through the C preprocessor. The preprocessor looks for lines beginning with # signs. Ignoring all other lines, it regards these as instructions. Preprocessor instructions include conditional compilation and direct substitution.

There are two kinds of substitution: #define and #include. These are similar to the define and include statements of Ratfor and are handled by much the same system mechanisms. The preprocessor instruction

```
#include "filename"
```

(where the quotes are required) will read file filename and copy its contents in place of the #include statement. When an inclusion is made, preprocessing restarts at the beginning of the included file. Therefore, an included file may have other #include statements in it. Recursive inclusion, in which file A contains the instruction #include "A", must obviously be avoided. While this requirement may seem self-evident and violations easy to spot, the sin of recursive inclusion can easily and almost invisibly turn up in circular references, in which file A contains #include "B" and file B contains #include "A".

The C language itself includes very few built-in functions. Practically everything useful, from input-output operations to evaluation of Bessel functions, is done by including library functions from one of many C libraries. These are inserted by a #include preprocessor instruction much like any other file, but with one key difference: the quotation marks are replaced by left and right angle brackets (the < and > signs). This arrangement permits the C libraries to be stored somewhere far away from the user's own directory structure. The angle brackets distinguish system-provided library files from any others and effectively tell the preprocessor to look for them in the appropriate place. For example, any C program that uses the curses screen window management package must declare

```
#include <curses.h>
```

Most of the common files required by users have names ending in .h and are referred to as *header files*, probably because their #include statements are conventionally placed at the head of the program file.

The preprocessor instruction #define replaces a given string of characters by another string of characters. The replacement technique is similar to that used with Ratfor. It is surprisingly clever; for example, it is possible not only to replace a function name but to have arguments substituted at the same time.

The C preprocessor allows declarations of structures, array sizes, variable definitions, utility functions, and various other useful program segments to be placed in separate files and to be copied into other programs where desired. Source code can therefore be arranged so that all the definitions and parameters that must be repeated in various program segments (e.g., array sizes) only appear in one place. Program alteration is thereby made easy, for a change made in a single place will automatically propagate to wherever it is needed, through `#include` and `#define` statements. Similar facilities are provided to the Ratfor and Fortran 77 programmer.

Compiling, Assembling, and Loading

High-level languages supported under Unix are commonly compiled in a multistep process which passes through C intermediate code. The C language is compiled in two passes, first from C itself to C intermediate code, then from C intermediate code to assembler language. Other languages, in particular Fortran 77, are processed by partial compilers which produce C intermediate code also. The translation of intermediate code to relocatable object code and the loading of object code are tasks carried out by a set of programs common to all languages in this family. The benefits of this structure are many. Construction of additional compilers is simplified, since they only need to go as far as C intermediate code; procedures written in different languages can often be intermixed; subroutine libraries can be shared; and system calls can be equally accessible from all. Best of all, only one version need exist of the machine-dependent parts of the system.

The **ld** Loader

The loader program **ld** produces executable machine language programs by combining relocatable object modules. Relocation amounts to final translation of relocatable object code into absolute, executable machine code. Numerous modules must be combined even when the source program consists of only a single text file such as a Fortran program, because the Fortran program commonly employs various library subroutines and system calls for such tasks as floating-point calculation, reading files, and sending characters to the screen. Typically, a Fortran or C program of only a few lines, say to read the keyboard input and echo it to the screen, will require combining dozens of individual program segments. The task of **ld** is to locate all the pieces, to link them together correctly, and to write the resulting machine language text into a file. The loader is invoked by the command

```
$ ld file1 file2
```

The files named in the command must be relocatable object programs produced by the assembler, or the names of object program libraries. The output is placed into a file named **a.out** unless the command is made to specify otherwise with the **-o** option, as in the command

```
$ ld -o outfile file1 file2
```

Libraries normally provided as part of the operating system do not have to be named in the command, they are considered to be included automatically. User-supplied libraries, on the other hand, must be named explicitly.

The **ld** program is used by most programmers without realizing that they are using it, because the loader is usually included as the final stage of language processing sequences such as **cc** and **f77**.

The **cc** and **f77** Commands

The Fortran and C compilers usually provided in Unix systems are **f77** and **cc**. Both produce output in the same language, the C intermediate code. This code is translated to the assembler language of the machine in use, by another program called (for historical reasons) "the second pass of the C compiler"; its file name is usually `/lib/c2`. C intermediate code is not implementation dependent: it is the same for every installation. On the other hand, the assembler language text is necessarily different for every hardware configuration because it reflects the machine instruction set on a line for line basis. The text obtained from the C second pass is finally translated by the assembler into relocatable object code, machine instructions which are final and absolute except for assignment of the memory locations where the program is to reside at execution time.

When the command **cc** is issued, a pipeline is created including the first and second phases of the C compiler followed by the loader. The pipeline is some half a dozen programs long, because the individual phases of C compilation involve several processes each. Indeed, the assembler itself is part of the pipeline. On issuing the command

```
$ cc sourcefile.c
```

the program sequence is executed and the object code corresponding to `sourcefile.c` is placed in a file called **a.out**. This default file name has nothing to do with the C compiler, but rather reflects the habits of **ld**, the final program in the pipeline. The exact structure of the pipeline, and whether any intermediate files are teed off, depends on the options included with the command.

The manner in which **cc** is set up permits numerous options. There are actually only a dozen (mostly of little interest), but there appear to be more because options and arguments are passed downstream to other processes in the pipeline if they are not recognized. Option names are so chosen that the several C compiler phases and the loader all recognize different ones. For example, the **-o** (output file name specification) option may be given with the **cc** command; it is not used by the C compiler itself but is passed on down the pipeline until it is finally recognized by the loader. Thus,

```
$ cc -o outfile sourcefile.c
```

produces the output in file `outfile`, the **-o** having been passed downstream until it reached the loader. A nearly full set of options is shown in Table 9.3. While not all the listed options are available under all Unix versions, additional options are often provided.

The **f77** command launches a process sequence similar to that of **cc**, but it uses the Fortran 77 compiler instead of the first phase of the C compiler to get started. In fact, it may even include **ratfor** as the starting process. Again, the number of options looks vast; but in reality it is much smaller than it seems, because unrecognized option symbols are passed downstream until they are understood by some other program. In principle,

TABLE 9.3. Language compiler options

`-c`	cc2	compile to object file, but do not load
`-d`	ld	define common storage in spite of `-r` option
`-e`<*name*>	ld	<*name*> is the entry point of assembled program
`-i`	ld	separate (shared) text and data address spaces
`-f`	cc2	use floating point interpreter (no hardware)
`-g`	cc2	generate `sdb` debugging information
`-l`<*name*>	ld	search library `/lib/lib`<*name*>`.a` first
`-m`	f77	use the M4 preprocessor ahead of **ratfor** and **f77**
`-o`<*name*>	ld	name the output file <*name*>, not `a.out`
`-onetrip`	f77	*do* loops are tested at the end of loop execution
`-p`	cc2	produce profile file and monitor execution
`-r`	ld	relocation symbols to be generated in output
`-s`	ld	strip symbol table and relocation symbols
`-u`	f77	all variable names undefined by default
`-u`<*name*>	ld	tabulate <*name*> as an undefined symbol
`-w`	f77	suppress compiler warning messages
`-x`	ld	keep only external symbols in symbol table
`-z`	cc2	check stack overflow at subroutine entry points
`-C`	f77	include subscript bound check in code
`-D`<*name*>	cpp	define <*name*> to C preprocessor, like `#define`
`-E`	cpp	run C macro preprocessor only, to standard output
`-E`<*name*>	f77	<*name*> is a string of EFL options
`-F`	f77	produce `*.f` files from `*.r`, don't compile
`-I`<*name*>	cc1	look for `#include` files in <*name*> before default
`-L`<*name*>	ld	before `-l`: search directory <*name*> before default
`-O`	cc2	optimize object code
`-P`	cc1	run C macro preprocessor, produce `*.i` files
`-R`<*name*>	f77	<*name*> is a string of **ratfor** options
`-S`	cc2	produce assembler language output in files `*.s`
`-U`<*name*>	cpp	remove any initial definition of <*name*> (see `-D`)
`-V`	ld	identify version of loader in use
`-W`<*p*>,<*a*>	cc2	pass argument <*a*> to processing phase <*p*>
`-`	as	all undefined symbols are taken as global

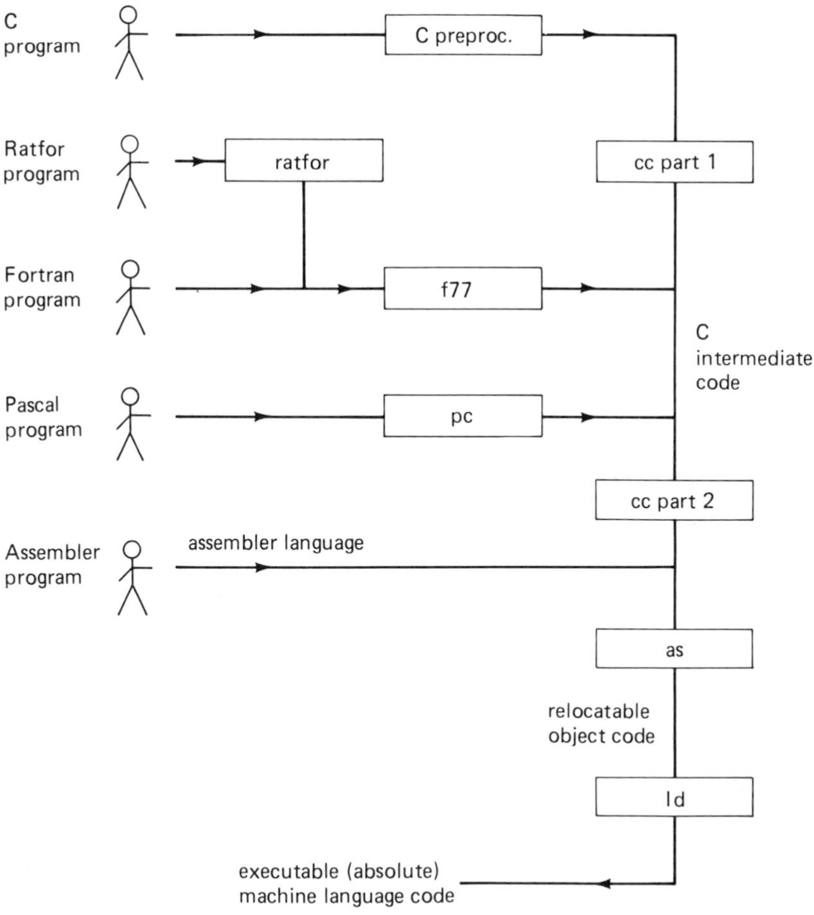

FIGURE 9.1. Processing path from programmer to machine language, for the commonly supplied languages under Unix.

the sequence is thus **f77**–second phase of **cc–as–ld**. The entire process structure is shown diagrammatically in Figure 9.1.

Additional high-level languages can be added to such a structure with no more than moderate effort; it suffices to devise a translator to convert the new language into C intermediate code. Since C intermediate code is not machine dependent, this translator will not be machine dependent either. New languages can thus become available on all hardware implementations almost at once.

The Process Option Hierarchy

Because options are passed downstream, most option names are unique in the entire suite of compiling, assembling, and linking programs. Both capital and lowercase letters must be used to accommodate the whole range of 30-40 options. Where simultaneous use of two options does not seem to make sense, option letters are occasionally duplicated. There is even an option **-W** for passing options on to specified downstream processes, should it ever be necessary to override the natural sequence.

A comprehensive table of options applicable to the Fortran 77 and C compilers, the assembler, and the loader appears below. In the table, the various options are shown along with the processes that recognize them; *cpp* is the C preprocessor, *cc1* and *cc2* denote the first and second phases of the C compiler. The table is as nearly complete as differences between system versions permit. The locally available manuals should be consulted for the finer details, should they ever be required.

Program Archives

Although the Unix file structure permits large numbers of files to be marshalled conveniently, there is still a need for grouping together archives (also called *libraries*) of subroutines. A typical high-level language program may use several hundred system-provided routines such as mathematical functions, input-output services, and data conversions. Many of these are quite short, but each one must take up at least one block of file space (512 or 1024 bytes) when stored in individual files. Furthermore, searching for so many separate files would slow operation considerably even if file space and directory clutter were not a consideration. The Unix system therefore allows so-called library files to be built. These contain internal directories which can be searched for the required routines.

Certain libraries exist in permanent form on every Unix system. But users may also build private libraries of frequently used functions. Libraries are maintained by the **ar** (archivist) program. It permits insertion, extraction, and moving of individual modules within a library or between a library and other files. It also permits cataloguing libraries.

When loading programs, some system-provided libraries are automatically included (e.g., Fortran mathematical routines). Others, including all user-created libraries, must be explicitly named to the loader. Apart from this fact, there is no distinction between system-provided and user-created libraries.

Berkeley Pascal

Of the several Pascal compilers now available under the Unix operating system, Berkeley Pascal is probably the most widely used. Initially built during 1976-1978 and subsequently maintained at the University of California, Berkeley, it is mature, well debugged software. The Berkeley Pascal subsystem includes both an interpreter and a compiler, an advantage for serious program development.

Structure of the Pascal System

The whole Berkeley Pascal system contains the six main commands **pi**, **px**, **pix**, **pc**, **pxp**, and **pxref**, as well as a few minor ones.

pi is a translator which converts the Pascal source code into an interpretive (intermediate) code; **px** is an executive program which reads the intermediate code and interprets it. In other words, **px** translates the intermediate code commands into binary machine instructions, one command at a time, and executes them immediately. **pix** is essentially a pipeline comprising **pi** and **px**.

The **pc** compiler can be used to produce executable modules, or it may be employed to create assembler language programs. These can be linked with other programs, possibly originating from other languages. Normally, **pc** expects to work on complete Pascal programs. However, incremental compilation is also possible.

pxp and **pxref** are utilities for supporting Pascal program development. **pxp** is an execution profiler which monitors the execution of a program and shows how many times each statement was executed. It can also be used to reformat Pascal source programs into readable form. **pxref** is a symbol cross-reference generator, useful in tracing variable names in large programs.

The Berkeley Pascal system introduces a few conventions of its own. File names ending in `.p` are taken to be Pascal source files. The file name `obj` is reserved for interpreter output and the name **a.out** for executable code.

Interpreted Pascal

The simplest way of running the Berkeley system is through the interpreter pipeline. If file `source.p` contains a Pascal program, then

```
$ pix source.p
```

causes the source program to be translated into intermediate code by **pi**, then to be interpreted by **px**. The next screen response should therefore be whatever output the program `source.p` may produce. Alternatively, the user may wish to do the job in two steps; the sequence is then

```
$ pi source.p
$ px obj
```

since **pix** subsumes both **pi** and **px**. The interpreter **pi** places its output into file obj by default. Of course, it is possible to move this file to a different name, in which case the new name would have to be substituted for obj in the **px** instruction. The two-step procedure is useful for development of large programs, where there is not much point in retranslating sections already known to work.

Code produced by **pi** may be stored in files and executed by **px** at a later time. To the user, files produced by **pi** appear to be executable. In keeping with the usual Unix shell conventions, the file obj can therefore be executed either by the command **px obj** or by **obj**. Furthermore, in the absence of any file name **px** assumes that obj is the desired file, so that simply typing **px** will have the same effect. **pi** is convenient and easy to use, but it may place some restriction on program size since everything has to be in memory at once. The limitation is not severe; even on small computer systems, about 1000–2000 lines of source code can be handled.

The interpretive Pascal subsystem consisting of **pi** and **px** provides for options in a style consistent with the Unix shell, so the command may be followed by a minus sign, a string of option letters as appropriate, and the file or files to be operated on. The available options are

-b<*n*>	set output buffer to <*n*> blocks (output buffer = one line)
-i	list include files in full (include statements only)
-l	source program listing to be generated (no listing)
-p	postmortem error backtrace and dump omitted (trace is done)
-s	standard Pascal language check (no checking is done)
-t	subrange bound testing is suppressed (tests are performed)
-w	warning diagnostics are suppressed (warnings are issued)
-z	profile counters are set up for later **pxp** run (no counters)

All the options (except for **b**) are toggles; they reverse whatever their previous settings may have been. The values given in parentheses are those assumed by default, to be reversed if desired. Options may also be invoked in the program itself, by including in the program text a special comment line. However, when used in a program, the options no longer act as toggles; they must be assigned firm ON or OFF values. Ordinary comments may follow in the same comment brackets, permitting the user to retrace his program logic at a later date. For example,

```
{$s+ Standard Pascal checking turned on here}
. . . . . . .
{$s Standard Pascal checking turned off here}
```

The **-l**, **-s**, **-t**, **-w** options are probably self-explanatory. A few brief comments on the others may be in order.

Berkeley Pascal permits sections of program text to be included via `include` statements, somewhat in the manner of C. The statement

```
#include filename.i;
```

will be replaced at translation time by the text contained in `filename.i`. The included files must have names ending in `.i`. They are not normally fully listed in the program listings; only the `#include` statement will be shown. The **-i** option causes them to be printed instead of the `#include`, if requested.

Since the interpreter is most useful for program development, an error backtrace (also called a *postmortem dump*) facility is provided. It counts the number of statements executed, indeed limits it, thereby preventing infinite loops. It also clocks the execution time and to some extent identifies runtime errors. If no backtracing is desired, it can be turned off with the **-p** option.

The **-z** option may be employed to turn on counters that subsequently allow execution profiles to be produced by **pxp**.

Ordinarily, Pascal output is buffered by print lines; that is, output characters are saved up until an end of line is encountered. The buffer size can be changed by the **-b** option to be larger or for the output to be unbuffered; it is unlikely that any but expert users will need to make much use of this facility.

Compiled Pascal

The **pc** compiler produces executable object code or, if preferred, assembler language code. It is thus possible to link Berkeley Pascal programs with programs originating in other languages at the assembler level. Program loading and execution follow the procedures as given above for C and Fortran 77, with a few differences that arise from the idiosyncrasies of Pascal language structure. The procedures involved are similar to those of Fortran 77, with **pc** instead of **f77** feeding the second pass of the C compiler (*cc2* in the above).

The **pc** compiler is primarily intended for use where programs have been more or less thoroughly debugged with **pi**. Hence, the options available are aimed at yielding good quality object code first, only secondly at providing debugging information. Fewer facilities are provided in **pc** than **pi** for finding programming errors.

The set of options provided with **pc** is wider than with **pi**. The options, with default values in parentheses, are

-b<*n*>	output buffer <*n*> blocks (buffer = one line)	*pi*
-c	compile partial program (full program expected)	

-C	subrange bound test (no tests are performed)	
-g	log debugger information (none logged)	
-i	list all include files (include statements only)	*pi*
-l	source program listing generated (no listing)	*pi*
-o<*name*>	output file name to be <*name*> (**a.out** is used)	*ld*
-O	object code optimizer to be used (not used)	*cc2*
-p	profiling counters for **prof** (none generated)	*cc2*
-s	standard Pascal check (no checking is done)	*pi*
-S	assembly language output (object code is produced)	*cc2*
-w	warning diagnostics (warnings are issued)	*pi*
-z	profile counters for later **pxp** run (no counters)	*pi*

Options marked *pi* are identical in effect to the corresponding options available with **pi**; they will not be discussed further. Those marked *cc2* or *ld* are passed downstream and therefore have the same effect as with the C compiler **cc** or the loader **ld**.

The subrange bound test option **-C** is similar to that provided by **pi**, except that the default is set the other way around: unless the user asks for it, no checking is done. This reversal will be seen to be consistent with the general approach of **pc**: good object code comes first, debugging second. The **-g** option provides for logging the information required by the Unix symbolic debugger.

It is possible to compile parts of programs (e.g., individual procedures or functions) separately and to use the resulting relocatable object code later. The **-c** option informs **pc** that a partial compilation is intended. Because Pascal allows considerable flexibility in creating data types, partial compilation is not as easy to arrange as in Fortran; similar data types must be similarly defined across the boundaries of separately compiled files. This problem is resolved in Berkeley Pascal by use of included files containing the necessary definitions. For details of partial compilation, the Berkeley Pascal manuals should be consulted.

Error Flagging

The interpreter **pi** and the compiler **pc** flag source code errors by drawing a line across the source program listing, with a label showing the error type and (where appropriate) an arrow to show the error location. For example, a missing *do* in a *for–do* loop is flagged by displaying

```
    37        for i := 1 to n begin
e --------------------------^----- Inserted keyword do
```

meaning: in source line 37, there exists a nonfatal error, which **pi** has attempted to cure by inserting the missing do. The label at the left of the ruled line identifies the error as one **pi** was able to correct well enough to allow execution. There are three categories of error flaggings: warnings w, nonfatal errors e, and fatal errors E. Warnings may be suppressed if there are many fatal errors in a program, on the reasonable supposition that many major errors are unlikely to be cured in one attempt. In any case, quite a few warnings may arise through secondary effects of major program errors, then just as commonly disappear by themselves when the errors are cured.

The error messages issued by Berkeley Pascal generally take the form of nearly-English text, so that no book of error codes is required to decipher them. However, clear messages are not necessarily correct messages. All that **pi** can tell with certainty is that something has gone wrong; its guess as to what may well be incorrect. In the above simple example, **pi** assumed that do should precede `begin`; it could not correctly guess that the user, in a moment of absentmindedness, had typed in the word *begin* when he really meant *do*. The incorrect guess will presumably manifest itself much later in the program as the absence of an end to match the `begin`!

Execution Profiling

The **pxp** execution profiler lists the Pascal program specified in the command and shows how many times each statement was executed. Such operation counts are useful in at least two important ways. First, program segments with zero execution count clearly have not been tested at all, suggesting that the test data should be altered or that program logic needs checking. Secondly, execution counts permit the programmer to identify those (usually few) segments of the program which account for the biggest part of execution time. Those, and few if any others, deserve to be reexamined with a view to code optimization. The profiling options available with **pxp** are

`-a`	all routines to be included in the profile (omit if unused)
`-t`	tabulate procedure and function calls (no table given)
`-z`	profile named included files, or all (no profile at all)

Note that if neither the **-t** nor the **-z** option is specified (i.e., neither a detailed profile nor a table is asked for), no profiles will be given; all that results is a listing of the program text.

Profiles produced by **pxp** include only those routines which were actually executed, but with the **-a** ("all") option **pxp** will also list those included in the program file but not run. The execution count for the latter will naturally be zero. However, it is often useful to have them included in printout. Profiling can be made selective by requesting the **-z** option, which permits a number of `.i` files to be named; only the named files will then be profiled. If no `.i` file names are given, the **-z** option is understood to ask for everything to be profiled. The **-t** option requests a summarizing table of procedure and function calls.

Program Tidying

When **pxp** is run without requesting any profile information, it will produce a program listing only. Pleasing and readable output is obtained by guiding **pxp** through its various options. These are

`-d`	suppress listing of declarations (all source text listed)
`-e`	substitute text for include statements (statements only)
`-f`	full parentheses for mathematics (minimal parentheses)
`-j`	left justify everything (nested blocks indented 4 spaces)
`-s`	strip comments in listing (comments are fully listed)
`-_`	underline keywords in listing (keywords are listed plain)
-<*n*>	indent nestings <*n*> spaces (default value is 4 spaces)

In producing listings, Berkeley Pascal works in lower case, except for any literally included text (e.g., text to be printed out). Keywords are thus reduced to lower case, as are variable names.

The various options are probably self-explanatory, except perhaps for **-f**. When analyzing mathematical expressions, **pxp** normally reduces parentheses to the fewest possible by exploiting the rules of operator precedence. Under the **-f** option, enough additional parentheses are included to enforce the correct order of computation even if the precedence rules of operators are ignored.

Listings produced by **pxp** contain date and time in the header. It should be noted that these do not show the time when the listing was produced, but constitute a version date stamp of the program. In other words, they show the time of most recent modification of the program file.

Basic

Unix systems support a variety of interpreted as well as compiled languages, with **bas**, a dialect of Basic, included as part of the Version 7 release. Basic is a simple, interpreted, programming language whose major advantage is immediate execution; every statement can be executed, and its results can be known, on the spot. Like standard Basic, **bas** is not generally well suited to ''serious'' computation where Fortran, Pascal, and C have a strong edge. But it serves very well for occasional calculations, in the role of a superpowerful desk calculator. Because it is assumed that Basic will normally be used only in a desk calculator role, **bas** lacks refinements that some other versions of Basic possess.

Only a very brief description is given here, intended to highlight the major features of **bas**; it is assumed that the reader is familiar with Basic itself.

Expressions, Names, and Statements

As might be expected, **bas** works in lower case. Otherwise its statements resemble those of standard Basic. Variable names in **bas** may be of any length and composed of a letter followed by letters and numbers. Although long names are permitted, only the first four characters are actually used. Hence, *voltage* and *volts* would both be considered identical to *volt*. Numeric values may be written in any of the notations acceptable to the **f77** compiler.

Expressions are formed by combining operators, names, and numeric values. The admissible operators are the usual arithmetic and relational ones, as well as the logical operators & (and) and | (or). Precedence rules for operations follow those of standard Basic and precedence may be forced by parentheses.

A statement may consist of a single expression which may (but need not) include an assignment operator. A statement consisting of an expression without any assignment operator (i.e., lacking an equal sign anywhere) is evaluated and the result is immediately displayed, making **bas** useful as a high-powered desk calculator. Most standard Basic statements are acceptable to **bas**.

A statement in **bas** may be prefixed by a line number, as is usual in Basic. Lines prefixed by numbers are stored in order of line numbers and are only executed in response to the `run` statement. The internal (numbered) statements may be examined with the `list` statement.

Running **bas**

When **bas** is invoked, a file name may be passed to it as an optional argument. This file will be read as input; when the file is exhausted, input is taken from the keyboard. One possible use of this arrangement is to load filed programs for execution with the `run` statement, but other uses—for example, automatic partial execution of some calculation—can be devised. No other options are provided with **bas**.

Internal statements in **bas** can be edited using the **ed** editor, which can be reached by way of the `edit` statement in **bas**. This statement reaches out of **bas** to the shell and requests the **ed** editor to be run. The file edited is always the file named in the **bas** command to the shell. In other words, if **bas** was set running with the command

```
$ bas progrm
```

then **ed** will edit the file `progrm`; there is no choice. Editing and debugging are thus possible with the full power of **ed**, without any separate editor to go with **bas**. The internal statements may be listed any time with the `list` statement and may be written to a file with the `save` statement. Both `list` and `save` permit one, two, or no arguments, so they may be issued in any of the three forms

```
list
list 20
list 20 40
```

In the first form, the entire file of internal statements is listed; in the second, only statement 20; in the third, all statements from 20 to 40 inclusive. The `save` statement works in the same way. If **bas** was invoked giving a file name, internal statements are saved in the named file; if no file name was given, they are saved in file `b.out`.

The mechanism provided in **bas** for reading external data is through a built-in function called `expr()`. Whenever this function is employed, it reads one line from the input and evaluates it as an expression. In other words, the statement

```
answ = data * expr()
```

will cause an expression (including simply a number) to be read from the input and to be used as if it had been written into the statement itself.

Assembler Language Programming

Assembler language has long been the traditional choice for operating systems programming. Since assembler language addresses machine registers directly, it gives the programmer absolute control over exactly what action will be taken and how. The number of operations to accomplish any particular task can therefore be minimized. For exactly the same reasons, assembler language programs are totally machine dependent and cannot be moved from one computer to another.

Assemblers under Unix

Within the Unix family of operating systems, the C language has largely replaced assembler language. Little can be done in assembler language that cannot be done in C, though that little is very important. A residual need for programming at the machine level will therefore always remain.

Since C does nearly everything necessary for system programming, no elaborate macro assemblers are needed under any operating system that supports C. Every different computer type of course requires a wholly new assembler. Most assemblers used with the Unix system are simple, often lacking capabilities for macros or symbol equivalences. The reason is inherent in the general design philosophy of Unix: nothing should ever be done in machine-dependent programs if the same task can be accomplished in a machine-independent fashion. In other words, a simple, straightforward assembler suitable for writing small programs ought to suffice because small machine language programs are the only kind that should ever be written!

Chapter 10

A Selected Command Set

Any command in the Unix system is merely the name of a program; in response to the command, the shell causes the correspondingly named program to be executed. Commands are therefore as fluid as programs resident in the system. Strictly speaking, it is no more possible to catalogue the available commands than to give a list of all programs. However, a set of standard programs always forms part of every Unix system release. These can be listed, and indeed the system manuals do so in full detail. What follows in this chapter is a selection from that rather daunting list, augmented by a few others found on many Unix systems but not "official" in the sense that they are not provided by AT&T Technologies (or Western Electric before them) as part of their system releases.

Definitions of Commands

For the novice user, and even for many practiced users who are not primarily system programmers, the multiple volumes of system documentation are heavy going at best. Although well enough written and nicely laid out, manuals often tell much more, and in much greater detail, than most users really want to know. Besides, the very volume of those encyclopedic tomes prevents ready reference. The System V basic documentation is well over four inches thick in its typeset form as published, and it consumes the better part of a box of paper when it is produced on the line printer. A full System V, Xenix, or 4.2 BSD are even more voluminous than that. When maintenance and installation instructions are included, the quantity of paper grows further; even small systems for personal computers are delivered with what looks like the Greater London telephone directory. The following brief summary of the major system-provided commands is therefore not intended to compete with the definitive system documentation, but rather to make it easier to consult as a quick reference.

The various commands are listed here in alphabetical order. A brief description of its action is given for each, as well as a summary of the command syntax and of the major options and qualifiers available. The lists of options are not complete in most cases, and many of the subtleties are omitted. A reference is also given in each case to the chapter of this book in which the most complete discussion of the command will be found. Only the chapter containing the fullest discussion is shown; further references will be found in the Index.

The several Unix system releases are not uniform in their command syntax, nor in the selection of commands provided. In the following an effort has been made to find the common elements in the various system versions, but this obviously cannot always be done; often enough, the command descriptions note differences. About ninety commands are listed here, less than half of what is listed in the Seventh Edition of the *Unix Programmer's Manual* and much less than half the command repertoire for either System V or 4.2 BSD. For a full description of each command, the user should of course turn to the system manuals; the object here is to present enough material to satisfy most users most of the time.

A Selection of Commands

Commands are listed in alphabetical order in the following. In the descriptions, optional items are always enclosed in square brackets, for example [*item*]. Items thus shown may be included in a command line or omitted. Items not enclosed in square brackets are mandatory. The ellipsis . . . means that the immediately preceding item may be repeated as many times as desired. For example,

cat [*option*] <*file*> . . .

indicates that the command verb **cat** may be followed (optionally) by some option qualifier; it must be followed by at least one file name <*file*> or several file names.

Words in angle brackets are generic identifiers, i.e., names of particular kinds of entities. Thus, <*file*> means a file name, <*user*> means a user login name, and so on. The most frequently occurring identifiers are probably *<file>* and *<directory>*.

ar

Function: Maintains archives and libraries.
Syntax: ar *<option>* [*<oldfile>*] *<archive>* *<file>* . . .
Usage: The archivist is used to insert, remove, or replace files in libraries. Its major use is to update libraries used by the linker in making up executable program modules. One of the characters **dmpqrtx**, preceded by a minus sign and possibly followed by one or more of **abciluv**, constitutes *<option>*; *<archive>* is the archive file, and *<file>* is the name(s) of the constituent file(s). Replacements or additions may be specified to occur either before or after the constituent file *<oldfile>*; if unspecified, they are placed at the end of the archive. The initial characters in *<option>* are

`d`	deletes named files from the archive
`m`	moves named files to the end of the archive
`p`	prints the named files as they are in the archive
`q`	(quick) appends to end of archive without checking position
`r`	replaces the named files by new ones, allows repositioning
`t`	tabulates (lists) constituents of the archive
`x`	extracts named files from the archive

The most important second characters, following those above, are

`a`	put *<file>* in archive after item *<oldfile>*
`b`	put *<file>* in archive before item *<oldfile>*
`l`	local directory (most archives are in directory `/temp`)
`u`	update (with `r`) replace only files newer than existing ones
`v`	verbose (i.e., with complete reporting of actions)

In older system versions no minus sign is required with <option>.
More in: Languages and Compilers (Chapter 9)

as

Function: Assembler, details dependent on computer.
Syntax: as [*options*] *<file>*
Usage: as assembles programs and produces object code executable after

loading with the loader **ld**. For obvious reasons, every type of computer requires a different assembler so a large variety of assemblers exists under Unix. Almost all accept one option:

`-o objfile` output goes to file `objfile`, not `a.out`

The other common option is `-m`, which invokes the **m4** macro preprocessor (part of many Unix systems). **as** and similar assemblers are intended to follow the C compiler. Few assemblers running under Unix are ambitious in macro processing and related facilities—after all, what the C compiler does not produce the assembler need not assemble. If any assembler language coding is really necessary (which rarely happens), the full system manuals should be read with care.
More in: Languages and Compilers (Chapter 9)

at

Function: Executes command file at a given time.
Syntax: at *<time>* [*<day>*] [*<file>*]
Usage: At or after the specified time, **at** reads the standard input and executes its contents as a shell script. (In some Unix versions a file name may be specified as the last element in the command). Time may be given in the 24-hour notation in all Unix systems, but many accept other reasonable formats, e.g., 8am, 7:30pm. The day, if included, can be given as a day of the week (sun, mon,. . ., sat) or as a date (Jun 12). Systems differ slightly on permissible date formats. Exactly when the file is executed depends on the frequency with which the local system checks its clock for such processes; delays of minutes are not uncommon. **at** uses the timekeeping arrangements of **cron**, so **at** processes are available to users with access to `crontab`.
More in: Facilities and Utilities (Chapter 6)

bas

Function: A Basic language interpreter.
Syntax: bas [*<file>*]
Usage: A dialect of Basic is interpreted. If the optional file name is given in the command, this file is read as input before the terminal keyboard. The dialect has some peculiarities which fit neatly into the general Unix framework. In part, they result from the view that there exist much better, and better integrated, languages than Basic for writing programs, but Basic will be employed by many users as a sort of powerful desk calculator.

More in: Languages and Compilers (Chapter 9)

cancel

Function: Cancels a waiting or running print job.
Syntax: cancel [<*request number*>] [<*printer*>]
Usage: A print job is removed from the print queue. Every printing request is assigned a number by **lp**; it may be cancelled by that number. Naming a printer cancels the job currently being printed on that printer. Either a request number or a printer designation must be given; the command without any arguments means nothing.
More in: Facilities and Utilities (Chapter 6)

cat

Function: Concatenates, then displays, files.
Syntax: cat <*file*> . . .
Usage: One or more files are joined end-to-end and fed into the standard output stream. If the output is sent to a file, as with `cat file1 file2 > file3`, then the destination file is cleared out first. Thus, the command `cat file1 file2 > file1` destroys `file1`, thereafter copies `file2` into a new file called `file1`. Caution is necessary: the file destruction really is performed first, so that the erstwhile content of `file1` is simply lost in this case. If no file names are given in the command, the standard input and output files are used.
More in: Facilities and Utilities (Chapter 6)

cc

Function: C language compiler, followed by loader.
Syntax: cc [*option*] . . . <*file*> . . .
Usage: Programs in the C language are compiled and loaded for execution. Valid options include all loader **ld** options except `-D`, and a number of options belonging to **cc** proper. The most important among the latter are

`-c` compile and assemble only (produce object file), do not load
`-S` compile only, leave assembler text in `.s` file

The files to be compiled should have their names end with `.c` if compilation is needed; assembler language files may also be included, provided their names end in `.s`. If loading is suppressed, output files with similar names but ending in `.o` are produced. If suffixes are not used, an output file name can be specified via the loader `-o` option; if none is specified, the resulting executable module is placed in file **a.out**.

Numerous other options are listed in the relevant chapter of this book. Caution: upper as well as lower case are used in the options, with different meanings.

More in: Languages and Compilers (Chapter 9)

cd

Function: Changes the working directory.

Syntax: cd [<*directory*>]

Usage: The current directory is abandoned and <*directory*> is made the current directory, provided of course it exists and provided the user has execute (i.e., search) permission for it. If no directory is specified, the login directory of the user is understood by default.

More in: Files in the Unix System (Chapter 3)

chmod

Function: Change file access permissions.

Syntax: chmod <*permission*> <*file*> . . .

Usage: Permissions are granted to read, write, or execute (r, w, or x), to the user who owns a file, the group to which its owner belongs, or others (u, g, or o). The <*permission*> can be specified in the command in two ways. It can be set absolutely, by choosing an appropriate combination of the following numbers and adding:

	user	group	other
read	0400	0040	0004
write	0200	0020	0002
execute	0100	0010	0001

For example, `chmod 0710 secret` permits the program **secret** to be openly accessed by the owner, to be executed but not read by members of the group, and not to be accessed at all by the general public.

Alternatively, <*permission*> in the command may be given symbolically, in the form <*who*> <*opr*> <*permit*> where <*who*> identifies the users (one or more of u, g, o; a may be substituted for ugo); <*opr*> is the operation to be performed (+, - or =), and <*permit*> is any combination of the permissions r, w, x. **chmod** examines the symbolic argument string and does the computation indicated above. The symbol `+` means that the new permissions are added to what is already there, `-` indicates removal, `=` requests replacement of what is already there. Note that addition and subtraction refer to permissions, not purely arithmetic operations; adding a permission where it already exists produces nothing new. For example, if after execution of `chmod 0710 secret` another **chmod** command is issued with the argument string shown below, the following results could be obtained:

`ug+r` produces 0750 (permission 0040 added)
`ug-r` produces 0310 (permission 0400 removed)
`ug=r` produces 0440 (0400 and 0040 replace everything)

Several permission changes can be placed in the same command line, separated by commas but without intervening blanks, as in `u=rwx,g=x` to produce 0710.
More in: Facilities and Utilities (Chapter 6)

cmp

Function: Compares two files.
Syntax: cmp [*option*] *<file1>* *<file2>*
Usage: The differences between files are noted, by displaying the byte and line numbers where the differences occur. If the files are identical, no action is taken. Two mutually exclusive options may be used:

`-l` show decimal byte number, and differing bytes
`-s` show nothing, return exit codes only

Exit codes: 0 means identical, 1 means different, 2 says there were some errors in the files.
More in: Facilities and Utilities (Chapter 6)

comm

Function: Finds and outputs common lines in two files.
Syntax: comm [*option*] *<file1>* *<file2>*
Usage: The two files, which should first have been ordered in ASCII sequence (e.g., by **sort**), are read and the lines in them sorted into three columns: (1) those occurring only in *<file1>*, (2) those only in *<file2>*, and (3) in both files. The option may be given as any combination of the

digits 1, 2, 3, preceded by a minus sign; each digit suppresses the corresponding column in the output. Two input files must always be specified; a minus sign instead of a file name means the standard input file.
More in: Facilities and Utilities (Chapter 6)

cp

Function: Copies a file.
Usage: cp *<file1>* *<file2>*
cp *<file>* . . . *<directory>*
Usage: In the first form, **cp** makes a copy of *<file1>* and calls it *<file2>*. In the second form, it copies one or more files into the specified directory, with their file names as they are. A file cannot be copied onto itself.
More in: Facilities and Utilities (Chapter 6)

csh

Function: Command shell with C-like syntax.
Syntax: csh [*options*]
Usage: csh is alternative to the Bourne shell. It takes more time to get started but runs a little faster because data tables are kept in a rapidly accessible format. **csh** starts by executing the shell commands in file .cshrc; if it is a login shell it starts up by executing file .login as a shell script and exits by executing .logout. About a dozen options are provided but not often used because everything the options can do can also be done by shell commands in .cshrc or by commands issued to **csh** once it has started.
More in: Unix Command Shells (Chapter 4)

cu

Function: Remote Unix calling and connection program.
Syntax: cu [*options*] *<destination>*
Usage: cu provides communication (calling up and logging in) to a remote Unix system. It manages an interactive conversation, with the remote system visible to the user and **cu** transparent most of the time. The main options are

-e	communicates with even parity (default: no parity)
-h	emulates half-duplex terminal if remote expects that

`-o`	communicates with odd parity
`-s`*<speed>*	communicates at *<speed>* baud if that speed is available

The *<destination>* may be a telephone number (for dial-out modems), a direct line name (for hard-wired lines), or a system name, or `-l` followed by a special file name. (Not all systems support all these.) Telephone numbers must consist of numbers only, except for equal signs = to signify waiting for a dial tone, or minus sign - to wait a few seconds.

The **cu** program transmits all keyboard conversation to the remote machine except for any line beginning with a tilde ~ character. These are interpreted as commands to **cu**:

`~.`	terminate the conversation, shut down cu
`~!`	launch a new local shell, have it listen
`~!` *<comm>*	have a new shell execute *<comm>*
`~%take` *<rem>* [*<loc>*]	copy remote file *<rem>* to local file *<loc>*
`~%put` *<loc>* [*<rem>*]	copy local file *<loc>* to remote file *<rem>*

If the target file is not named, the same file name is used, prefixed by the appropriate working directory name.
More in: Facilities and Utilities (Chapter 6)

date

Function: Displays current date and clock time.
Syntax: date
Usage: If its output is redirected to a file, this command records the time and therefore can be useful for determining when some particular event happened. The kernel uses the system clock for a great many things, from timed processes to file date stamping. It is therefore important to persuade the system manager (if persuasion is needed!) to keep accurate time. Managers please note: different Unix versions accept input times and dates in different formats (e.g., year first or last, seconds included or not).
More in: Facilities and Utilities (Chapter 6)

diction

Function: Improves phrase usage in writing.
Syntax: diction [*options*] *<filename>*
Usage: diction is a stylistic improver of writing. It looks for bad things in a text file, using a list of other people's vices. Options are of two sorts. The first kind specifies how macro definitions, long lists, and **troff** com-

mands are dealt with; most people needn't worry. The second kind is important:

`-n` suppresses the standard file of nasty vices
`-f`*<file>* uses the user-provided *<file>* of things that need attention, in addition to (or instead of) the standard file

The options are a little nonstandard, each must carry its own minus sign. Users probably will wish to tailor the system-provided phrase blacklist to their own favorite mistakes.
More in: Text Preparation and Processing (Chapter 8)

df

Function: Shows amount of free disk space.
Syntax: df [*<filesystem>* . . .]
Usage: The amount of unused disk space remaining on the specified file systems is shown. If no file system is named, free space on all the accessible and mounted systems is displayed. For most users, **df** is handy to determine the remaining space on small external media such as floppy disks. Caution: some systems report the number of 512-byte slices, some the number of kilobytes.
More in: Facilities and Utilities (Chapter 6)

diff

Function: Finds the differences between two files.
Syntax: diff [*options*] *<file1>* *<file2>*
Usage: The two files are compared on a line by line basis. Differences between the two files are listed in such a form as to exhibit how *<file1>* can be made into *<file2>*. The available options are characters, preceded by the usual minus sign:

`-b` ignore trailing blanks in lines being compared
`-e` produce **ed** script
`-f` produce backward **ed** script
`-h` hurried job, compare only a few neighboring lines

The `-e` option is truly useful: it can be used to keep a whole trail of file versions very compactly. One need only store the root file, plus a set of successive **ed** scripts that will change one to the next. The reverse script

unfortunately can only be read by eye; **ed** does not know how to operate backwards.
More in: Facilities and Utilities (Chapter 6)

du

Function: Shows the amount of disk space used.
Syntax: du [*option*] [<*directory*> . . .]
Usage: The amount of file space tied up by all files listed in <*directory*> and its subdirectories is determined. If no directory name is given, the current directory is assumed. Without options, all subdirectory names are listed and totals for subdirectories are shown. There are two options:

`-a` all file sizes (not just subdirectories) are listed
`-s` summary only: no names are listed, only the grand total

Only one option character may be given, preceded by a minus. For historical reasons, the disk space is usually listed in units of 512 bytes, which equal disk blocks in older systems (e.g., Seventh Edition) and half-blocks in more recent ones (System V and its derivatives). Some systems, however, report kilobytes.
More in: Facilities and Utilities (Chapter 6)

echo

Function: Echoes arguments
Syntax: echo [`-n`] *arguments*
Usage: echo displays exactly what arguments the shell will employ, wherever argument strings get complicated. It is particularly handy where wildcard constructions are used, since these are fully expanded; also in checking aliases and macros. The `-n` option, available in most systems based on Version 7, suppresses the newline character normally appended to the output of **echo.**
More in: Unix Command Shells (Chapter 4)

ed

Function: The standard Unix text editor.
Syntax: ed [–] [<*file*>]
Usage: All the usual program preparation, documentation, and text prep-

aration functions are provided in **ed**, except immediate screen display. The - (minus sign) option suppresses character counts. If *<file>* is given in the command line, the relevant file is read in for editing; otherwise, **ed** begins with an empty editing buffer. There are many commands in **ed**, with various options and variants; in point of fact, **ed** is an interactive subsystem within the Unix operating system.
More in: Editing with **vi** and **ed** (Chapter 7)

eqn

Function: Mathematical preprocessor for **troff**.
Syntax: eqn
Usage: eqn accepts quasi-verbal descriptions of equations or formulae and turns them into **troff** request sequences. Closely related to **neqn** (intended to work with **nroff**) but much cleverer, it is normally used in a pipeline with output taken directly to **troff**.
More in: Text Preparation and Processing (Chapter 8)

ex

Function: Interactive editor.
Syntax: ex [*options*] [*<file>* . . .]
Usage: This editor is related to **ed** but much more comprehensive because it includes both line-oriented and screen editing. Most **ed** facilities are duplicated by **ex**; **vi** is a subset of this editing system. Options include

`-`	silent, all interactive prompts and feedback suppressed
`-r`	recovery mode: rescues named files after system or **ex** crash
`-R`	Read-only (file cannot be accidentally overwritten)
`-v`	starts up as **vi** (which is included within **ex**)

One or more files may be named in the command. They will be concatenated as required.
More in: Editing with **vi** and **ed** (Chapter 7)

file

Function: Determines file type.
Syntax: file *<file>* . . .
Usage: A series of tests is performed to try classifying what type *<file>*

is—object, source, or whatever. If it is a text file (i.e., if it only contains valid ASCII characters), **file** tries to determine in what language. It is not always successful in that attempt.
More in: Files in the Unix System (Chapter 3)

find

Function: Finds a file or files of a particular kind.
Syntax: **find** *<directory>* . . . *filespec* . . .
Usage: The directory specified in the command is searched, along with all its subdirectories in their proper hierarchical order. For every file reachable by starting at the specified directory, the Boolean expression *filespec* is evaluated. Over a dozen different forms of file specification are possible; each is given as a logical function preceded by a minus sign, possibly followed by a parameter. The most important functions are

`-atime` *<n>*	all files accessed within the last *<n>* days
`-group` *<group>*	files belonging to a specified user group
`-mtime` *<n>*	all files modified within the last *<n>* days
`-name` *<file>*	specific name(s); * and ? are taken as wild-cards
`-newer` *<file>*	files newer than the file *<file>*
`-print`	outputs the currently examined file pathname
`-type` *<t>*	*<t>* = d or f (directory or plain files)
`-user` *<user>*	specific user; *<user>* may be login name or number

The various kinds of file specification can be combined logically. The logical intersection (AND) is understood if two or more specifications are given in a row; `-o` is taken to mean logical union (OR); the exclamation mark ! means negation. The curious part is that **find** does nothing with the information about files. Output is available with the `-print` function which always evaluates to *true*, but which will only be reached if everything ahead of it in the chain of expressions was true. Thus,

```
$ find /usr -name dict.d -print
```

will print the full name of any file called `dict.d` anywhere in the directory structure that begins with `/usr`. Logical combinations can produce complex searches and can find the desired files even over a very large set of directories.
More in: Files in the Unix System (Chapter 3)

format

Function: Formats floppy disks or other magnetic media.
Syntax: **format** [*options*] [*<device>*]

Usage: Sector and block markers are written onto the magnetic surface. This command is not well standardized; in some Unix systems formatting is done by **mkfs**, while in others the **format** command also makes a file structure. In small systems using floppy disks, the **format** and **mkfs** functions are often separate. Options are in any case dependent on the hardware system.
More in: Files in the Unix System (Chapter 3)

f77

Function: Fortran 77 compiler
Syntax: **f77** [*option*] . . . <*file*> . . .
Usage: The **f77** command compiles Fortran 77 text and, unless prevented by options, pipelines the resulting code to the loader **ld** to produce an executable module. Valid options include: all options accepted by **ld** except `-u`, all options accepted by the second phase of the C compiler, and some applicable to **f77** only. The most important among these are

`-onetrip`	*do*-loops execute at least once (check at end of loop)
`-u`	make all undeclared variables undefined (debugging)
`-w`	suppress all warnings
`-w66`	suppress all warnings about Fortran 66 compatibility
`-C`	subscript-out-of-bounds check done at execution time
`-F`	translate Ratfor to Fortran, do not proceed farther
`-R`<*string*>	pass <*string*> to **ratfor** as option for `*.r` files

f77 expects Fortran text, unless the file name has a suffix that implies otherwise: `.r` for Ratfor, `.c` for C, `.s` for assembler. The `.f` suffix may be used to identify Fortran. Each file is compiled and/or assembled according to its suffix. The loader output is placed in file **a.out**, unless a file name is specified (see **ld** options), or unless files were identified by suffixes; in the latter case, the output is placed in a file by the same name, but with the `.o` suffix.

f77 implements a practically full Fortran 77, with some desirable extensions. Sufficiently legible diagnostics are produced to obviate any need for a book of error codes.
More in: Languages and Compilers (Chapter 9)

grep

Function: Filters input lines, looking for a pattern.
Syntax: **grep** [*options*] <*character string*> <*file*>

Usage: grep reads the specified file, looking for a specific character string in each line. Only one input file name is permitted in the command, but numerous files will be read if the name contains wild-card characters. Without options, the input lines which contain the specified string are copied into the standard output. Options are, as usual, one or more characters preceded by a minus sign:

- `-c` print only the number (count) of lines with matches
- `-l` list (once) every file name in which a match is found
- `-n` number lines with line numbers from input file
- `-v` output all lines where no character strings match

The rules for forming character strings are exactly the same as for the **ed** editor. Class, wild-card, and repetitive constructions are all allowed; most character strings need to be protected with quotes or reverse slants to avoid their being misinterpreted by the shell. **grep** must be one of the least obvious command names; even after finding out that it stands for *Global Regular Expressions Print*, one never remembers.
More in: Facilities and Utilities (Chapter 6)

kill

Function: Halts (aborts) a currently running process.
Syntax: kill *<process>*
Usage: Any currently running process may be halted, by giving its process identification number *<process>* as the argument of this command. The process identification number is shown whenever a background process is set running; alternatively, process identification numbers can be determined by using the **ps** command.
More in: The System Kernel (Chapter 5)

ld

Function: Linking loader.
Syntax: ld [*option*] *<file>* . . .
Usage: This command links together several object programs with any necessary libraries, producing an object module. The object module may be executed, or (if used with the `-r` option) it may be used later as a component in another run of **ld**. The output is left in a file named **a.out** unless a file name is given in the `-o` option.

The files specified may be relocatable object code, or libraries. They are concatenated in the order they are named. If libraries are included, it is important to note that **ld** will search each library exactly once as it proceeds from left to right through the list of files. Only those library programs are loaded which are required by the files listed ahead of the library. Program order within libraries is therefore important: calling programs must precede the programs they call. "Backward" references among library modules are left unresolved.

The loader permits a variety of options, expressed by character strings with a preceding minus sign. The following are the most useful:

`-i` load text and data into separate address spaces
`-o` if a name follows `-o`, it is used as the output file name
`-s` strip debugging aids from object code, to save space

These options are standard between the various breeds of system; others, of which there are many, vary. A detailed list is given as Table 9.3 in Chapter 9, *Languages and Compilers*.

Several language compilers within the Unix system pipe their output to **ld** automatically. In such cases, options can usually be passed through from the compiler command to **ld**.
More in: Languages and Compilers (Chapter 9)

line

Function: Copies one line.
Syntax: line
Usage: One line is copied from standard input to standard output. **line** differs from **cat** in automatically exiting when an end of line occurs. It is used in shell scripts to collect keyboard input.
More in: Unix Command Shells (Chapter 4)

ln

Function: Adds a further directory entry for a file.
Syntax: ln *<file1> <file2>*
Usage: ln creates a directory entry which refers to the ordinary file *<file1>* by the alternative name *<file2>*. File name *<file1>* must follow the normal Unix file conventions; *<file2>* may be a file name, or it may be abbreviated to a directory name only. In the latter case, the full name *<file2>* is understood to be the given directory name, suffixed by the last component of name *<file1>*. In some Unix systems, *<file2>* may be omitted; the

current directory is then understood to be meant. In other systems, both names must appear. The old and new names have equal validity for all further work; there is no "real" or "original" name. **ln** only creates synonymous names for files; it does not create duplicate files. Creation of synonymous names across file systems (i.e., to removable volumes) is forbidden, as is creation of synonymous names for directories.
More in: Files in the Unix System (Chapter 3)

login

Function: Logs in a new user.
Syntax: login [<*user*>]
Usage: A new user can log in without the old user explicitly logging out. If no user name <*user*> is given in the command, the system asks for it. A password is always required to log in, and is asked for unless the user password has been set to blank. System managers often assign blank passwords when authorizing new accounts, to allow new users to choose their own passwords.
More in: Getting Started (Chapter 2)

lp

Function: Line printer spooler.
Syntax: lp [*option*] . . . [<*file*> . . .]
Usage: The files named are queued for printing on the line printer. Options are given by a character string prefixed by a minus sign. The most important option characters are

`-c`	copy the file immediately (any later changes do not print)
`-m`	report by mail when the print job is complete
`-n`<*no*>	print <*no*> copies of the file
`-r`	remove (i.e., delete) the file after placing it in queue
`-w`	write to terminal when printing done (mail if logged off)

The `-r` option, which is not available on many newer systems, removes the file after queueing it for printing, not after printing it. Thus, some time may elapse during which there exists no printed copy as yet, nor a file any longer.
More in: Facilities and Utilities (Chapter 6)

lpr

Function: Line printer spooler.
Syntax: lpr [*option*] . . . [<*file*> . . .]

Usage: This name is a synonym (now archaic) for **lp**; systems based on the Sixth or Seventh Editions may accept **lpr** but not **lp**.
More in: Facilities and Utilities (Chapter 6)

lpstat

Function: Displays the current status of printing requests.
Syntax: lpstat [*options*]
Usage: Where printers are remote, **lpstat** avoids useless trips to see whether a print job has finished yet; in all systems, it reports printing request numbers. (The latter must be known to cancel a print request.) The most useful options are

`-o`[*list*]	status of printers shown in list (all, if no list)
`-s`	summary, showing defaults and available printers
`-u`[*list*]	status of requests belonging to users listed

Items in lists can be separated by commas, or by commas and whitespace if the entire list is in quotes. The list must begin immediately after the option letter. If several options are specified, simple concatenation of letters may not work; for example, `-so` is unambiguous but `-os` is mistaken as an inquiry after printer `s`; `-o -s` always works.
More in: Facilities and Utilities (Chapter 6)

ls

Function: Lists contents of directories.
Syntax: ls [*options*] <*file*> . . .
Usage: Every directory file named in the command has its contents displayed; every nondirectory file named shows information as specified by the options. If no name is given, the current directory is listed. Options may be combined, and must be preceded by a minus sign. The most important ones are

`-a`	list all entries, including names beginning with . (dot)
`-d`	list only the names for directory files, not their contents
`-l`	long form: permissions, number of links, owner, size, etc.
`-r`	list in reverse order (alphabetic, or time if `t` given)
`-s`	give size of files in terms of 512-byte blocks
`-t`	list by last modification time, not alphabetically
`-u`	use time of last access, not modification, with `t` and/or `l`

Under the `-l` option, each file is classified by a character identifier as follows:

b	block special file
c	character special file
d	directory file
p	named pipe (*fifo* special file)
-	ordinary file

The next three characters show read/write/execute permission, for the file owner; the next three, permissions for users in the same group; and the next three, for everybody else. The characters mean

r	read permission granted
w	write permission granted
x	executable (directories: searchable)
s	executable, with SUID set

The s identifier means that the process will be allowed to read and write files as if it were run by the owner of the executable file. It can therefore read and write files for which the process owner does not have read/write permissions. This temporary privilege terminates with the process.
More in: Files in the Unix System (Chapter 3)

mail

Function: Sends mail to others or reads mail.
Syntax: mail [-t] <*user*> . . .
mail [*option*]
Usage: This command has two forms: one for reading mail, the other for sending. To send mail, the addressees <*user*> . . . are named; all subsequent input on the standard input file is considered to be the message, up to the next occurrence of a line containing only a period (. character) or up to the next control-D. The message is prefixed by the sender's name and time of transmission and is left in the addressee's mailbox. The -t option, where available, lists all addressees. Mail thus takes the format of a multiply addressed interoffice memo.

Messages are read, the most recent one first, by **mail** without an addressee's name. As each message is displayed, the user is expected to specify how to dispose of it. (Note: most **mail** systems have no prompt; they simply sit there silently waiting for the user to say something.) Valid user requests are

d	delete this message, go on to the next one
m [<*user*>]	mail the message to <*user*> (default: same user)

p	repeat display of this message
q	quit reading mail, leave unread mail in mailbox
s [<*file*>]	save this message in <*file*> (default: `mbox`)
w [<*file*>]	save message, as with `-s` but without header
x	exit without changing the mailbox file
-	repeat display of previous message
?	give summary of valid responses (* in some systems)
! <*comm*>	execute the shell command <*comm*>, then continue
newline	(RETURN key) go on to next message
EOT	(control-D) quit, same as q

The mail-reading form of this command permits options to be specified:

`-f` <*file*>	read the <*file*> as if it were the mailbox file
`-p`	display mail without pausing for disposal instructions
`-q`	quit mail immediately on an interrupt (DELETE key)
`-r`	examine mail in reverse order, old **mail** first

Options can be concatenated, and must be preceded by a minus sign. While messages are being displayed, the display can be halted with an interruption (DELETE key), which stops the current message only, not the **mail** command.
More in: Facilities and Utilities (Chapter 6)

man

Function: Display or print the Unix Programmer's Manual.
Syntax: man [*option*] [<*chapter*>] <*section*> . . .
Usage: The *Unix Programmer's Manual* is searched for the requested <*section*> or sections. The search is confined to a particular chapter if a chapter number is given; otherwise, the entire manual is searched and all sections with the specified name are output on the standard output file. Options may be specified as a character string preceded by a minus sign. The most useful options are

`-n`	output using **nroff**
`-w`	show pathnames of the manual sections, but display no text

If no options are given, the effect is that of `-n`; either an already formatted text is output, or (if there is no such) **nroff** is used to format it. This command appears in most systems based on the Seventh Edition and in some derived from the Berkeley 4.2 BSD version. How sad that it is usually absent from System V derivatives, which may have a **help** command instead (an insipid, watery substitute for the real manual).
More in: Facilities and Utilities (Chapter 6)

mesg

Function: Blocks incoming messages.
Syntax: mesg [*option*]
Usage: Without option, the present state of the message switch (*yes* or *no*) is reported. To turn off incoming messages ("do not disturb") or to accept them again, the command is used with the option `n` (no) or `y` (yes). Note: no minus signs prefix the options for this command.
More in: Facilities and Utilities (Chapter 6)

mkdir

Function: Makes new directories.
Syntax: mkdir *<directory>* . . .
Usage: New directories are created, provided the user has write permission in the parent directory. Any new directory is set up with read, write, and execute permissions granted as prescribed by the current system defaults and by the user's own `umask` setting (if any). It is up to each user to protect his files differently if he wishes.
More in: Files in the Unix System (Chapter 3)

mkfs

Function: Makes a file structure.
Syntax: /etc/mkfs *<specialfile>* *<prototype>*
Usage: mkfs writes a new file structure (directory tree) onto a magnetic medium. In some Unix systems, it also formats the medium (i.e., writes block and sector markers); in others, formatting is done separately. Either way, making a new file structure irretrievably destroys anything previously on the volume (disk or tape). The device is accessed through its special file *<specialfile>*.

In the simplest form of **mkfs**, *<prototype>* is simply a decimal number which specifies how many blocks of file space the new file structure is to cover. More generally, *<prototype>* is a file containing a string of instructions to define the new file structure. The flexibility provided by this command is enormous; almost any conceivable file characteristic may be specified in *<prototype>*. The destructive power of **mkfs** is also enormous, for it can destroy whole diskfuls of files at a single blow.

In the standard System V Unix, **mkfs** is restricted to the system manager and is located in directory `/etc`. Some other system versions and com-

patible systems have user-accessible, possibly different or restricted, **mkfs** commands.
More in: Files in the Unix System (Chapter 3)

more

Function: Displays one screenful and waits.
Syntax: **more** [+<*line*>] [+/<*pattern*>] <*file*>
Usage: **more** sends contents of <*file*> to the screen, much as **cat** does; but whenever a screenful has been sent, **more** stops and waits. Pressing the space bar on the terminal sends another screenful. Display normally starts at the beginning of the file but may begin at a particular line number as specified by the +<*line*> option. Display may begin at a place where the character pattern <*pattern*> first occurs; if so, display can continue as usual if the space bar is pressed, or restart at the next occurrence of the same pattern if the `n` key is pressed. There are other options; they mostly deal with how lines are counted to determine whether the screen is full.
More in: Facilities and Utilities (Chapter 6)

mount

Function: Mounts a file system.
Syntax: **/etc/mount** <*specialfile*> <*directory*> [`-r`]
Usage: This command connects the file directory of a disk, tape, etc. volume physically mounted on the device addressed through <*specialfile*> to the Unix file system, by attaching the volume root directory as <*directory*>. The latter must previously exist and should be empty. The file volume must have a Unix file structure; if it does not, using **mount** may cause a system crash. If the `-r` option is specified, the volume is mounted for reading only. This command may be issued without any arguments; it will then display what devices are currently mounted.

In standard System V Unix, **mount** is restricted to the system manager and is located in directory `/etc`. Some other system versions and other systems have user-accessible mount commands, slightly different or differently restricted.
More in: Files in the Unix System (Chapter 3)

mv

Function: Moves (i.e., renames) files.
Syntax: **mv** <*file1*> <*file2*>
mv <*file*> . . . <*directory*>

Usage: In the first form, the name of <*file1*> is altered to <*file2*>. If there already existed a <*file2*>, it is removed (destroyed) first. In the second form, the specified <*file*>s are moved to the <*directory*> named. **mv** cannot be used to destroy a file by moving it onto itself.
More in: Files in the Unix System (Chapter 3)

neqn

Function: Mathematical typesetting.
Syntax: neqn [-d<*x*><*y*>] [<*file*> . . .]
Usage: neqn is a preprocessor for driving **nroff**, capable of being used with terminals. There is another program **eqn** which is preferable for use with **troff**, although **neqn** may be used. Input is read from the specified files or from the standard input if no files are shown in the command. Output is directed to the standard output. All input is passed to the output unmodified, except for (1) lines delimited by the command lines .EQ and .EN, and (2) character strings encased in two delimiter characters <*x*> and <*y*>, if any such are set by including the -d option in the command line. The lines to be modified are processed by including such **nroff** or **troff** commands as appropriate to reformat the equations or mathematical expressions, so far as the hardware device (phototypesetter or printer) is capable of forming mathematical expressions.
More in: Text Preparation and Processing (Chapter 8)

nice

Function: Run a task at reduced priority.
Syntax: nice [<*priority*>] <*command*> [&]
Usage: To keep the execution of <*command*> from interfering with terminal work, it can be made to run at reduced priority. If no <*priority*> is specified, the priority that would otherwise be assigned to the command is incremented by 10 (high numbers mean low priority). If <*priority*> is given, it must be a number preceded by a minus sign. (The minus identifies the number as being an option; it has no arithmetic significance.) The detached job symbol & is not required, but must be included if the terminal is to be freed for other work. The system manager is entitled to improve the priority of a command, normal users can only push it farther into the background.
More in: The System Kernel (Chapter 5)

nroff

Function: Text formatter.
Syntax: nroff [*options*] [<*file*> . . .]
Usage: Text files are reformatted in accordance with commands embedded in the text itself. These set margins, justify and fill lines, indent paragraphs, number and title pages, and otherwise provide text formatting services. A large number of options is allowed. Each option must be individually preceded by a minus sign; all the options must be listed before any of the files. The main options are

`-m` <*name*>	use macro library `/usr/lib/tmac/tmac.`<*name*>
`-n` <*n*>	number the first page <*n*>
`-o` <*n1-n2,n3,n4-n5*>	print only pages *n1* to *n2*, *n3*, and *n4* to *n5*
`-s` <*n*>	stop every <*n*> pages to allow paper changing
`-T` <*name*>	use output device of type <*name*>

The <*file*>s listed are processed in the order given; if no files are listed, the standard input is used. A single minus sign will also be understood to signify the standard input. The standard manuscript-preparation macro library ms is located in `/usr/lib/tmac/tmac.s` and is (in accordance with the above) accessed by `-ms`. Many systems provide other macro packages. They usually reside in `/usr/lib/tmac` or `/usr/lib/macros`; well-organized systems will provide access to the latter via the `-m` option.
More in: Text Preparation and Processing (Chapter 8)

od

Function: File dump program
Syntax: od [*options*] <*file*> . . .
Usage: File content is dumped to standard output. If no file name is given, the standard input is used. Dumping is done on either a byte (character by character) or 16-bit word basis. Two options are available for dumping by bytes, four for dumping by words:

`-b`	*bytes*:	shown as three-digit octal numbers
`-c`	*bytes*:	as ASCII characters or octal numbers
`-d`	*words*:	as unsigned decimal numbers
`-o`	*words*:	as six-digit octal numbers
`-s`	*words*:	as signed decimal numbers
`-x`	*words*:	as four-digit hexadecimal numbers

With the `-c` option, all printable ASCII characters are represented by themselves; nulls, backspaces, form feeds, newlines, carriage returns and tabs echo as `\0`, `\b`, `\f`, `\n`, `\r`, `\t`; all others are shown in octal. The options are mutually exclusive; only one may be specified at a time.
More in: Facilities and Utilities (Chapter 6)

passwd

Function: Changes password, or installs one.
Syntax: passwd
Usage: The user is asked for both old and new passwords, and the new one is installed. Passwords are refused if they are too short or contain unacceptable characters. If the current password is blank (which counts as no password at all), the **passwd** command is used to install a new one. Blank passwords are often assigned by system managers to newly authorized users.
More in: Getting Started (Chapter 2)

pc

Function: Berkeley Pascal compiler.
Syntax: pc [*options*] <*file*>
Usage: pc compiles Pascal, producing either assembler code or object code, as specified by the options. It may be considered to feed into the second pass of the C compiler, so that options not recognized by **pc** will be passed on to the assembler and the loader **ld**. The Pascal accepted is close to the ISO standard. The input file name must end in `.p`, so that **pc** may recognize it as a Pascal source file.

The compiler **pc** is intended for compiling programs debugged with the interpreter **pi**, which provides more facilities for finding program errors. The set of options provided with **pc** is wider than with **pi** and is biased toward yielding good object code. Options are specified by giving a string of option letters, preceded by a minus sign. Option letters may be concatenated into a single string. Both upper and lowercase characters are used in **pc** options; they are not interchangeable. The available options are

`-b`<*n*>	output buffer <*n*> blocks (buffer = one line)
`-c`	compile partial program (full program expected)
`-C`	subrange bound test (no tests are performed)
`-g`	log Unix debugger information (none logged)
`-i`	list all `include` files (list `include` statements)

-l	source program listing generated (no listing)
-o *<name>*	output file name to be *<name>* (**a.out** is used)
-O	Object code optimizer to be used (not used)
-p	profiling counters for **prof** (none generated)
-s	standard Pascal check (no checking is done)
-S	assembly language output (object code is produced)
-w	suppress warning diagnostics (warnings are issued)
-z	profile counters for later **pxp** run (no counters)

If options are not specified, actions or values given in parentheses are assumed.

Parts of programs (e.g., individual procedures or functions) may be compiled separately, the resulting relocatable object code being linked and loaded later. For details of partial compilation, the Berkeley Pascal manuals should be consulted. **pc** is part of the Berkeley Pascal system; it is not part of the standard AT&T Unix software.
More in: Language and Compilers (Chapter 9)

pg

Function: Backward and forward paging screen display.
Syntax: pg [*options*] *<file>* . . .
Usage: Copies *<file>*s to the terminal screen, one screenful at a time, with the ability to page backward as well as forward (unlike **more** which only pages forward). Important options are

-f	truncate lines if over screen width, do not fold
-s	show up messages in reverse video if possible
-*<number>*	make the screen "page" *<number>* lines (default 23)
+*<number>*	start display at line number *<number>* of *<file>*

When **pg** starts it immediately shows one screenful of text. Thereafter it will page as requested by user commands: a number *<a>* followed by a single letter followed by a suffix. The number specifies the address (sometimes in lines, sometimes screens) where to display next; if unsigned, *<a>* is an absolute place in *<file>*, if signed then relative to the current cursor location. Major commands are

<a>	displays a new screen as specified by *<a>* in screens
*<a>*l	displays a new screen as specified by *<a>* in lines
h	gives an abbreviated helpful list of commands
q	quits running **pg**
! *<cmd>*	starts a shell and passes *<cmd>* to it as a command
$	displays the last screenful of the file

The default value for *<a>* is 1, so simply striking RETURN moves on one screenful. A temporary exit to the **vi** editor is possible by `!vi` *<file>*. Editing and displaying can therefore be intermixed. This facility is particularly useful if the text displayed by **pg** is a filtered version of *<file>*.
More in: Facilities and Utilities (Chapter 6)

pi

Function: Berkeley Pascal interpreter.
Syntax: pi [*options*] *<file>*
Usage: pi interprets Pascal, producing intermediate code which can be executed by means of the **px** execution monitor. The code produced is placed in a file named `obj`. The Pascal accepted is close to the ISO standard. The input file name must end in `.p`, so that **pi** may recognize it as a Pascal source file.

pi options are stated in the usual style. The command may be followed by a minus sign, a string of option letters as appropriate, and the file name or names which are to be operated on. The available options are

`-b`*<n>*	set output buffer to *<n>* blocks (buffer = one line)
`-i`	list `include` files in full (list `include` statements)
`-l`	source program listing to be generated (no listing)
`-p`	postmortem error backtrace and dump omitted (trace is done)
`-s`	standard Pascal language check (no checking is done)
`-t`	subrange bound testing is suppressed (tests are performed)
`-w`	warning diagnostics are suppressed (warnings are issued)
`-z`	profile counters are set up for later **pxp** run (no counters)

The option values given in parentheses are those assumed by default, to be reversed if desired. Options may also be invoked in the program itself, by including in the program text a special comment line.

pi is often used to debug programs which, when finished, are compiled into executable binary code with **pc**. In general, **pc** produces better optimized, faster running programs with lower memory requirements, while **pi** runs quicker and provides better debugging aids.
More in: Languages and Compilers (Chapter 9)

pix

Function: Berkeley Pascal interpreter and executor.
Syntax: pix [*options*] *<file>*
Usage: pix interprets and executes Pascal. It is the combination of the **pi**

interpreter and the **px** execution monitor; command descriptions for these should be consulted for details.
More in: Languages and Compilers (Chapter 9)

pr

Function: Print-formats files.
Syntax: pr [*option*] . . . <*file*> . . .
Usage: Listings are produced in the standard output file (usually the terminal screen) of one or more named input files. Each file starts on a new page. The page starts with a header including date and file name. Options for **pr** are listed separately, each with its proper preceding plus or minus sign; the characters are not concatenated. The main options of importance are

`-l`<*n*>	sets page length to be <*n*> lines (default = 66)
`-m`	lists all files simultaneously, one per column
`-`<*n*>	produces <*n*>-column formatted output
`+`<*n*>	begins printing at page <*n*>
`-w`<*n*>	sets page width to be <*n*> characters (default = 72)

The right number of columns should be set up if the `-`<*n*> option is given, that is, <*n*> should be the number of files, or an integer multiple of it, or an integer submultiple. Note: during the running of **pr**, interterminal message passing is disabled.
More in: Facilities and Utilities (Chapter 6)

prep

Function: Separates file into words.
Syntax: prep [*options*] <*file*> . . .
Usage: Input files are copied to the standard output, one word per line. Words are reduced to lower case only, numbers and punctuation are stripped, whitespace is eliminated. Useful options are

`-i`<*file*>	ignore (weed from output) all words in <*file*>
`-o`<*file*>	only include in output words listed in <*file*>
`-p`	punctuation marks are to constitute words too

The files for the `-i` or `-o` options must be in **prep** format, one word to a line.
More in: Facilities and Utilities (Chapter 6)

ps

Function: Displays process status.
Syntax: ps [*options*] [<*process*> . . .]
Usage: Status information is provided about the currently active processes. If a process identification number <*process*> is given, information is given about the named process(es). Of the ten or eleven available options, the most valuable are

`-a`	all processes associated with a terminal
`-e`	everything—all processes in the system
`-f`	full form, including the relevant commands,
`-l`	long form, with lots of other information

In System V and its derivatives, **ps** requires minus signs in front of the option letters; in Seventh Edition based systems it does not, contrary to most other commands. The long (`-l`) and full (`-f`) listings fill the screen with voluminous though somewhat different information. Of likely interest to users are: state of each process (S), the user identification number (UID), process identification number (PID), the identification number of the parent process (PPID), the terminal controlling the process (TTY), the cumulative execution time (TIME), and the command that initiated the process (CMD). The state reports give single characters with the following meanings:

I	intermediate	T	stopped
R	running	W	waiting
S	sleeping	Z	terminated
0	nonexistent		

In short form, **ps** shows only part of the information, but usually quite enough.
More in: The System Kernel (Chapter 5)

pwd

Function: Pathname of working directory.
Syntax: pwd
Usage: The full pathname of the working directory is displayed at the terminal (standard output). Users with many files do occasionally lose track of where they were and where they are going; also useful for finding out where in the Unix file structure the current working directory is located.
More in: Files in the Unix System (Chapter 3)

px

Function: Berkeley Pascal execution monitor.
Syntax: px [<*file*>]
Usage: px executes Pascal intermediate code produced by **pi**. If no file name is given, `obj` is assumed. **px** is most often used as part of the **pix** command, which is a combination of **pi** and **px**.
More in: Languages and Compilers (Chapter 9)

pxp

Function: Berkeley Pascal reformatter and profiler.
Syntax: pxp [*options*] <*file*>
Usage: Produces an execution profile of a Pascal program, i.e., shows how many times each source line was executed. The execution count is shown on a reformatted program listing, so that by suppressing the execution information, **pxp** may also be used as a program reformatter/beautifier. The input file name must end in `.p`, so that **pxp** may recognize it as a Pascal source file.

Options available with **pxp** are communicated in the normal style, that is, each option is specified by a single option letter and options may be concatenated into a letter string. A minus sign must precede the string. Two classes of options apply with **pxp**, those concerned with profiling and those concerned with formatting the listings. The options are

`-a`	all routines included in the profile (omit those not used)
`-d`	suppress listing of declarations (all source text listed)
`-e`	substitute text for `include` statements (statements only)
`-f`	full parentheses for mathematics (minimal parentheses)
`-j`	left justify everything (nested blocks indented 4 spaces)
`-s`	strip comments in listing (comments are fully listed)
`-t`	tabulate procedure and function calls (no table given)
`-z`	profile named included files, or all (no profile at all)
`-_`	underline keywords in listing (no underlining)
`-`<*n*>	indent nestings <*n*> spaces (4 spaces)

If options are not specified in the command line, action will be taken as shown in the parentheses above. If neither `t` nor `z` is specified (i.e., neither a detailed profile nor a table is asked for), no profile will result, only a listing of the program text. All listings produced by **pxp** contain in the heading the date and time of most recent modification of the program file (not the time at which the listing was produced). Listings are produced

in lower case, except for any literally included text (e.g., text to be printed out). Both keywords and variable names are reduced to lower case, if they were not so already.
More in: Languages and Compilers (Chapter 9)

ratfor

Function: Translates Ratfor to Fortran.
Syntax: ratfor [*options*] <*file*> . . .
Usage: The files named in the command, which must be Ratfor language text, are translated into Fortran. The resulting output is deposited in the standard output file. Options available with **ratfor** are prefixed with a minus sign; they are

`-h` quoted strings are given as Holleriths, like Fortran 66
`-C` comments are copied to output, and neatly reformatted
`-6c` c in column 6 for continuation line (else & in column 1)

ratfor can also be invoked under **f77**; in that case, any options must be passed via the `-R` option of **f77**.
More in: Languages and Compilers (Chapter 9)

rm

Function: Removes files from the system.
Syntax: rm [*options*] <*file*> . . .
Usage: Removes (i.e., deletes) the named files from the current working directory, provided the user has the appropriate permissions. Confirmation is asked for, by a `y` from the terminal, for every file without write permission. Options are characters, which may be concatenated, prefixed by a minus sign. They are:

`-i` asks for a `y` response before removal of any file;
`-r` asks for `y` for every entry if removing a directory file;
`-f` forces removal without any questions asked.

More in: Files in the Unix System (Chapter 3)

rmdir

Function: Removes directories.
Syntax: rmdir <*directory*> . . .

Usage: Removes directories from the system. Directories are not removed unless they are empty. Otherwise, operation is similar in principle to the **rm** command. No options are available with this command.
More in: Files in the Unix System (Chapter 3)

sh

Function: Command decoder.
Syntax: sh *<file>*
Usage: sh is the standard Unix command decoder; in fact, **sh** is the decoder that receives and understands all the commands listed in this chapter. Its standard input is from the keyboard if no *<file>* is specified; it is then an interactive decoder. Shell scripts may be passed to the shell as file names, as standard input reassignments with the **<** symbol, or by making the scripts executable.
More in: Unix Command Shells (Chapter 4)

size

Function: Shows object file size.
Syntax: size [*<file>*] . . .
Usage: The size of one or more files is determined and delivered to the standard output. The decimal number of bytes of each of the three portions of an object file is shown, as well as the total size. The file name may be omitted; **a.out** is then understood.
More in: Facilities and Utilities (Chapter 6)

sleep

Function: Suspends itself for a specified length of time.
Syntax: sleep *<time>*
Usage: Execution of this command is delayed by *<time>* seconds, thereby introducing a known time delay. If placed in a loop, **sleep** is useful for periodic activities like checking the mailbox; outside a loop, it is good for signalling quitting time or timing three-minute eggs.
More in: Unix Command Shells (Chapter 4)

sort

Function: Sorts the lines in one or more files.
Syntax: sort [*option*] [+*<pos>* [-*<pos>*]] [*<file>*]

Usage: The lines in the file(s) *<file>* are sorted and written to the standard output. If no *<file>* is given, the standard input file is assumed. By default, the lines are sorted in ASCII sequence. The options are stated in strings, each beginning with a minus sign. The first string may contain one or more of the letters `cmu`, the second may choose from `dfiMnr`, the third either or both of `bt`. The options denote

`-c`	check if file is already sorted, no output if it is
`-m`	merge files only, the files are already sorted
`-u`	"unique", i.e., discard extra copies of duplicate lines
`-d`	dictionary sort (only letters, digits, and blanks count)
`-f`	forget case differences (i.e., consider A = a)
`-i`	ignore everything but ASCII 040-176 in non-numeric sorting
`-M`	sort three-character months so `Jan` < `Feb`, ignore case
`-n`	numeric strings at line starts sorted by arithmetic value
`-r`	reverse the sorting order
`-b`	blanks at the start of a line are ignored;
`-t`*<x>*	the field separator character is defined to be *<x>;*

The column options [`+`*<pos>*] and [`-`*<pos>*] restrict the sort to consider the field from after the first (`+`) to after the second (`-`) position. A position has the form `f[. c]`, where `f` is the number of full fields left of the position, `c` the number of columns to its left within its field. In addition, each position or position pair (i.e., each sorting key area) may be qualified by the alphabetic options of the second group (the options `cmu` are global to the whole sort). Thus multiple sort keys, modified sort keys, and various sub-options are possible. Caution: The Seventh Edition and System V descriptions of this command differ in several significant details.
More in: Facilities and Utilities (Chapter 6)

spell

Function: Tries to find spelling errors.
Syntax: spell [*options*] [*<file>* . . .]
Usage: *<file>*, or in its absence the standard input file, is read to find all the words in it. These are compared against a spelling dictionary. Three options, concatenated characters preceded by a minus sign, are available:

`-b`	British spellings are given preference (*colour*, *recognise*)
`-v`	verbose: anything slightly dubious is listed in detail
`-x`	lists every plausible stem for doubtful words

Spellings are checked but syntax is ignored. For example, no message is issued if *its* replaces *it's*. The spelling dictionary can be updated and most installations are well advised to do so; however, the updating must be controlled so no errors slip into the certified correct spellings! Because updating is possible, **spell** may vary a good deal between installations.
More in: Text Preparation and Processing (Chapter 8)

struct

Function: Translates Fortran to Ratfor.
Syntax: struct [*option*] . . . <*file*>
Usage: struct translates the <*file*> named in the command, which must be Fortran language text, into Ratfor. The output goes to the standard output file. The translation is not unique, and may be guided by options, the most useful of which are

`-a` maps sequences of `elseif`'s into a (non-Ratfor) `switch`
`-b` avoids multilevel `break` statements, uses go `to`'s
`-i` does not map computed go `to`'s into `switches`
`-n` avoids multilevel `next` statements, uses go `to`'s
`-s` expects standard card-image (not free formatted) input

struct can be confused by some of the more esoteric (and badly structured) constructions available in Fortran 77, such as multiple subroutine entry and return points.
More in: Languages and Compilers (Chapter 9)

stty

Function: Sets expected terminal characteristics.
Syntax: stty [*options*]
Usage: Matches the expectations of the Unix kernel software to the characteristics of the terminal—a matter complicated by the fact that one might also set up the terminal to match the expectations of the kernel. The number of options in **stty** verges on the incredible. Unfortunately, **stty** has undergone drastic changes, in command syntax as well as specific options, between the various Unix versions; furthermore, derivative systems may show variations. For this command, it is best to consult the locally valid system manuals and to have a talk with the system manager if there is one.

When setting up a terminal, it is important to make sure all the option switches on the terminal are set to correspond to the settings made by

stty. On many terminals the switches actually set input bits for a microprocessor. It may be necessary to turn the terminal off and on again after a few seconds, thereby forcing the microprocessor to read the bit settings.
More in: Unix Command Shells (Chapter 4)

style

Function: Checks the writing style of a document.
Syntax: style [*options*] <*file*>
Usage: Parses the sentences of the document in <*file*> and reports on sentence structure, readability indices, and sentence variation through the document. Also gives detailed parses for individual sentences, if desired. The options specify which sentences are to be printed out for examination and whether a full sentence-by-sentence parse is desired. The option sequence is nonstandard, each option must have its own minus sign.
More in: Text Preparation and Processing (Chapter 8)

tail

Function: Copies last part of a file to standard output.
Syntax: tail [*options*] [<*file*>]
Usage: Copies the file content, beginning at a designated place and continuing to the end of the file. The option specifies the number of lines (or blocks, or characters) as `+`<*n*> if counted from the beginning of the file, `-`<*n*> if counted from the end; the number <*n*> may be followed by one of the characters `l`, b, or c to denote lines, blocks, or characters. If the options are omitted, a small part of the tail end, about half a screenful, is fetched by default.
More in: Facilities and Utilities (Chapter 6)

tar

Function: Archiver and backup copier for removable media.
Syntax: tar [*options*] <*file*> . . .
Usage: Tape archiver program, more recently adapted to floppy disks and tape cartridges. It creates and modifies archives or extracts files from them. The options admissible consist of one of the characters `crtux`, followed by one of `f`vw. The first group specifies the activity:

c creates a new archive and writes the specified files to it
r appends files to the end of the archive

t lists all the names of the files in the archive
u updates, appending new or recently modified files only
x extracts files from the archive

The second option group shows how the work is to be done:

f <*dev*> uses <*dev*> as device special file instead of default
v works verbosely, reporting all activity in detail
w queries every action and waits for confirmation

When extracting from an archive, or when appending to it, **tar** works recursively: if <*file*> is a directory, the files contained in it are moved.
More in: Files in the Unix System (Chapter 3)

tbl

Function: Table formatter.
Syntax: tbl [<*file*> . . .]
Usage: tbl is a preprocessor for **nroff** or **troff**. All input text is taken from the named files or from the standard input if no files are named in the command. The input is passed through to the standard output, except for lines encased in the command lines `.TS` to `.TE`; the latter are preprocessed by writing **nroff** or **troff** commands.
More in: Text Preparation and Processing (Chapter 8)

tee

Function: Pipe fitting in Unix pipelines.
Syntax: tee [*option*] <*file*> . . .
Usage: The standard input is transcribed to the standard output, with an extra copy deposited in <*file*>. There are two useful options, each of which must carry its own minus sign (if both are used):

`-a` append to <*file*>, do not overwrite
`-i` ignore any interruptions while transcribing

More in: Unix Command Shells (Chapter 4)

test

Function: Testing of file names or shell variables.
Syntax: test <*expression*>

Usage: The *<expression>* is evaluated and the exit status of **test** is accordingly returned as true or false. Expressions are formed by combining simpler expressions with logical operators `-a` (and), `-o` (or), ! (not). Elementary expressions are of three kinds: file identification, string analysis, and arithmetic comparison. File tests take the form

-*<ch>* *<file>*

where the character *<ch>* describes the file, following the conventions of the **ls** command, with one of `rwxfdcbp`. Additionally, `s` (size greater than zero) may be used. Tests show true if *<file>* exists and has the required characteristic. String comparisons are of three forms:

-*<ch>* *<string>*	string length is zero or nonzero (*<ch>* `z` or `n`)
<st1> = *<st2>*	strings *<st1>* and *<st2>* are identical
<string>	*<string>* is not null

Arithmetic comparisons take the form *<n1>* *<op>* *<n2>*, where *<op>* is a Fortran-style comparison operator: `eq`, `ne`, `ge`, `gt`, `lt`, `le`.
More in: Unix Command Shells (Chapter 4)

time

Function: Times execution of a command.
Syntax: **time** *<command>*
Usage: Useful for finding out how much time a program takes to run; *<command>* may be any valid command understood by the shell. The elapsed time, processor time, etc. are displayed, in seconds. Caution: timings can vary quite a bit depending on what other jobs are running on the system.
More in: Facilities and Utilities (Chapter 6)

tr

Function: Character translation.
Syntax: **tr** [*options*] *<string1>* *<string2>*
Usage: The standard input file is transformed and written into the standard output file, with every character in *<string1>* removed and replaced by the character in the corresponding position in *<string2>*. This command is useful for changing upper to lower case, or similar character-for-character transformations. There are three options:

-c use as *<string1>* the ASCII characters not listed (complement)
-d delete all characters listed in *<string1>*
-s squeeze all repeated characters from *<string2>* to singles.

The strings may be made up using conventions similar to the expressions built in **ed**. Unique to **tr** is the notation [*<x>***<n>*] which, if used in *<string2>*, means *<n>* repetitions of *<x>*; [*<x>**] denotes many repetitions of *<x>*, useful for padding out *<string2>* to make its length match *<string1>*.
More in: Facilities and Utilities (Chapter 6)

troff

Function: Phototypesetter-based text formatter.
Syntax: troff [*options*] [*<file>* . . .]
Usage: Text files are reformatted in accordance with commands embedded in the text itself and are transmitted to the phototypesetter. **troff** functions similarly to **nroff**, except that the range of options is wider because the output hardware device is more flexible.
More in: Text Preparation and Processing (Chapter 8)

tty

Function: Displays the terminal name.
Syntax: tty
Usage: This command determines the pathname of the terminal special file, thus identifying the terminal type. It is useful for checking whether the system is healthy, a fast and harmless way to make it do something and produce a little output. In shell files, **tty** provides a way of identifying from what terminal activity originated.
More in: Facilities and Utilities (Chapter 6)

umask

Function: Sets or reports the user file-creation mask.
Syntax: umask [*<o><g><a>*]
Usage: Masks (denies) file permissions. The specified permissions code is taken away from what is granted by default when new files are created. The three octal digits for *<o>* owner, *<g>* group, *<a>* all others, are

made up by combining read = 4, write = 2, and execute = 1.
More in: Unix Command Shells (Chapter 4)

umount

Function: Unmounts a file system.
Syntax: /etc/umount *<directory>*
Usage: umount disconnects the root directory of a disk, tape, etc. volume from the Unix system, by releasing *<directory>*. The latter is returned to whatever use it had before the corresponding mount command.

In standard System V Unix, **umount** is restricted to the system manager and is located in directory `/etc`. Numerous other system versions and systems have user-accessible, but often slightly different or restricted, **umount** commands.
More in: Files in the Unix System (Chapter 3)

uniq

Function: Finds repeated adjacent lines in a file.
Syntax: uniq [*options* [+*n*] [-*m*]] [*<infile>* [*<outfile>*]]
Usage: The input file *<infile>* is read and copied to *<outfile>*; if no names are given, the standard files are used. Adjacent lines are compared while copying. If no options are given, all second and further copies of repeated lines are discarded. Specifying some number *m* in -*m* causes *m* fields to be skipped in each line before comparing begins; giving +*n* causes *n* characters to be ignored in the first field examined. Options are concatenable characters preceded by a minus sign:

-c count repetitions of each line, and display their number
-d copy over only the duplicated lines, one copy of each
-u copy over only the unduplicated lines

The utility **sort** must be used first if the files in question are not already sorted.
More in: Facilities and Utilities (Chapter 6)

uucp

Function: Unix-to-Unix file copier.
Syntax: uucp [*options*] *<sourcefile>* *<destination>*

Usage: Provides file transfers between Unix systems connected through almost any communication medium. *<sourcefile>* and *<destination>* are file identifications, usually on two different systems. Files on the local system may be identified by the usual pathname rules. Files on a remote system may be given as pathnames, preceded by the system name and an exclamation mark (e.g., `remote! /usr/joe/bxt`). The abbreviation ~*<name>* may be used to stand for the login directory of user *<name>*. The key options are

`-c` copy from original file, do not copy to a spooling file
`-d` make all necessary directory entries for the copy
`-m` mail notification to the requestor when the job is done

Copying to and from remote systems creates security problems of hair-raising complexity. Most system managers are a bit protective about permissions granted for remote copying.
More in: Facilities and Utilities (Chapter 6)

vi

Function: Screen editor for text preparation
Syntax: **vi** *<file>*
Usage: Screen editor with variable and independently controllable screen window size and placement, with cursor-controlled editing functions. **vi** is a very powerful editor with a large command set, often used in place of **ed** for text preparation. It is a subset of the **ex** editor, whose listing may be consulted for options and related detail. *<file>* is opened for editing when **vi** is invoked; it may be overwritten with edited text when exiting.
More in: Editing with **vi** and **ed** (Chapter 7)

wc

Function: Counts characters, words, and lines in files.
Syntax: **wc** [*options*] [*<file>* . . .]
Usage: Word counting program, used to assess the size of text files. If several files are named, both individual and cumulative totals are shown. Characters, words, and lines are counted if no option characters are shown; otherwise, any one or combination of the three may be selected by the option characters `c`, `w`, `l`. If used, the option characters may be concatenated and must be preceded by a minus sign. If no file name is given,

the keyboard is taken as the default input device, and the typed input is counted until a control-D is sent.
More in: Facilities and Utilities (Chapter 6)

who

Function: Shows who is on the system.
Syntax: who [am I]
Usage: Without option, **who** displays the terminal pathnames, user identification names, etc. of everybody currently on the system. It is essential prior to using the **write** message passing facility, to determine whether the intended message recipient is logged in. With the option, information is displayed for the requestor only, a convenience for author identification in shell scripts. **who** is useful as a harmless activity to check whether the system is alive; possibly good also for amnesia sufferers.
More in: Getting Started (Chapter 2)

write

Function: Sends immediate message to specified user.
Syntax: write *<user>* [*<terminal>*]
Usage: The command line causes the intended recipient *<user>* to be alerted that a message impends. All lines typed at the keyboard after the **write** are immediately transmitted to the recipient, interrupting whatever else he may have been doing (with a few exceptions). A terminal name may also be given, a convenience if the recipient is currently logged in at several. Transmission is terminated when a control-D is typed. Two-way communication can be set up, provided some form of agreed "over and out" protocol is used to avoid both parties sending or listening at the same time.
More in: Facilities and Utilities (Chapter 6)

Summary of Common Commands

Most Unix systems accept similar, or almost similar, commands. To give a broader overview of what is available, the following summary listing shows the most common user-accessible commands in the Seventh Edition, 4.2 BSD, and System V versions of Unix. It should be understood, of course, that not all the commands exist in all three versions, and that any one command may in any case be available or not as the local installation wishes.

Commands treated in detail above are marked with an asterisk.

adb		general-purpose debugging program
apply		applies a command to a set of arguments
apropos		locates commands by keyword lookup
ar	*	maintains archives and libraries
as	*	assembler, details dependent on computer
at	*	executes command file at a given time
awk		pattern scanner and processor language
backup		system backup (incremental)
banner		prints banner headline in large letters
bas	*	a Basic language interpreter
basename		strips directory and suffix from file name
batch		queues batch jobs for eventual execution
bc		arbitrary-precision arithmetic language
cal		prints calendar for any year or month
calendar		diary or reminder service
cancel	*	cancels a waiting or running print job
cat	*	concatenates, then displays, files
cb		C program beautifier
cc	*	C language compiler, followed by loader
cd	*	Changes the working directory
cflow		generates C program flow graph
checkeq		checks **eqn** requests in **troff** files
checknr		checks **nroff** and **troff** files
chfn		changes **finger** entry
chgrp		changes group
chmod	*	changes file access permissions
chown		changes file ownership
clear		clears terminal screen
cmp	*	compares two files
col		filters out reverse line feeds
colrm		removes columns from a file
comm	*	finds and outputs common lines in two files
compact		compresses (packs) files
cp	*	copies a file
cpio		archival copying program
cron		clock daemon, controls process timing
crypt		encryption/decryption of text files
csh	*	command shell with C-like syntax
csplit		splits a file into several by context
ctags		creates a tags file from C sources
cu	*	remote Unix calling and connection program

cut		cuts out specified parts of each line
cxref		generates cross-references for C programs
date	*	displays current date and clock time
dc		desk calculator simulation
dd		converts and copies a file
delta		changes SCCS files
deroff		removes **nroff**, **troff**, **tbl** and **eqn** requests
df	*	shows amount of free disk space
diction	*	improves phrase usage in writing
diff	*	finds the differences between two files
diff3		three-way differential file comparison
dircmp		compares directories, like **diff** for files
dirname		finds directory portion of file pathname
du	*	shows the amount of disk space used
dump		dumps files to backup medium incrementally
dumpdir		produces directory for dump tape or diskette
echo		echoes arguments as understood by the shell
ed	*	the old standard Unix text editor
efl		extended Fortran language processor
egrep		extended version of **grep**
env		finds out and alters shell environment
eqn	*	mathematical preprocessor for **troff**
error		analyzes compiler error messages
ex	*	interactive editor, which includes **vi**
expand		expands tabs to spaces
explain		interactive thesaurus to accompany **diction**
expr		evaluates arguments as an expression
f77	*	Fortran 77 compiler
factor		factors numbers into primes
false		no action, but *false* exit status
fgrep		fixed-string version of **grep**
file	*	determines file type
find	*	finds a file, or files of a particular kind
finger		mreports names and statistics on users
fmt		simple text formatter
fold		folds long lines to fit output device width
format	*	formats floppy disks or other magnetic media
fp		Functional Programming Language translator
ftp		transfers files to another system
get		generates readable (ASCII) from SCCS file
graph		draws a graph (as file for plot filters)
grep	*	filters input lines, looking for a pattern
groups		shows group memberships
head		gives first few lines of file
help		helps user with command syntax interactively
hostname		sets or displays name of current host system

id		shows user and group (real and effective) IDs
indxbib		builds inverted index for a bibliography
join		joins files line by line, comparing fields
kill	*	halts (aborts) a currently running process
last		shows last logins of users and terminals
lastcomm		shows last commands executed in reverse order
ld	*	linking loader
learn		computer-aided instruction about Unix
lex		generates lexical analysis programs
line	*	copies one line
lint		verifies C programs for syntax
lisp		Lisp interpreter
ln	*	adds a further directory entry for a file
login	*	logs in a new user
logname		returns the user's login name
look		finds lines in a sorted list
lookbib		finds references in an **indxbib** bibliography
lorder		finds ordering relation for object (**ar**) library
lp	*	line printer spooler
lpq		see **lpstat** (4.2 BSD)
lp	*	line printer spooler, see **lp**
lprm		removes line printer jobs, see **cancel**
lpstat	*	displays current status of printing requests
ls	*	lists contents of directories
lxref		Lisp cross-reference program
m4		general macro processor
mail	*	sends mail to others, or reads mail
make		maintains program or other files
man	*	displays *Unix Programmer's Manual* pages
mesg	*	blocks incoming messages
mkdir	*	makes new directories
mkfs	*	makes a file structure
mkstr		creates error message file from C sources
more	*	displays one screenful and waits
mount	*	mounts a file system
mt		manipulates magnetic tapes
mv	*	moves (i.e., renames) files
mvdir		moves (i.e., renames) directories
ncheck		finds names given i-numbers
neqn	*	mathematical typesetting preprocessor
netstat		shows network status
newgrp		changes user to a new group
news		displays system news announcements
nice	*	runs a task at reduced priority
nl		numbers the lines in a file
nm		displays object file symbol table

nohup		runs program regardless of disconnection
nroff	*	text formatter for fixed character pitch
od	*	file dump program, characters or words
pack		packs file, exploiting redundancy
passwd	*	changes password, or installs one
paste		merges lines from files as columns
pc	*	Berkeley Pascal compiler
pcat		lists a file compressed with **pack**
pdx		Pascal debugger
pg	*	backward and forward paging screen display
pi	*	Berkeley Pascal interpreter
pix	*	Berkeley Pascal interpreter and executor
plot		graphics filters for various terminals
pmerge		Pascal file merger
pr	*	print-formats files
prep	*	separates file into words
prof		displays program execution profile data
prs		outputs an SCCS file
pstat		displays almost anything in system tables
ps	*	displays process status
ptx		generates a permuted index
pwd	*	pathname of working directory
px	*	Berkeley Pascal interpreter and monitor
pxp	*	Berkeley Pascal reformatter and profiler
pxref		Pascal cross-reference program
quot		gives summary of files of each user
ranlib		converts archives to random libraries
ratfor	*	translates Ratfor to Fortran
rcp		remote file copy
red		**ed**, restricted to current directory
refer		finds literature references for documents
reset		resets terminal to a sensible state
restor		restores incrementally from backup medium
rev		reverses lines in a file
rm	*	removes files from the system
rmail		handles mail received via **uucp**
rmdel		removes an SCCS file alteration (delta)
rmdir	*	removes directories
rsh		restricted (Sys V) or remote (4.2 BSD) shell
sact		shows activity in SCCS file editing
script		makes typescript of terminal session
sed		stream editor
sh	*	command decoder
size	*	shows object file size
sleep	*	suspends itself for a specified length of time
soelim		eliminates . so from **nroff** input

sort	*	sorts the lines in one or more files
sortbib		sorts bibliographic database
spell	*	tries to find spelling errors
spline		interpolates smooth curve
split		splits a file into pieces of fixed size
strings		finds printable strings in object files
strip		removes symbols and relocation bits
struct	*	translates Fortran to Ratfor
stty	*	sets expected terminal characteristics
style	*	checks the writing style of a document
su		substitutes different user id temporarily
sum		sums and counts blocks in a file
sysline		displays system status on terminal
tabs		sets terminal tabs
tail	*	copies last part of file to standard output
tal		talks to another user
tar	*	archiver, backup copier for removable media
tbl	*	table formatter
tee	*	pipe fitting in Unix pipelines
test	*	testing of file names or shell variables
time	*	times execution of a command
tip		connects to a remote system
touch		update alteration or access date of a file
tp		manipulates tape archives
tr	*	character translation
troff	*	phototypesetter-based text formatter
true		no action, but *true* exit status
tsort		sort with constrained partial ordering
tty	*	displays the terminal name
umask	*	sets or reports the user file-creation mask
umount	*	unmounts a file system
uname		displays current system name and version
unexpand		replaces strings of spaces with tabs
uniq	*	finds repeated adjacent lines in a file
units		converts units of measurement to others
unpack		restore text form of packed files
uptime		shows how long system has been up
users		compact list of users on the system
uucp	*	Unix-to-Unix file copier
uulog		maintains or removes **uucp** activity log
uuname		displays the names of other known systems
uusend		sends a file to a remote host
uustat		enquires about **uucp** status and controls jobs
uusub		monitors the **uucp** network
uux		Unix-to-Unix command execution
val		validates an SCCS file

vi	*	screen editor for text preparation
vlp		formats Lisp programs for **nroff**
vmstat		reports virtual memory statistics
w		reports who is doing what, see **whodo**
wait		awaits completion of process
wc	*	counts characters, words, and lines in files
what		shows what modules were used for a file
whatis		describes what a command is
whereis		locates source, binary, etc. for program
which		locates file including aliases and paths
who	*	shows who is on the system
whodo		reports who is logged in and doing what
write	*	sends immediate message to specified user
xargs		permits argument substitution in commands
xstr		extracts strings from C programs
yacc		''yet another compiler-compiler''
yes		infinite source for *yes*'s (e.g., in pipes)

Chapter 11

An Annotated Bibliography

The literature now available on the Unix operating system includes some fifty or sixty books as well as a substantial number of articles and technical papers. Many of the technical papers will prove to be of little interest to the system user whom this book is intended to serve, because they deal with specialized internal details. On the other hand, texts and handbooks are likely to be of greater importance. An attempt has therefore been made to cover the textbook and monograph material thoroughly, while listing only a small fraction of the periodical literature.

Books

The Unix user today finds a good selection of books available at several levels. Accordingly, this annotated bibliography groups them by their general character and objectives, into introductory and advanced; overviews and treatments of specialized topics; Unix proper and closely related topics such as the C language. The annotations, which naturally reflect the author's personal opinion and reaction, are intended to serve the serious user of Unix, the user who requires access to a range of system utilities and needs to know how to coordinate their use.

Reasonably full bibliographic data appear for every book listed, including the ISBN. Where several editions, forms of binding, or other variants are known to exist, the ISBN given is usually that of the paperback or "student" edition.

Elementary Books

Books listed under this heading are intended for people with no understanding of computers who suddenly find themselves faced with Unix. For some incomprehensible reason, their authors mostly seem to think a lack of computing experience also implies a lack of intelligence; much of the material is slow-paced and repetitious. The books are listed alphabetically by author's surname.

Birns, P. M., Brown, P. B., Muster, J. C. C.: *Unix for people. A modular guide to the UNIX operating system: visual editing, document preparation, & other resources*. Englewood Cliffs, NJ: Prentice-Hall, 1985. ISBN 0-13-937442-6. xiv + 533 pp.

The term "modular" means that the book is organized as class notes to accompany 30 lessons. It would probably go over well as a teaching aid, but both its folksy writing and its slow pace make it hard to read. Despite the great length and relative completeness of this book, its usefulness is probably limited to formal courses, with exercises and assignments to keep the reader from straying.

Lomuto, A., Lomuto, N.: *A Unix primer*. Englewood Cliffs, NJ: Prentice-Hall, 1983. ISBN 0-13-938886-9. xvi + 240 pp.

A very simple book directed at people with no computing experience whatever. Its content is largely confined to using Unix files and the **ed** editor. The book contains little cartoons to break the tedium of reading and it provides plenty of white space for readers to doodle in.

Shirota, Y., Kunii, T. L.: *First book on Unix for executives*. Tokyo: Springer-Verlag, 1984. ISBN 4-431-70003-X. xi + 154 pp.

The phrase "for executives" presumably implies intelligent, literate people with little computing experience and no desire to acquire any. If that is its intended audience, the text of this book is well pitched; but the two-color cartoons of rabbits might have been better used elsewhere. An informative two hours' read while waiting for an airplane.

Thomas, R., Emerson, S., Yates, J., Campbell, J.: *The business guide to the Unix system*. Reading, MA: Addison-Wesley, 1983. ISBN 0-201-08848-7. xxi + 474 pp.

The introductory chapter, with its inevitable photographs of terminals, is followed by an outline of the file system and editors; then the text formatting facilities of Unix and communication utilities. The book is organized as a series of self-tutoring lessons, which progress very slowly through large numbers of excessively detailed examples. Zero knowledge of computers is assumed.

Thomas, Rebecca, Yates, Jean: *A user guide to the Unix system*. Berkeley, CA: Osborne/McGraw-Hill, 1982. ISBN 0-931988-71-3. xi + 508 pp.

This book is intended to serve the beginning user. It covers only a small portion of the available Unix system utilities but gives examples of all the commands which it does treat, in a beautifully clear form. Occasionally, however, the examples are so lengthy and extensively detailed as to verge on the boring. A useful summary list is given of those commands that do appear in the book. Unfortunately, the user is assumed to be interested only in the treatment of text files through basic system utilities, so that programming language support (C, Fortran, etc.) is not even mentioned; the strong text processing facilities included in Unix software, such as **nroff**, appear tantalizingly in marginal notes but are never treated as working tools. Thomas and Yates thus provide the neophyte a good introduction but do not accompany the reader very far in learning to use the system.

Waite, M., Martin, D., Prata, S.: *Unix primer plus*. Indianapolis, IN: Howard W. Sams, 1983. ISBN 0-672-22028-8. 414 pp.

Written for the true beginner, this book contains a general description of Unix structure, an introduction to text editing, and a brief mention of the programming languages available. Like the Lomuto and Lomuto book, it is designed not to overstress its audience. Little if any computing experience is expected of the reader, while frequent changes in writing style, cartoons, and two-color printing all contribute to easing understanding.

Waite, M., Martin, D., Prata, S.: *Unix System V primer*. Indianapolis, IN: Howard W. Sams, 1984. ISBN 0-672-22404-6. 431 pp.

A rewriting of the authors' previous book, with added material on the C shell and the **ex** editor. Most of the text is not heavily altered so both the positive and negative aspects of the former book are repeated.

General Books

Books aimed at the computer-literate with no Unix experience, the intended audience of this book, are no longer in short supply. They vary in their character and content, of course, but the selection now available is good. As above, the following are listed alphabetically by author's surname.

Banahan, M., Rutter, A.: *Unix—the book*. Wilmslow, Cheshire: Sigma Technical Press, 1982. vi + 265 pp. (Distributed by Wiley). ISBN 0-905104-21-8. vi + 265 pp.

Containing a great deal of material in very brief form, this book is of reference value to anyone prepared to live with its two shortcomings: it is written in a distinctly unfunny style presumably intended to be humorous, which quickly becomes wearying for the reader, and its glued binding of poor quality begins shedding pages almost before leaving the bookstore. The text processing facilities and utility programs that form part of Unix software are covered in detail; so is the C language. Curiously, other more common programming languages barely rate a mention. System startup, shutdown, and maintenance occupy a chapter. All in all, a good reference book for the experienced programmer willing to accept gratuitous insults from the authors, but not an easy book for beginners.

Bourne, S. R.: *The Unix system.* Reading, MA: Addison-Wesley, 1982. ISBN 0-201-13791-7. xiii + 351 pp.

Written by a member of the original Unix software team, this book deals extensively with the shell, with document preparation, and with a selection of utility programs. It contains a chapter on the C language and gives much useful detail on system programming. Although beginning users will find it readable, this well-written book really addresses itself to the experienced programmer without previous Unix experience.

Brown, P. J.: *Starting with Unix.* Reading, MA: Addison-Wesley, 1984. ISBN 0-201-10924-7. xii + 221 pp.

This book is accurately titled; it really is for beginners, but for beginners with high objectives. It assumes that the reader knows little about Unix and not very much about computers in general; but it moves on briskly toward the goal of sophisticated use. Although the chapter on programming is disappointing, the general level of the book is high and the material well chosen. The author deserves particular commendation for including a brief chapter on all the mysterious things that can go wrong, along with some advice on how to try curing them. Light, almost amusing in its style, this book is a pleasure to read and a valuable mine of information.

Budgen, D.: *Making use of Unix.* London: Edward Arnold, 1985. ISBN 0-7131-3519-0. vii + 194 pp.

Clearly intended for experienced computer users new to Unix, this book contains a wealth of information about Unix and its derivatives, about using the system and living with its idiosyncrasies, as well as about software engineering and system management. It is well written and solidly packed with facts—perhaps even so solidly packed that beginners may not find it palatable. The experienced computer user would probably have preferred a little more detail about program development tools, and perhaps a summary of commands, but these can be found in other books.

Christian, K.: *The Unix operating system.* New York: John Wiley, 1983. ISBN 0-471-87542-2. xviii + 318 pp.

This well-organized book is subdivided into two parts, suitable for beginners and advanced programmers. The beginners' part occupies the first 138 pages, covering about the same subject matter as most other introductory books: shell, login procedures, file management, text processing, and so on. The advanced programmers' part occupies about 120 pages. It is mainly devoted to the facilities available for applications software development (rather than to the needs of the system manager). The book is well designed and produced, but a bit expensive.

Gauthier, Richard: *Using the Unix system*. Reston, VA: Reston Publishing Co. (a Prentice-Hall Company), 1981. ISBN 0-8359- 8164-9. xiv + 297 pp.

Gauthier's book can be read by the novice, but it can be difficult going for anyone who does not possess a good deal of prior experience with interactive computer systems. Oriented to system managers and users rather than to system programmers, it contains little internal detail but does give a substantial amount of information on how to set up, manage, and maintain a Unix system installation. Most of the text is directed at the system (in the narrow sense), so that many of the programs commonly wanted by users (e.g., **nroff**) are not covered, and languages used in computing (e.g., Fortran) are not even mentioned. While examples are given for almost all the material treated, the level of the material varies from very elementary to very advanced. A set of review questions is provided for each chapter, with suggested answers at the back of the book.

Kochan, S. G., Wood, P. H.: *Exploring the Unix system*. Hasbrouck Heights, NJ: Hayden, 1984. ISBN 0-8104-6268-0. vii + 371 pp.

A good introduction and overview of the Unix system, suitable for beginners who have some acquaintance with computing. Sufficient to allow the neophyte to get started, but includes in the bargain chapters on system administration and software development—not enough to be expert, but plenty for a start. Marred by bad printing on bad paper, which are more than compensated by the good content.

McGilton, H., Morgan, R.: *Introducing the Unix system*. New York: McGraw-Hill/Byte (McGraw-Hill Computer Books), 1983. ISBN 0-07045001-3. xx + 556 pp.

The main strength of this book is its detailed treatment of text processing (editing, formatting, and manipulation), to which over two-thirds of its text is devoted. The remainder of the book consists principally of four or five introductory chapters, which are suitable for beginners, and a useful chapter directed to system managers. There is also a short chapter on the Berkeley Unix system. In contrast to most other books, no summarizing chapter of system commands is provided. The book is rich in well-chosen examples and therefore probably better for initial study than for use as a reference work.

Miller, C. D. F., Boyle, R. D.: *Unix for users*. Oxford: Blackwell, 1984. ISBN 0-632-01182-3. x + 210 pp.

An excellent book for the mature scientific user, covering the facilities available in Version 7 Unix admirably. Most topics are treated with brevity and, especially pleasing in a book of this kind, with wit; but the brevity may mean additional reference sources must be consulted. Examples, though extremely short, are plentiful and well chosen. System management is discussed in the context of medium or large computer centers, not personal computers. A book to be recommended warmly, but not as the only book on the shelf.

Prince, V.: *Le système Unix*. Paris, France: Editests, 1983. ISBN 2-86699-003-X. 128 pp.

This first book on Unix to appear in the French language gives a well-organized overview of the major commands and includes introductory chapters to help the beginning Unix user to get started. It attempts to cover too many commands in too little detail so that a large gap remains between excessive brevity here, excessive garrulity in the full system manuals. Useful, however, to readers unable to make good use of the English-language literature on the subject.

Topham, D. W., Truong, H. V.: *Unix and Xenix: a step by step guide*. Bowie, MD: Brady, 1985. ISBN 0-89303-918-7. [ix] + 508pp.

Like many beginners' books, this one concentrates on the system proper and does not even admit language compilers exist. Shell programming, on the other hand, is well introduced. The book is divided into a large number of short chapters and may be attractive as a course textbook, with one chapter about the right amount of material to cover in an hour.

Walker, A. N.: *The Unix environment*. Chichester: John Wiley, 1984. ISBN 0-471-90564-X. xi + 151 pp.

A lightly presented, chatty book written in that curious, somewhat idiosyncratic English which parts of the academic computer community like to affect; contains elements of both technical manual and personal reminiscence. The content is broad and clearly the result of a good deal of experience; it is most likely to be appreciated by experienced computer users with a leaning to scientific work. Novices may find it expects a bit too much prior knowledge to form a serious working tool.

Whiddett, R. J., Berry, R. E., Blair, G. S., Hurley, P. N., Nicol, R. J., Muir, S. J.: *Unix; a practical introduction for users*. Chichester: Ellis Horwood, 1985. ISBN 0-85312-950-9. 195 pp.

A good overview for the serious beginner, with enough solid content to keep the experienced coming back on occasion. Unfortunately, only the basic system is treated, nothing is said about its use for purposes other than text processing. Tidy in its British brevity, but as they say about Chinese food—half an hour after you have eaten, you're hungry again.

Manuals and Standards

Every Unix system comes—or certainly should come—with a full set of manuals detailing every aspect of system operation and use. These are generally tied to specific systems; two, however, have been published in the open literature. Because they describe generic systems rather than specific implementations, they tend to standardize the systems themselves. Standards, on the other hand, deliberately set out to define what implementations should contain.

Bell Telephone Laboratories, Inc.: *Unix programmer's manual. Revised and expanded version.* New York, NY: Holt, Rinehart and Winston, 1983. Vol. 1: ISBN 0-03-061742-1, xvi + 425 pp. Vol. 2: ISBN 0-03-061743-X, vii + 616 pp.

This book is the openly published version of the 7th edition of the Unix system documentation, somewhat amended and revised. Its original version, edited by B. Kernighan and M. D. McIlroy, has been the authoritative support manual for the Unix system as used at Bell Laboratories since 1979. In machine-readable form, this pair of large quarto (22 cm by 28 cm) volumes was furnished as part of the normal Unix Seventh Edition itself, thus available at almost every installation (though often in a form edited and altered to bring it into line with the software locally installed). Indispensable for system maintenance, it is also a valuable reference for users; but it is not satisfactory as a beginner's book. Most people employ it as an encyclopedia, to look up specific details from time to time.

AT&T: *Unix programmer's manual* [Steven V. Earhart, ed.]. New York: Holt, Rinehart and Winston, 1986. *Vol 1: Commands and utilities.* ISBN 0-03-009317-1, xxix + 524 pp. *Vol. 2: System calls and library routines.* ISBN 0-03-009314-7, xxxv + 465 pp. *Vol. 3: System administration facilities.* ISBN 0-03-009313-9, xiv + 142 pp. *Vol. 4: Documentation preparation.* ISBN 0-03-011207-9, xiii + 355 pp. *Vol. 5: Languages and support tools.* ISBN 0-03-011204-4, xvii + 618 pp.

This five-volume set, over 2200 pages in all, is to Unix System V what its 1983 precursor was to the Seventh Edition: the definitive and encyclopedic book that tells all. Mercifully, it is published as normal-sized octavo paperbacks instead of large bundles of gigantic pages like its older brother. It is organized into volumes well enough separated by logical subject area to permit easier reference than was possible before—and a good thing too, because many system releases based on System V reach the public with manuals furnished only in printed form, without machine-readable copies. The general format and layout of this book resembles the conventions established by the Seventh Edition (and earlier) and much of the material is, for obvious reasons, similar. Volumes 2 and 3 generally resemble the earlier book, while Volume 3 is more of a novelty. If it seems that the average user might not wish to know its contents, beware: there are many single-user systems based on System V now running on personal computers, so that administrative operations like file cleaning can become unavoidable even to the otherwise uninterested user! Volume 4 is little changed from its earlier counterparts, aside from descriptions of the newer mm and mv macro packages. In Volume V, it should be noted that System V supports C, Fortran 77, and Ratfor; there is no Pascal and no longer any Basic.

AT&T: *System V interface definition.* Issue 2. Indianapolis, IN: AT&T, 1986. *Vol. I:* ISBN 0-932764-10-X. ix + 320 pp. *Vol. II:* ISBN 0-932764-10-X. ix + 463 pp.

A chunky two-volume paperback intended mainly for the Unix applications programmer. The system variables, system calls, and conventions for handling most programmer-accessible parts of System V are detailed in a format reminiscent of the *Unix Programmer's Manual.* Many of its pages closely resemble their conterparts in that five-volume work. Although not written to be a user manual, this book can very well do double duty in that role. It is small enough to be actually owned and consulted by individuals, and it is surprisingly readable in spite of its forbidding title. Organized differently from the traditional Unix manuals, this book proceeds by layers: Volume I defines the rock-bottom system, including system calls and basic library routines; Volume II builds on it. To the user, Volume II is particularly handy because it sets out the command structure and such environmental factors as the terminal capabilities file and the terminal screen manager.Most unfortunately, the layered structure of the book means that the high-level facilities of main interest to users are often missing: no compilers, no text processing. This book strives to be a definitive document in much the same way as the IEEE P1003 standard; but it does differ a little bit from the latter. In addition, it also hints at the directions AT&T is likely to wish to steer System V and (presumably) other Unix versions yet to come.

Institute of Electrical and Electronics Engineers, Inc.: *IEEE trial-use standard portable operating system for computer environments.* IEEE Std 1003.1. New York: IEEE, 1986. (Distributed by Wiley-Interscience.) ISBN 0471-85027-6. 207 pp. (+3 unpaginated).

A draft American national standard for the major internal parts of Unix. Covers process, system, and input-output primitives; files, file directories, and filing systems; parts of the C language library; password conventions, encryption and management; data interchange (**tar**) format for moving files between computers. The objective of this standard, like most standards, is to define precisely which systems, and in in what circumstances, can be stated to conform to the published description. Because Unix is a trade name, the name POSIX has been registered as a trade mark by the IEEE to identify any conforming system.

/usr/group: *The /usr/group standard.* Santa Clara, CA: /usr/group, 1984. No ISBN, ca. 162 pp. unpaginated.

The first draft of a standard for system calls, created by a committee of interested individuals from a broad cross-section of companies and institutions with an interest in Unix. This committee subsequently gave rise to IEEE working group P1003, creators of the IEEE standard.

Buck, D. L.: *Reader's guide to the 1984 /usr/group standard.* Santa Clara, CA: /usr/group, 1984. No ISBN, ca. 80 pp. unpaginated.

Annotations to accompany the draft standard by /usr/group. The standard itself strives to be purely factual, free of opinion and explanatory material; the necessary accompanying matter is in this separate volume.

Specialized Books

The following are not necessarily difficult to read, in fact some are downright easy. However, they all deal with specialist topics ranging from text processing to system maintenance. They are arranged alphabetically by first author's surname.

Arthur, L. J.: *Unix shell programming*. New York: Wiley, 1986. ISBN 1-83900-0. xv + 261 pp.

The first book to concentrate exclusively on shell programming, this volume addresses itself to comparatively inexperienced Unix users. A pity, then, that the typography is at times confusing and the writing often hard to follow, that several commands discussed exist neither in System V nor the Seventh Edition, and that others have a syntax different from what the author uses. There are some interesting examples and a lot of valuable material, but the book will not be easy going for most people.

Bach, M. J.: *The design of the UNIX operating system*. Englewood Cliffs, NJ: Prentice-Hall, 1986. ISBN 0-13-201799-7. xiv + 471 pp.

A serious and detailed book devoted to the structural details of the kernel, the Unix file structure, and the management of processes. The principal stress is on System V (Release 2 and also Release 3—the author is at Bell Laboratories) but Berkeley releases are considered as well. This definitive book is well written and easy reading for anyone who satisfies the prerequisites: at least one good course in operating systems and some acquaintance with programming in C.

Blackburn, L., Taylor, M.: Pocket guide: UNIX. London: Pitman, 1984. ISBN 0-273-02106-0. [ii] + 62 pp.

Spiral-bound booklet of postcard size printed in small type and designed to stand up for consultation next to the terminal keyboard. Very wide coverage of Unix commands and facilities, considering the compact format. Somewhat too tutorial for anyone who uses Unix on a regular basis. Typographically less than ideal—commands and headings are not set off sufficiently to be easy to find (this problem might be cured with a colored felt-pen). Good for beginners and rare or irregular users.

Bolsky, M. I.: *The Unix system user's handbook*. Englewood Cliffs, NJ: Prentice-Hall, 1982 (?). ISBN 0-13-937764-6. 100 pp. (incl. covers).

A spiral-bound booklet of the form sometimes called a "reference card" by the computer community, this one is intended to be kept near the terminal for ready reference. It summarizes the main points of keyboard use and goes into excessive detail about the **ed** editor. About two-thirds of the book is composed of pages taken from the Unix manual without alteration; the result is far too extensive detail for a reference card and far too short for a reference manual (because only some commands are given). The selection of commands is curious—for example, **ln** and **more** are nowhere to be found but esoterica like **news**, **teach**, and **uuto** take up a good bit of space. Summary: there are better books and shorter reference cards!

Bolsky, M. I.: *The* **vi** *user's handbook*. AT&T Bell Laboratories, 1985 (?). No ISBN. 67 pp. (incl. covers).

A spiral-bound booklet similar in form to the same author's *Unix System User's Handbook* and *C Programmer's Handbook*, but curiously enough not published, or so it would seem, by the same publisher. The **vi** editor is covered fully in this "reference card", perhaps too fully; the material is all there but it is not always easy to locate the desired item among the mass of details. A booklet obviously intended to be kept at the terminal—but only a qualified success in that way, since its bulk at least rivals that of the manual pages which describe **vi**.

Dunsmuir, M. R. M., Davies, G. J.: *Programming the UNIX system*. New York: Wiley, 1985. ISBN 0-470-20192-4. 176 pp.

A guide to systems programming aimed at beginners in that esoteric art. Definitely a second-level Unix book, this one presupposes a reasonable understanding of the Unix system structure and of the C language. The book is well written but reading is made difficult by the bad photo-reduced typography.

el Lozy, M.: *Editing in a Unix environment: the* **vi/ex** *editor*. Englewood Cliffs, NJ: Prentice-Hall, 1985. ISBN 0-13-235599-X. xiv + 226 pp.

A comprehensive tutorially organized book, this one includes all the normal Unix editors and their relatives: **vi**, **ed**, **ex**, **sed**, **awk**. There are useful notes on differences between versions. Accurate and thoughtful presentation of a large amount of information. Caution: this is intentionally *not* a book about text processing, only about editing! **nroff** and other formatting programs are hardly even mentioned.

Foxley, E.: *Unix for super-users*. Wokingham: Addison-Wesley, 1985. ISBN 0-201-14228-7. xiv + 213 pp.

An excellent guide for managers, particularly of small systems, who need to administer a Unix system but do not wish to become system programmers. Management of user accounts, system backup procedures, bringing the system up and taking it down again, are accompanied by notes on performance and security problems. Not specific to any particular hardware or Unix version, it must still be accompanied by personal notes and system manuals.

Kernighan, B. W., Pike, R.: *The Unix programming environment*. Englewood Cliffs, NJ: Prentice-Hall, 1984. ISBN 0-13-937681-X. x + 357 pp.

An excellent book for people with extensive computing experience who do not have any knowledge of Unix, this thickish volume stresses shell programming, interfacing to system calls, and input/output from the C language. There is a good deal of useful information about the file system and a detailed, well documented, example of program development in C which covers over fifty pages. Anybody inclined to learn serious shell programming or to get started in programming in C should take this book seriously. A substantial level of maturity as a programmer and as a system user are prerequisites.

Kochan, S. G: *Programming in C*. Hasbrouck Heights, NJ: Hayden, 1983. ISNB 0-8104-6261-3. [ix] + 373 pp.

C has been called a "write-only language" because its great flexibility and its rich range of operators easily seduce programmers into writing marvellously brief, clever, and altogether unreadable code. Kochan's book is to be recommended because he takes a very disciplined approach; anyone writing C in the way he suggests is likely to produce well-structured and maintainable programs. Fortran programmers will probably like this book.

Krieger, M.: *Word processing on the UNIX system*. New York: McGraw-Hill, 1985. ISBN 0-07-035498-7. xix + 380 pp.

Detailed exposé, backed by voluminous examples, of the text formatting facilities, macro libraries, and text-oriented utilities of Unix. The treatment of **nroff** is extremely thorough, though curious shortcomings still remain. The `-ms` macro package is described in very great detail. Incredibly, the **vi** editor is only mentioned in the introductory pages—to say that the all but obsolete **ed** line editor is far preferable! **spell** is given short shrift, and many good Unix utilities like **diction** are simply ignored. A good book to consult for **nroff** and **troff**, perhaps.

Rochkind, M. J.: *Advanced Unix programming*. Englewood Cliffs, NJ: Prentice-Hall, 1985. ISBN 0-13-011800-1. xv + 265 pp.

A rare and welcome book by a system programmer, a breed notorious for its inability to communicate with ordinary mortals. While highly specialized, this volume is quite readable and tells all about the Unix kernel; about system calls, how they are used, and how they vary between versions of the Unix system; and about system programming practices. Knowledge of the C language is assumed, as is a good familiarity with the use of Unix.

Strong, B., Hosler, J.: *Unix for beginners: basic word processing skills with* **vi.** New York: John Wiley, 1986. ISBN 1-80664-1.

Strictly devoted to word processing for beginners, this book does little not implied by its title and does it in a series of "lessons" which are probably best employed as a teaching aid in secretarial schools. Leaving aside the obvious fact that **vi** is an obsolete word processor though a good computer editor, typists are more likely to profit from this book than computer users.

Weber Systems, Inc.: *XENIX user's handbook*. Cleveland, OH: Weber Systems, 1984. ISBN 0-938862-44-8. 308 pp.

Madly practical to the point of reproducing screen menus and checklists of keys to press, this how-to book deals exclusively with Microsoft Xenix as installed on the IBM PC/XT: installation, maintenance, and administration. Though some of it merely duplicates system manuals, it is detailed and likely to prove helpful to people who suddenly find themselves system managers of such tiny installations.

Thomas, R., Rogers, L. R., Yates, J. L.: *Advanced programmer's guide to Unix System V*. Berkeley, CA: Osborne/McGraw-Hill, 1986. ISBN 0-07-881211-9. vi + 575 pp.

A big book for the system programmer and for the serious applications programmer, this one contains much of the fruit of experience and a great many useful hints. The main topics treated are programming in C with the standard subroutine library, the use of system calls, and shell programming. There is a profusion of examples. On the negative side, this is a slow-paced book, dragging its way from one example to the next with deliberate lassitude.

Yates Ventures, Inc.: *The Unix system encyclopedia*. Los Altos, CA: Instrumentation Interface Incorporated, 1984. ISBN 0-917195-00-0. 448 pp.

A magazine-format vendor directory interlaced with a great deal of advertising and some editorial matter, the latter appropriate to a mid-market personal computer magazine and uneven in quality.

Books on Allied Subjects

Quite a few books have appeared in recent years on subjects closely allied to Unix but not actually about the system itself. A selection of these—obviously not complete in any sense—follows.

Bolsky, M. I.: *The C programmer's handbook*. Englewood Cliffs, NJ: Prentice-Hall, 1985 (?). ISBN 0-13-110073-4. 85 pp. (incl. covers).

A spiral-bound booklet of the kind called a "reference card" by the computer community and intended to be kept near the terminal for ready reference. Much too cryptic to learn about C from, but a good reference summary for the programmer.

Hume, J. N. P., Holt, R. C.: *Pascal under Unix*. Reston, VA: Reston Publishing Co. (a Prentice-Hall Company), 1983. ISBN 0-8359-5445-5. xii + 386 pp.

A good elementary textbook on how to program in Pascal, suitable for introductory courses in computer programming. The approach to Pascal is by a sequence of nested subsets, a clean-cut pedagogic tool. The Unix component is a short chapter on how to get programs up and running, in less depth than the *Getting Started* chapter of this book. Not really a book that can be told by its title!

Kernighan, B. W., Plauger, P. J.: *Software tools*. Reading, MA: Addison-Wesley, 1976. ISBN 0-201-03669-X. iii + 338 pp.

The major utilities (and a few kernel-level functions) provided in the Unix system are described by giving the underlying processing algorithms and developing Ratfor programs to implement them. Full of examples, program segments, and avuncular advice on good programming practices, this book is easy to read right through but harder to dip into for bits and pieces, because chapters tend to build upon each other. A small (incomplete) Ratfor translator is included as part of the book.

Kernighan, B. W., Plauger, P. J.: *Software tools in Pascal*. Reading, MA: Addison-Wesley, 1981. ISBN 0-201-10342-7. ix + 366 pp.

An extensive update of the 1976 book, with algorithms illustrated in Pascal rather than Ratfor. Some additional material is provided but the Ratfor translator of the earlier volume is unfortunately missing.

Kernighan, B. W., Ritchie, D. M.: *The C programming language*. Englewood Cliffs, NJ: Prentice-Hall, 1978. ISBN 0-13-110163-3. x + 228 pp.

This definitive book on C is well written and illustrated with a profusion of examples. It is indispensable for anyone intending to develop Unix system programs but optional (to put it mildly) for the casual user.

Periodicals

There are several magazines devoted exclusively to the Unix system and closely related topics. Most of these are listed below. Of course, various other periodicals also carry articles of Unix interest from time to time.

World Unix & C. New York: Springer-Verlag. ISSN 0176-9383. Quarterly, begun 1980.

Quality newsletter of twenty or more pages, with lots of news about software and hardware suppliers. A large part of it is composed of product announcements; some advertising is carried.

Unix Review. San Francisco: Review Publications Co. No ISSN. Monthly, begun 1983.

Trade magazine moderately light on editorial matter and heavy on glossy advertising of an informative sort. About 100–125 pages an issue. Subscriptions free to industrial executive personnel responsible for purchasing or specifying purchases.

Unix/World. Mountain View, CA: Tech Valley Publishing. ISSN 0739-5922. Monthly, begun 1984.

A glossy addition to the drugstore computer magazine shelves. Carries extensive advertising for hardware as well as software. Editorial content thin, mostly product descriptions or reviews. The magazine seems to be undecided about the sophistication as well as the composition of its audience. About 125 pages per issue.

The UNIX System V software catalog. AT&T Technologies, Inc. Reston, VA: Reston Publishing Co (a Prentice-Hall Company). (No ISSN; individual issues are treated by the publisher as books and are assigned ISBNs). Semiannual.

A semiannual listing of software available from a variety of vendors and known to be operable with Unix System V. The listings are more strongly oriented to business data processing than scientific or technical computation. Typical size about 250 pp., as a paperbound book of letter-sheet (8.5 in. by 11 in.) format.

Articles

The range of books on Unix is wide, indeed wide enough to provide almost all the information the neophyte user is likely to need. Periodical literature therefore serves the specialist, though review articles and bibliographic reviews are of more general interest as well. This very brief overview of the periodical literature is confined to papers of general or bibliographic interest; no specialist or research items are included.

Bourne, S. R.: Unix time-sharing system: The Unix shell. *Bell System Technical Journal,* vol. 57, no. 6, pt. 2, pp. 1971–1990, July–Aug. 1978.

This clearly written article describes how the Unix shell appears to the user. It is a little lacking in detail and too compact for reference, but the description is good and the summary of commands is useful.

Cherlin, E.: The Unix operating system: portability A plus. *Mini-Micro Systems,* vol. 14, no. 4, pp. 153–154, 156, 159, Apr. 1981.

The Unix system is transportable but still requires at least the writing of device drivers, parts of the kernel, and a C compiler. It has served as a model for several operating systems for 8-bit machines. The greatest portability difficulties arise in interrupt handling and memory management.

Greenberg, R. B.: The Unix operating system and the Xenix standard operating environment. *Byte*, vol. 6, no. 6, pp. 248–264, June 1981.

Historical origins of the Unix system, a review of its design goals and characteristics, largely from the viewpoint of microcomputer users.

Johnson, S. C.: Language development tools on the Unix system. *Computer,* vol. 13, no. 8, pp. 16–24, Aug. 1980. [16 refs.]

Software tools are described which make the writing of program generators relatively easy. (Program generators accept task specifications in user-oriented terms and produce programs in standard languages for performing the tasks).

Kernighan, B. W., Lesk, M. E., Ossanna, J. F., Jr.: Unix time-sharing system: Document preparation. *Bell System Technical Journal,* vol. 57, no. 6, pp. 2115–2135, July–Aug. 1978. [20 refs.]

An overview of the text processing facilities standard under the Unix operating system—**troff**, **nroff**, **tbl**, etc.—and how they fit together.

Kernighan, B. W., Mashey, J. R.: The Unix programming environment. *Computer*, vol. 14, no. 4, pp. 12–24, April 1981. [38 refs.]

A survey article, well written and easy to read. Describes the principal system features and outlines the range of Unix software tools available. Of interest mainly to newcomers to the system, though some details may be news even to old hands.

Lions, J.: Experiences with the Unix time-sharing system. *Software Practice and Experience,* vol. 9, no. 9, pp. 701–709, Sept. 1979.

Describes the author's experience in a university teaching environment.

Morgan, S. P.: The Unix system: making computers easier to use. *Bell Laboratories Record,* vol. 56, no. 11, pp. 308–313, Dec. 1978.

A broad general description, possibly of value to readers of this book, but certainly of interest to a broader audience.

Quaterman, J. S., Silberschatz, A., Peterson, J. L.: 4.2BSD and 4.3BSD as examples of the UNIX system. *ACM Computing Surveys,* vol. 17, pp. 379–418, Dec. 1985.

A description of the major characteristics of the two most recent Berkeley release versions of Unix, placed in a wide historical and technical context. Bibliographic notes and almost two pages of references to publicly available literature place this article on the recommended reading list.

Ritchie, D. M.: Unix time-sharing system: a retrospective. *Bell System Technical Journal,* vol. 57, no. 6, pp. 1947–1969, July–Aug. 1978. [15 refs.]

An overview of the Unix system and of its early technical history. Well written and pleasantly readable, though no longer up to date.

Stiefel, M. L.: Unix. *Mini-Micro Systems,* vol. 11, no. 4, pp. 64–66, Apr. 1978.

A general description is given of the Unix operating system, noting that commercial versions are now available. The review is optimistic and sees few flaws in Unix.

Appendix

The ASCII Character Set

The various sorting, text processing, and character handling operations for which Unix utilities are available assume that characters are ordered in the sequence prescribed by the ASCII character set. An ASCII (American Standard for Computer Information Interchange) character is defined as a string of 7 bits which represents a printable character or a nonprintable control function. For example, `1 101 000` represents the printable character `h`, while `0 001 000` represents the *backspace* function. For ease in reading, the binary digits are often written in groups of three, and even more frequently each group of three is given its natural numerical interpretation, that is, an octal representation is used. Thus `1 101 000` is normally written as `150`, the groups `101` and `000` having been interpreted as the octal numbers `5` and `0`, respectively. Decimal and hexadecimal representations, in which `1 101 000` appears as `104` or `6a`, are also commonly used.

Since an ASCII character is exactly seven bits long, 128 distinct characters can be formed. These are given in Table A.1, *The ASCII Character Set*.

Perhaps surprisingly, there are some installation-dependent differences between printed symbols and the corresponding ASCII bit configurations. For example, `043` (`0 100 011`) is rendered as the crosshatched "pounds" sign in American practice and as the "pounds sterling" symbol on many printers in Britain. Some other British printers and terminals substitute the "pounds sterling" sign for the dollar sign. There is no ambiguity, however, about the alphabetic and numeric characters, nor about the mathematical operators.

TABLE A.1. The ASCII Character Set

Nonprinting			Printable characters					
000	*nul*	^@	040		100	@	140	`
001	*soh*	^A	041	!	101	A	141	a
002	*stx*	^B	042	"	102	B	142	b
003	*etx*	^C	043	#	103	C	143	c
004	*eot*	^D	044	$	104	D	144	d
005	*enq*	^E	045	%	105	E	145	e
006	*ack*	^F	046	&	106	F	146	f
007	*bel*	^G	047	'	107	G	147	g
010	*bs*	^H	050	(	110	H	150	h
011	*ht*	^I	051	)	111	I	151	i
012	*nl*	^J	052	*	112	J	152	j
013	*vt*	^K	053	+	113	K	153	k
014	*np*	^L	054	,	114	L	154	l
015	*cr*	^M	055	-	115	M	155	m
016	*so*	^N	056	.	116	N	156	n
017	*si*	^O	057	/	117	O	157	o
020	*dle*	^P	060	0	120	P	160	p
021	*dc1*	^Q	061	1	121	Q	161	q
022	*dc2*	^R	062	2	122	R	162	r
023	*dc3*	^S	063	3	123	S	163	s
024	*dc4*	^T	064	4	124	T	164	t
025	*nak*	^U	065	5	125	U	165	u
026	*syn*	^V	066	6	126	V	166	v
027	*etb*	^W	067	7	127	W	167	w
030	*can*	^X	070	8	130	X	170	x
031	*em*	^Y	071	9	131	Y	171	y
032	*sub*	^Z	072	:	132	Z	172	z
033	*esc*	^[	073	;	133	[	173	{
034	*fs*	^\	074	<	134	\	174	|
035	*gs*	^]	075	=	135	]	175	}
036	*rs*	^^	076	>	136	^	176	~
037	*us*	^_	077	?	137	_	177	*del*

Character Names

Perhaps surprisingly, the names of all the ASCII characters are not well known. The letters and numerals are called by their natural names, of course; but that only accounts for 62 of the 128 characters. Of the remainder, about half are not printable in the sense that they do not correspond to any prescribed pattern of ink on paper. The first 32 characters

TABLE A.2. Special characters in the ASCII set

Oct	Mark	Name	Alternative or popular names
040		space	blank
041	!	exclamation point	exclamation mark
042	"	quotation mark	double quote
043	#	number sign	pound sign
044	$	dollar sign	currency symbol
045	%	percent sign	
046	&	ampersand	
047	'	apostrophe	closing single quote, solidus
050	(	opening parenthesis	left parenthesis
051	)	closing parenthesis	right parenthesis
052	*	asterisk	star
053	+	plus	
054	,	comma	
055	-	hyphen	minus, dash
056	.	period	decimal point, dot
057	/	slant	slash, virgule, oblique stroke
072	:	colon	
073	;	semicolon	
074	<	less than	left-arrow, left angle bracket
075	=	equals	equal sign
076	>	greater than	right-arrow, right angle bracket
077	?	question mark	
100	@	commercial at	at
133	[	opening bracket	left [square] bracket
134	\	reverse slant	backslash, reverse slash
135	]	closing bracket	right [square] bracket
136	^	circumflex	caret, up-arrow
137	_	underline	underscore
140	`	opening single quote	[single] back quote
173	{	opening brace	opening (left) curly bracket
174	|	vertical line	logical or, vertical rule
175	}	closing brace	closing (right) curly bracket
176	~	tilde	

(octal 000 to 037) and the last entry in the table (octal 177) are nonprinting control functions, the remainder are special characters (punctuation marks and the like).

The punctuation marks and other special characters in the ASCII set have clearly defined names (as laid out in the relevant standard) and are popularly called by various additional names. Names of the special characters, officially correct as well as popular, are shown in Table A.2, *Special Characters*.

The nonprinting characters have standard names also, but they are frequently called *control characters*, because they are formed by pressing a key while the CONTROL key is held down. For example, the backspace character (octal 010) is called backspace (*bs*) or *control-H*. In the relevant

ANSI standards documents, the control characters are given the following names:

^@	*nul*	null	^P	*dle*	data link escape
^A	*soh*	start of heading	^Q	*dc1*	device control 1
^B	*stx*	start of text	^R	*dc2*	device control 2
^C	*etx*	end of text	^S	*dc3*	device control 3
^D	*eot*	end of transmission	^T	*dc4*	device control 4
^E	*enq*	enquiry	^U	*nak*	negative acknowledge
^F	*ack*	acknowledge	^V	*syn*	synchronous idle
^G	*bel*	bell	^W	*etb*	end transmission block
^H	*bs*	backspace	^X	*can*	cancel
^I	*ht*	horizontal tabulation	^Y	*em*	end of medium
^J	*lf*	line feed	^Z	*sub*	substitute
^K	*vt*	vertical tabulation	^[	*esc*	escape
^L	*ff*	form feed	^\	*fs*	file separator
^M	*cr*	carriage return	^]	*gs*	group separator
^N	*so*	shift out	^^	*rs*	record separator
^O	*si*	shift in	^	*us*	unit separator

The names given here are in accordance with the ANSI standard. They differ from names as used by the Unix community in four cases. The control-J character is usually called newline (abbreviated *nl*) by Unix programmers, the control-L character is sometimes called newpage (*np*). Control-Q and control-S (*dc1* and *dc3*) are often called *X-on* and *X-off*, respectively, because they control transmission of characters to the terminal screen.

Subject Index

Command Index

For commands which do not appear in this index, please check the alphabetical sequence on pages 258–304.